Grace Will Lead Me Home

A true story written by

Paul Gerhard Tittel

with Karen Webb

Rejoice in the Lord always: and again I say, Rejoice.

Philippians 4:4

Table of Contents

Acknowledgements

Endorsement

Prologue

Chapter One: Father and Mother

Chapter Two: America

Chapter Three: Back to Germany

Chapter Four: Life in the Duplex

Chapter Five: The New House

Chapter Six: Boyhood Adventures

Chapter Seven: War comes to Hartenstein

Chapter Eight: The Russians

Chapter Nine: The Great Escape

Chapter Ten: Liberty

Appendix

About the Author

Acknowledgements

I am indebted to so many wonderful people who helped me bring this manuscript to completion. As I have said before, it is not easy with age to use the pen and put something constructive on paper. Others who have written later in their lives, like Billy Graham, point to this fact as well.

Those who read my book "Never Alone" wanted to hear more how the Lord guided me, protected me, and held his loving and caring hand over me in all circumstances. To Him belongs all honor, praise, and glory in all I did and still do. "Bless the Lord, O my soul and all that is within me, bless His Holy Name."

To Karen Webb who worked with me on this manuscript enthusiastically and was very dedicated through all the steps of the way and almost to the end. Unfortunately some unknown force pulled her away and was not able to complete it. Thank you, Karen for all your help.

To Pastor Matthew Borosso who took time away from his busy schedule to edit the manuscript in a timely fashion, thank you.

To Bill Russell and his wife Joyce who gave me on numerous times encouragement to bring the manuscript to completion. Helped me in selecting the cover of the book. Thank you so very much.

To Dr. John McKnight who after reading "Never Alone", inspired me to write this manuscript. Thank you, Dr. McKnight.

Endorsement

"Grace Will Lead Me Home" is an expansion of the book "Never Alone", A chronicle which I published in 2015. It had to be brought to light because you, the reader wanted to know and read more about God's grace, love and His leading me in many ways of my life. "Grace Will Lead Me Home" has two chapters almost identical from the book "Never Alone" of whom Dr. John McKnight writes: "Many, many thanks for writing 'Never Alone a Chronicle'. When I picked it up to read, I couldn't stop. So enthralling is the account it provides. The personal experience of a boy whom the Communist Party would rather have had dead is a fascinating record of suffering, courage, determination and ultimately, liberty. Its value is enlarged by the ease with which it reads and its clarity of expression. For those of whom have never heard and for the rest who may forget, this story had to be told and ought to be read. I am glad that I did. Thanks for the pleasure and enlightenment it has been to me. I hope that many will read this new volume."

John McKnight, Pastor
Reformation Bible Church
Darlington, MD 21034

Prologue

To see Him from a distance, one would think nothing of it—a young boy walking through the country side with a knapsack. It was early July and the flowering meadows that sat below the hills of evergreen forests looked like a picture perfect postcard. But for this boy it was far from a perfect day, it was the middle of a long arduous journey, and the beauty of the countryside was far from his thoughts.

As he traveled along a farm path he stopped and looked around him at the many forest covered hills. A look of doubt and a sigh of despair followed. Upon closer examination one could see that this wasn't a young boy at all. Barely 4 feet tall and weighing only 72 pounds, his navy shorts, and white and blue checkered shirt hung on him as if they were a hand-me-down from an older brother. His protruding cheek bones and skeletal structure spoke loudly of years of malnourishment. His sunken eyes held a steely gaze, showing that he had suffered and lost much more than he would ever tell at the age of 16.

"Come on, keep going, you can make it," Paul said to himself under his breath as he continued moving forward. He followed no specific route, but always headed in one direction - west. The sun was beginning to set, and he knew that time was running out. He had to find the border. Looking ahead, into the setting sun, he spotted a young man walking towards him. "Could you tell me where West Germany is?" He asked. The man turned and pointed to a mountain that was remarkably different from all the other fir and pine covered hills. This one had mostly deciduous trees. It was very plain to see and an easy landmark for him to follow. After thanking him, he continued on, now, more certain of his direction.

Having been caught once already by the East German border guards he knew that if he were caught again his journey and his life would most likely be over. Learning from his previous mistakes, he moved swiftly into the forest of pines wanting to avoid the border guard's watchful eye. The soldiers viewed the fields from a higher vantage point with their binoculars, and didn't bother trying to peer into the thick forests below. Here he safely traveled through the evergreens as the mountain with deciduous trees drew closer.

Dusk had fallen as he climbed up the side of the mountain—the one he had not let out of his sight while hiking during the last hour. His heart was beating faster, not just from the steep incline, but from the anticipation of what he was about to do. Nearing the top there were several benches posed to overlook the scenic valley below. It was a quiet summer night, and here he found three women sitting and enjoying the evening together. As Paul approached them, he thought, "Maybe I'm already over the border?" So he asked them loudly, "Is this West Germany?!" The women didn't say a word but pointed down the hill. He turned and looked to where they were pointing. One hundred yards away 4 border guards were hurriedly, clambering up from their seated positions, running towards him with their loaded rifles. Obviously, they had heard his question and had the answer for him too. The guards started yelling at him to "Stop!" The women were yelling at him to "Run!" He did neither…he flew.

Not far from where the women sat, grew a thick undergrowth of shrubbery that extended towards them from the forest. It was in this direction that Paul ran with all the might his little legs could muster. He leapt into the air and dove headfirst into the underbrush. Because of his slight build it wasn't very difficult for him to crawl through it. However, the soldiers couldn't follow him because they were too big—they would have to find another way. Once past the undergrowth he ran like a rabbit, quickly dodging tree limbs and rocky outcroppings. He paused for a breath but not for long. Although the border guards had a hard time following him, they could still shoot in his direction. He heard the bullets as they whizzed by his ears and shattered the bark off the trees that were near him.

He continued running until he was exhausted. Seeing a low lying bush ahead, he dove underneath it. Crawling out the other side, he found that he was sitting at the edge of a little ravine with a small brook at the bottom. He laid down by the shrubbery trying to catch his breath. Swirls of grey mist enveloped him. Images of his family and scenes from the war over the last 5 years played out before him. Tears slowly streamed down his face. He heard a guard dog barking in the distance. A final whisper fell from his lips as the black abyss of exhaustion took hold, "If this is it. I give up. ...so be it."

Chapter One: Father and Mother

With a white knuckled grip Carl Rudolf Tittel held onto the ice cold metal railing. The vibration of the steam turbine engines could be felt through the iron of the handrail. He looked out over the vast expanse of black ocean before him. Stars shimmered with a brilliance he had never seen before on land. It was late January and the temperature at night was frigid. Watching the smoke like vapor of his breath spread out before him, he knew the fresh air had done him good. He inhaled deeply—the last waves of radiating pain from a migraine dissipated from the right side of his head. Reaching up with his hand, he gently rubbed the area feeling the deep scar. Here, where shrapnel should have taken his life, it took only a piece of his skull instead. Six years had passed since serving in the German army during WWI. He closed his eyes, tilted back his head and sighed as the memories came rushing back…like a flood…he couldn't stop them even if he wanted to.

########

It was August 1915, Alsace France, and the heat in the trench that he stood in was unbearable. His uniform drenched with sweat, clung to him like a second skin. He looked down the line at his fellow comrades. Some, new to the war had eyes wide with fear, while other old *guns* slept clutching their rifles. A lieutenant, in charge of a platoon of 50 men, he had just received orders to take his company up a steep forested hill reclaiming territory that had been lost to the French in a previous battle.[1] Watching as his men passed the order down the line—at his command they would climb from the trenches and proceed, hopefully to victory over this small piece of cursed earth. Some would pay for it with the ultimate price, and for other *lucky* souls an injury would move them from the front to the safer haven of hospital care and maybe even a ticket home.

The responsibility weighed heavy on the shoulders of the eighteen year old. Many young men were in his situation—finding themselves promoted in rank swiftly because of the prolific amount of casualties. There was no other way. He looked ahead, up the steep incline, hoping to catch a glimpse of what they were about to encounter. All that stood before them was the quiet of the forest showing only trunks of tall trees with little undergrowth. Scattered throughout the hillside were small pockets of shattered forest from the previous battle. Turning to his men, he met their gaze, and gave the signal they were waiting for—raising his arm he pointed towards the hill. Leaping out of the trench, he marched forward with his Gewehr rifle held tightly in his hands.

They continued half way up the mountain with no encounters. "It looks like we're going for a walk in the park." Carl thought to himself…a hazy, dreamy thought of home came to mind…there were beautiful mountains near his home town. Stopping, he realized the heat was getting to him. Grabbing his canteen he poured water into his mouth and over his face. He turned back to look down the hill at the men who followed him. They were more than soldiers, they were his friends—having been through so much together— he felt an overwhelming sense of love and pride for them. And with that thought, Carl became one of the *lucky* ones.

########

Seven days later, after waking up from what he thought was a severe hangover, he squinted through blurry eyes and saw one of his sergeants from his company sitting on the end of his bed.

"Lars," Carl whispered in a weak voice.

"You had angels watching over you my friend." Lars said shaking his head with an enormous smile. "Hey, nurse!" he yelled. "Sleeping Beauty just woke up!"

The nurse looked at Lars from the other end of the large white room where she was talking to another patient. She picked up her clip board and ran discreetly down the aisle between cast iron beds filled with wounded soldiers all in different physical states—some healing some dying.

"Lars you know better." she spoke softly, "Other soldiers are sleeping."

"Oh a little excitement is good to get the blood pumping, Greta." He winked at her and she blushed. They obviously had a rapport more than nurse and soldier.

"So what happened to you?" Carl's voice becoming clearer the more he spoke. His question was for Lars whose arm was wrapped in a sling. Meanwhile, Greta adjusted Carl's pillows and examined the bandage on his head.

"Lieutenant, this is what you get when you want to play hero," Lars spoke in a cocky voice. "Like walking into a line of fire to pick up the body of your commanding officer - after having seen him blown 15 feet in the air by an exploding artillery shell…(Lars pauses for a moment and looks to the ceiling to reflect, then continues) I thought you were probably dead, but I did it anyway. And this? (pointing to his arm in a sling)—It's just a graze. I could have been sent back to the front sooner but they thought I could maybe talk you out of the coma you were in. Guess it worked, huh?"

Carl chuckled, then winced, as Greta removed his bandages. His head still pounded fiercely.

"I know God is real because you're still alive, Carl," said Greta. Carl turned to look at her. "No one should have survived this injury" she said emphatically. "But by God's grace you did." Greta reached for his hand and squeezed it, then continued to apply the new bandage to his head.

"So tell me Lars, what happened to me? The last I remember I was in Alsace France on a tree covered hill…then…"

"Then Boom!" said Lars. "The forest erupted—in front of us, above us —from everywhere. Tunisian sharp shooters and militia were hidden in the trees. With their black skin and black uniforms they were perfectly invisible. They had artillery too, entrenched at the top of the hill. The first gun shots were aimed at you because they were looking for uniformed officers. Don't know how they missed you being in front and out in the open like you were. I saw you standing with your canteen in hand as the first bullets whizzed by—the sharp shooters missed, but not the shrapnel from the howitzer shell that landed near you.[2] I thought you were a dead man for sure when I saw you fly through the air." Lars smiled and shook his head. The thought of Carl flying was somehow comic relief to what should have been the end of his friend's life.

The smile left his face as he continued, "I couldn't bear seeing you lay there. So I went out from the cover of the tree I was crouched behind. I dove into the hole left by the exploding artillery. Dragging you next to me, I threw you over my shoulder, almost dropped you when a bullet grazed my arm, but made it down the hill to the trenches. There I found that you still had a pulse and for the first time in a long time I thanked The Maker. The rest of the company dug in and then we called for our long range artillery. After bombarding the top of the hill they flushed the Tunis out of the trees and back over the mountain—yes we regained the hill."

"Lars, that's so good to hear and that was awfully heroic of you—I owe you my life—but, are you sure you weren't using me as a shield to cover your back as you retreated down the mountain?" Carl asked with a serious look on his face.

Lars looked soberly at Carl then tilted his head back as a fountain of laughter erupted from his mouth. His blue eyes almost overflowing with tears, he held onto his sides because it was so gut wrenchingly funny. Carl just grinned and chuckled, knowing laughter would be too painful with his wound. Greta joined in too. Such a bond had been formed between the two of them from the atrocities they had faced together. There was never a doubt that they always held each other's best interest at heart.

After the laughter had quieted, Lars mentioned the journey back through the front lines, to first aid tents, then by train to the hospital where they now sat. "The doctor showed me your x-ray and you have about 3 inches of your skull missing. I always thought you were hard headed and this proves it—for some crazy reason the shrapnel ricocheted off your head!"

Carl smiled. Just seeing Lars and hearing his banter put him at ease.

"Okay gentlemen, visiting hours are over." Greta said in her stern nurse voice as she gathered up the paper from the bandages.

"Yah, yah," said Lars as he stood up to leave.

"You can visit again in the morning…after breakfast." Greta added.

"Wait," said Carl as he reached out his hand to catch Lars' robe. "How many?"

Lars knew what he meant. He knew his friend's heart. He looked at Greta, who nodded, then back at Carl. "Sixteen," short and quick he said the word.

"And wounded?" Carl asked.

"Twenty-one— including you and me." Lars looked at the floor as he spoke. Such gravity had now entered the room.

"Thank you my friend…thank you for everything," Carl said quietly. His hand fell back to his side and within a few moments he was sound asleep.

Lars looked down at Greta, "Will he be okay?"

"The doctor will look at him tomorrow and run some tests, then we'll know for sure. But after having seen so many head wounds…and now that he's awake…I know he's going to be just fine."

########

A month had flown by and gradually Carl regained his strength and equilibrium. Lars had to return to the front since he was fit for duty. They said their goodbyes with promises of contacting one another after the war. Because of the severity of Carl's injury, after his recovery he would soon be sent back home to civilian life.

The doctors ran many tests. During his weeks of therapy Carl heard the word "miracle" escape from their lips several times. He almost had a clean bill of health—except for maybe the occasional headache, migraine or possible seizure after the injury—the doctors warned him of.

"Don't worry about what might happen, enjoy every day the good Lord gives you." One doctor told him encouragingly.

Finally, with tests completed, and papers signed, Carl sat on his hospital bed waiting for Greta. She would soon wheel him out of the hospital to a waiting taxi that would take him to the train station. Reaching into his kit bag he pulled out a small mirror. His hair had grown out several inches since he'd been admitted. He lifted it up from the right side of his head to look at the large indentation and scar the shrapnel had left. It was quite a hole but his thick black hair covered it so well that only he knew it was there. After combing his hair back into place and putting the mirror away, he looked over to the small box of his belongings. So many letters from home, church friends and family had been so faithful to write him, even his pastor. This brought to mind Pastor Otto—the local Lutheran pastor - who had come to his beside to pray for him while he was still bed ridden. Pastor Otto told him that his parents had put in a special request that a local pastor visit him so his home pastor had forwarded this request onto him, to which he gladly replied.[3] Carl was thankful for his visits. He also thought of the women from his home church in Zwickau who had regularly sent him care packages filled with dried fruit, nuts and bread.[4] He couldn't wait to get home and thank them all for their thoughtfulness.

Suddenly, Greta came with a burst through the double doors pushing the wheelchair in front of her. "All aboard!" she said in a loud whisper, glancing back and forth to see if she had woken anyone.

Excited for the journey home, Carl quickly slipped into his wool army coat, hopped into the wheelchair, and flipped the foot rests down. Greta set his belongings on his lap. "I thought this day would never come," said Carl.

"I knew you would make it." Greta patted him on the shoulder as she steered him down the hallway. A few minutes later they were outside and parting ways. He thanked her for her kindness and care and told her that he hoped things worked out between her and Lars. Sitting down in the backseat of the cab, he turned to wave as they drove away, and watched as she stood at the curb waving back enthusiastically.

"Such a sweet girl." Carl thought. "Lars is lucky."

########

The train ride went smoothly, with only several stops, reaching Zwickau late in the morning. The time had passed swiftly. The scenery was beautiful - being early October the trees on the mountains were brilliant in color. His mother had written him that they would be waiting for him at the train station. They would walk with him back to their hometown of Eibenstock. As the train approached the platform, he saw his mother and father huddled together—their eyes scanning the train doors as everyone began to exit. A lump formed in his throat. He worked hard on controlling the outburst of emotion he felt—at least until he embraced them both. Slowly, like turtles following each other, the train full of people unloaded. Finally, he stepped out onto the crowded platform.

"Ma, pa!" he yelled.

They came running to embrace him. He felt their arms covered in heavy woolen coats surround him. They held him, patted his back, his father touched his cheek. He held onto them tightly as they all cried in a huddle. Each wept for different reasons but mostly for the overwhelming joy of being with each other again. His mother reached up and moved his hair over to look at the scar. "Oh my son," she gasped. "Mom, I'm fine. It just looks bad." Carl said while rolling his eyes to his dad—knowing he would understand how he felt.

"Come now, mama. The boy is hungry. We need to get him home to your Sauerbraten and rye bread." His father winked at him, picking up his duffle bag.

Not to be outdone by his father, his mother grabbed the small box from his hand that contained all the letters he'd received while at the front. She held it under one arm, took Carl's other arm, and with her head held high, proud to have her boy home, the three of them walked arm-in-arm through the station.

As they made their way through the town, Carl could hear people yelling from windows, "Carl, welcome back! Welcome Home!" Zwickau was not their hometown but it was where they went to church every Sunday. Word travelled fast in Lutheran circles…sometimes faster than the mail. They smiled and waved back at the warm welcomes.

As they passed the local bakery, the door jingled and out bustled Mrs. Webb onto the sidewalk in front of them. Clara was not only renowned for her culinary skills but she also kept a tidy ship while in charge of the Ladies Aid at their church. A rotund woman whose size was only outdone by that of her heart, was said to have sent 100's of packages to help feed the men on the front lines. Having no children, she adopted each soldier as one of her own.

"Clara!" said Carl. "Thank you so much for your care packages. It was like Christmas every time I opened one."

"Carl Rudolf Tittel, it is so good to see you home my dear! We prayed over the food before we mailed it hoping angels would bring it straight to your hands."

"And they did." Carl said while embracing her and giving her an affectionate kiss on the forehead.

"Here," said Clara as she handed him a basket of sandwiches made with Kriegsbrot bread[5], and a container of beer. "Something for the journey home."

"You are always so thoughtful—thank you Clara," said Emil, Carl's father.

"It may be a time of rationing but we always have something to share," said Clara.

"I'll bring the basket back Sunday," Carl's mother, Anna. "God bless you for taking such good care of my sons." Tears welling up in her eyes.

"Yes, still one left to see safely home—Martin will continue to receive them until he gets a welcome home hug right here (as she pointed to the ground in front of her shop) just like Carl." She said emphatically.

"Now off with you. I know Carl needs his rest. God bless you till we meet again." Then as quickly as she appeared she disappeared returning to her shop to wait on customers.

"That woman has done so much for so many. It's amazing what she does in so little time," Anna said as she watched Clara wait on customers through the glass window of her shop.

"One would think if Germany did win the war that part of the credit would go to her," added Emil, half joking, half serious.

"I don't think that's too farfetched of an idea pa." Carl said grinning as he stepped between them. Slipping his arms one at a time into each of theirs while he held onto the basket, he continued, "So tell me now, how are my brothers and sisters?"

As they continued their trek home, Anna and Emil shared the lives of Carl's other siblings—starting with Max—the oldest, then Martina, Anna named after his mother, Paul, Emil named after his father, Martin, Clemens and little Johanna. He had been gone almost a year, so much had happened. Eibenstock being 20 miles away gave them plenty of time to share the details of each of their lives.

########

Seeing the afternoon sun pass overhead, they decided to take a break near the Filzbach river to enjoy the meal Clara had prepared for them. Sitting in the grass, after the meal, they passed the jar to each other sharing sips of beer. Surrounding them were the colors of fall, the rich blue sky, and the warm autumn sun. Carl remembered what he had just lived through and how miraculous it was to be sitting with his parents and having a picnic. Overcome with emotion, he said quietly to them, "God is so good, God is so good." Tears slipped down his cheeks—he wiped them off with the sleeves of his coat.

"Yes, I know son, I know." His father responded with tears in his own eyes. "Now we continue to pray for your brother Martin's safe journey home from the great war." Putting his hand on Anna's knee, she closed her hand over his and gripped it tightly in agreement.

########

Upon arriving home, Anna opened the door to their small but accommodating house. Like a salmon upstream, she waded through the swarm of children rushing out to greet their brother. She hollered to them before stepping inside, "Be careful now, not too long, give your brother a rest. Martina and Anna hurry in to help with supper!"

After everyone had taken their turn embracing him and welcoming him home, Carl and Clemens sat on benches outside the house and talked. Clemens was only 2 years younger and they shared a special bond. Talking with his brother brought joy back into his heart. He had forgotten how good it felt to be with his younger sibling. It made him think of Lars and Martin too—how he wished they were here. Hopefully the war would be over soon.

########

A year passed while Carl found work doing odd jobs in town at a local paper mill while the war continued on. By the spring of 1917 with few job prospects, and college enrollment starting, he knew what he wanted to do. Even as a young child, before the war, he was quite an experienced calligrapher for his young age and his drawing skills were better than most. His parents supported his decision having seen his work—they knew this was his gift. In the spring of 1917 after passing the entrance exams, Carl made the decision to attend a local trade school majoring in art. He studied hard and if he did well in his classes he would graduate in the spring of 1920.

More good news came the following year on November 11, 1918—the war finally ended. A few weeks later, Martin returned home from the front unscathed. When he came through the door and they locked eyes, Carl knew without speaking, all that his brother had been through. They hugged each other and wept, and from that moment on neither spoke of the war or their time on the battlefield—that part of their life was over. Now was the time to set their sights on the future, something their mother constantly reminded them of by reciting Jeremiah 29:11 to them daily.

Lars had also written him. How good it was to hear from his old friend. He and Greta had married as soon as the war ended. They were now living happily in his hometown. Carl looked at the back of the small picture Lars had sent along with the letter—both of them were smiling and waving. It was signed "Best of luck, Lars and Greta." How something so small could bring such hope to his heart—even in such trying times people still fell in love and were happy. If Lars and Greta found it, maybe, just maybe there was a chance for him too…His mother's voice came to his ears:

For I know the thoughts that I think toward you, saith the LORD, thoughts of peace, and not of evil, to give you an expected end.

########

While Carl was in school his brother Clemens continued to find work in the area, but it was difficult. His father tried to get him a job in the textile industry where he worked, but there were no openings. Everything looked so bleak.

After the war, inflation hit Germany hard and money was worth practically nothing.[6] Most work was done for food or bartering one skill for another with little pay. Often over late night beers they would talk about what many other Germans were talking about...America. Stories came flooding back from immigrants who had already made the journey— jobs, money, opportunities, that at the time, Germany could not offer. So, the brothers continued working hard, saving every penny to pay for the steerage, one way ticket of $102. Often Clemens would ask Carl sullenly, "Should we still go to America? How will we ever afford it?" Carl would always reply, "One penny at a time, my brother, one penny at a time."

Clemens continued to find menial labor and Carl did calligraphy while he was in school for local businesses which gave him something to put into his savings. He was supposed to get a pension from the government after being wounded in the war, but the government had no money, so he had no pension.

Besides working and dreaming of a better life, Carl and his family, were involved in many church activities. The Lutheran church, since its founding in 1517 by Martin Luther had become an important part of German culture and history. Church services on Sunday were a time when families gathered to worship and commune together. Music was a central theme of the service, and in many families children sang in the choir, played an instrument or did both. Many large celebrations took place at the church.

It was no surprise in the summer of 1919 when an announcement came from the Lutheran church in Hartenstein (a small nearby town) inviting the Tittel's and the rest of their congregation to a special celebration. For Carl's family it was something to look forward to. The 4 1/2 hour walk was short compared to the walk they usually took to their home church in Zwickau every Sunday. So they put on their best clothes and headed to the town of Hartenstein. All of them that is, except Max. Max had decided he'd had enough walking and did not want to attend church anymore. Whether it was the hard times they lived in or just becoming an adult, his parents knew it was time for him to make his own decisions and live with the consequences. So they told him that was fine, but he would need to find another place to live if he couldn't abide by their rules. So Max moved onto a farm and worked as a farm hand. Sorely missed, but always loved, the family traveled on without him.

It was July, and everything was lush and green and full of life. Several of them joined together, walking arm-in-arm, while singing their favorite hymns. His parents smiled as they listened to Carl's voice. Even though he was completely tone deaf and couldn't carry a tune it didn't stop him from loudly worshiping the Lord. As Carl walked along singing boldly with his

family he had no idea that he was about to become *lucky* once more.

Hartenstein was a small town with a population of about 3,500. It rested on steep hilly slopes at the foot of the Erzgebirge, (the Ore mountain range). It was a picturesque place with castles dating back to the 11th century.

A common vacation spot for many Germans, many of its buildings and shops were hundreds of years old. For one resident it was the most beautiful place in the world. Marie Anna Loescher loved where she lived. From the beautiful castles and surrounding mountains to the musical family she was a part of, she could honestly say her life was perfect…except for one thing. She wanted a family of her own and not just a family—a large family. Although doctors had warned her and her parents from an early age that having children could jeopardize her health. (She had been born with a heart condition and several doctors had said she could have a shortened lifespan or possibly die if she had children.) Marie continued to hope…

"What do they know anyhow," she said out loud to herself. "A girls gotta have dreams," so thought the young 18 year old. But hope did seem far away. All the young men that she had even a bit of interest in had left for America.

She sat up in bed and reached for her robe. Wrapping it around her she went to her closet. Today was a special day. The church was having a celebration and it was her first time singing a solo. She wanted to wear something special. Musical talent ran deep in her family and she enjoyed using her gifts—especially in Sunday worship. Singing, playing the lute, piano, and the recorder—her parents had taught her well and this was evident every Sunday. Her brother Hans was well known for playing the pipe organ and along with her father's brother built them. She reached into the closet and pulled out a lovely white dress with a red sash. She laid it, still on its hanger, across her chest and looked into the full length mirror that hung on the back of the closet door. "This is it," she said confidently as she swirled in a circle.

########

Carl and his family had arrived early at the church. He was glad because he wanted to get a good seat—hopefully the front row. Before entering, they stopped at an open faucet nearby to get a drink and wash their hands, feet, and faces, refreshing themselves from the long hike. They could have eaten some of the food they brought with them for the return journey but waited in anticipation for the big meal that would be served after the service. It was customary for the hosting church to put out a good spread of food and drinks. After resting for a bit Carl followed his family into the church. A few people were already seated. Women and children sat on the left, men on the right - it was an old custom but no one complained. Turning to look behind him as he walked up the aisle, he saw a small set of wooden stairs that led up to a balcony, and a pipe organ that he was sure would have a beautiful sound when played later. He continued walking, following behind his father and brothers, and sat down in the front row next to Clemens. His mother and sisters sat across from him on the other side. Gradually the church filled to capacity. The organist began to play the introductory piece, followed by the choir singing the first verse of "Lord, Keep Us Steadfast in Your Word." Then it happened. At the start of the second verse. He had heard stories of men being smitten by a woman with one look. But this was not a look, it was a sound.

Lord Jesus Christ, your power makes known,

A tremendous sound. It melted his heart, it made him want more, he was enraptured by an angel he could not see.

For you are Lord of lords alone.

Everything in him, every sound piece of logical thinking in his brain begged him not to do it.

"You had to sit up front idiot—don't do it!" he thought, trying to reason with himself.

Defend your holy Church that we,

Yes, he was smitten. He felt he had no choice. He turned, ever so slowly and looked up to the balcony. There standing in sunbeams that sparkled through one of the many stained glass windows, was an apparition, something from a dream. No verbal description could recreate what he was seeing. Body parts did strange things. His heart leapt into his throat… and his brain…his brain evaporated…then his mouth fell slightly open and stayed that way.

May sing your praise triumphantly.

As last note from the last stanza faded into quiet. That's when he lowered his gaze and noticed over 100 sets of eyes staring back at him. One old gentleman two pews back chuckled to himself. He slowly turned around to face the altar. Yes, he was a dead man, smitten through and through, and he hadn't even met her yet.

########

The sermon lasted an eternity. As ushers finally came to excuse them row by row, Carl reversed his opinion he previously held about sitting in the front row—at least he could be one of the first to leave. Dare he glance up one more time to the balcony above? This thought flashed through his mind as he walked down the aisle, waiting in line to shake the pastor's hand. He dared. He looked. She looked down at him and smiled…and he knew. Just like that, he knew they would be husband and wife someday.

Marie calmed herself. She almost giggled. "What a silly handsome young man," she thought. She noticed him at the end of her solo. She knew someone was staring at her while she sang but she dared not look, perchance losing her focus on the words and melody. After she sang the last note, she caught a glimpse of his face as his gaze shifted from her to the rest of the congregation staring back at him. He looked dumbfounded. As if he had never heard someone sing before. She giggled, audibly this time. As he passed underneath the balcony she noticed him looking at her again. She boldly looked back and smiled. At that moment something happened to her heart—it skipped a beat. "Could he be the one," she mused? Minutes later at the front of the church, the two met in person. Carl was pacing back and forth thinking of what to say, when Marie snuck up behind him and tapped him on the shoulder. He spun around. "You look deep in thought," she said mischievously. "I'm Marie Loescher." She said as she held out her hand.

Carl shook her extended hand. Looking down at her he noticed what a wisp of a woman she was, but in her eyes he saw strength and determination. "Carl Tittel," he replied, as he released his hand and continued to smile down at her. They talked for hours. Not bothering to enjoy the meal with others they sat together and conversed about everything from their faith, to politics and art. They talked about their families – Carl running through the long list of his siblings before ending with the names of his parents – Emil and Anna. Marie came from a smaller family. She pointed out her two brothers – Hans and Gerhard and her parents, who were all sitting at the same table under a nearby tree.

"My parent's names are Paul and Anna. Our mothers share the same name – that might get confusing if they're ever in the same room together," Marie smiled. Carl nodded in response. She noticed that some people were getting ready to leave and others were beginning to clean up. "Will he ask me or not?" she wondered.

Finally, as Carl's family approached him to start their long walk home, he brought up the topic Marie had been waiting for. "Would you mind if I came over next Sunday to see you again?" Carl asked sheepishly.

"I would be delighted," she said as she shook his hand goodbye. She turned to join her own family as they waited patiently for her, for their short walk home.

Carl watched her walk away. He tried to keep a picture of her face in his mind. But at the moment all he could remember was that the red sash of her dress perfectly matched the color of her lips.

Next Sunday he would approach Paul Loescher and ask permission to see his daughter. Permission was granted. Ten months of dating was followed by his graduation from business college, then their wedding. It was a month of celebration for Carl and his family. It all happened so quickly, but everyone knew that it was meant to be. As the wedding bells chimed in the church where they first met, Carl lifted the veil from Marie's face and couldn't help but think that he was the *luckiest* man alive. "No," he thought, "…blessed. I am so blessed, because I'm looking at the face of an angel."

1. Ultimately no one ever made any significant progress and especially not enough to justify the thousands of men on both sides who died over a couple of yards or meters in most cases. (http://www.getalsaced.com/alsace-france-in-world-war-one.html)

2. When the once-fluid fronts of World War 1 degraded into trench warfare, all sides sought methods for dislodging the entrenched enemy. Artillery was one such weapon and it proved highly critical against all manner of targets - infantry, fortifications, tanks. As such, field guns and howitzers proliferated the various fronts that began to spring up by the time of early 1915.

    http://www.militaryfactory.com/armor/detail.asp?armor_id=792

3. Author's note: The lines of communication between Lutheran churches and fellow parishioners were sometimes faster than the postal service. A means of communication and aid that stretched far back into the past and would reach far into the future of Carl's family.

4. Concerning German soldiers from WW1: Fruits and desserts were not provided. The subsistence was meager, but it taught the soldier frugality and endurance which would prove useful in the front. The soldier was expected to add to his meal from his own pocket, particularly breakfast and supper. The meager rations forced families to send food, money and creature comforts to their loved ones, thus greatly reducing the expenses of the government. In addition, the families of the soldiers were forced to become a part of the military machine by playing a very important role in the subsistence and comfort of each of "their" soldiers. This carefully crafted idea was not an accident, and it worked quite well throughout the war. In the American Army, anything sent from home was a

luxury, but in the German Army it was viewed as a necessity. http://www.greatwar.com/scripts/openExtra.asp?extra=10

5. During the winter of 1914, the German people began eating K-Bread (Kriegsbrot - war bread). This type of bread replaced wheat with potatoes as the main ingredient. The best food was sent to the front lines to ensure the soldiers had enough energy to fight. This meant that the civilian population had to do without.

   http://olc.spsd.sk.ca/DE/history20/unit1/sec4_03.html

6. After World War I, Germany was deep in debt. Soldiers back from the war needed money for pensions. War widows needed compensation. Reparations to France and Britain were enormous. And no other country would lend it money. So Germany's central bank printed a bunch of money and loaned it to the government. The result was possibly the most destructive case of inflation in history. http://www.npr.org/sections/money/2011/09/14/140419140/the-economic-catastrophe-that-germany-cant-forget

Chapter Two: America

"No." And I mean NO! Marie yelled, fists clenched at her sides.

Carl was looking into the eyes of a very determined woman. "Marie, we've discussed this. There's no other way." He tried to reach for her but she turned away.

"Discussing is one thing. Actually doing it is another. Our families…our church…our friends…Hartenstein—our home, how can you even think of leaving it all behind. You must have a hole in your head!" Marie turned to face him before realizing what she had just said.

"As a matter of fact I do," Carl retorted grinning.

"Oh Carl, this is no time to jest."

"I know love, I know," Carl pulled her close and this time she didn't resist.

"I've tried for over a year to find a steady job that pays money, and all I can find are a few calligraphy signs and some commissioned pen and ink drawings. Not nearly enough to raise a family on. Germany's economy is so poor, there are jobs but no money to be found anywhere—rather too much money. People in the cities shop with wheelbarrows full of it because of hyperinflation. Then there's the food rationing…Marie...I know America will be much better."

He held her in his arms as she rested her head on his chest. Brushing a hair from her face, he looked down at her pleading eyes. "I promise, Marie, once we are all in America, if for some reason it's not any better than here in Germany, we will come back."

"I will hold you to that promise Carl Tittel." She gently pushed herself away from him and leaned over the crib to check on Elisabeth—hoping her outburst hadn't woken her from her afternoon nap.

She looked down at her sleeping baby and reflected back on the past two years. It was hard to believe so much time had passed since their wedding on that beautiful June day. Because of the economy, and Carl's parent's house being full with his siblings, her parents offered them to live in their house until they got on their feet. Everything was so perfect then, especially when she found that she was expecting over a year later. Elisabeth was born in May, 1922. The pregnancy and birth were without difficulty—contrary to doctor's opinions. Many prayers were said on her behalf and praises sung at Elisabeth's christening, thankful for the health of both mother and child. Marie could hardly believe that she was already 2 months old.

A month after their wedding in June of 1920, her older brother Hans announced that he had met a girl from Neustadt—a town not far from Hartenstein—and they planned to be married in August that same year. It was a rush of a wedding to plan for, but it came off beautifully. Helene or Lene as they called her, had also become an invaluable friend. It was no surprise that when Marie made known she was expecting, soon after, Lene was too. Gertrud was born exactly a month after Elisabeth. She was happy to know Elisabeth would have a cousin close in age to play with. While they didn't live with his parents as she and Carl did, Hans and Lene lived only a few blocks away in a small apartment. Hans worked for his father making slippers and house shoes. It was a small family run business that even through the hardship of the times they lived in, it still offered an income for both of them.

Marie came back to the present as she pulled the covers over Elisabeth's shoulders, Carl remarked, "She looks so much like you, Marie, another angel on the earth."

Marie turned and looked at Carl with a smile, "Thank goodness for that."

He was glad her sense of humor had returned so quickly.

She went and laid across the bed, the same one where she dreamed of the life she now lived. "God really does answer prayers," she thought. "Except for going to America—she didn't like God's answer for that one," looking at Carl trying to smile.

Carl flung himself on the bed next to her, which made her body bounce in the air several inches. She laughed. He loved to see her laugh. He laid on his side taking in her beauty.

"So now what, Mr. Tittel?" she asked as she watched his face grow with excitement at the question.

"Now begins the process of applying for our American passports. This will take a while, so we need to start right away. America has passed a new law allowing only a certain amount of immigrants into the country each year.[1] Applying for passports now will probably mean we won't be able to travel until next year—1923. This isn't a bad thing, because Elisabeth will be older and the trip won't be so hard on her. As you know, Clemens and I have been saving for our fares and travel expenses for quite some time now and he has enough to cover his costs. I've saved enough for the 3 one way tickets for us too. Your brother Hans is still working on his fair, but he still has time."

"It's not the money that concerns me so much, Carl, but the 4 months alone without you, while I wait to make my own passage with Elisabeth."[2]

"I know I'll be missing you just as much, but the time will go by quickly, you'll see. It's the adventure of a lifetime, Marie, and I can't imagine any other person I would want to share it with. I'll write you regularly and let you know what to expect especially at Ellis Island." Carl sat up and swung his legs over the edge of the bed. "You've read the letters from my cousin Johann who made the trip over last year. His sponsor has a large dairy farm in Buffalo, Minnesota and they're looking for more workers."

Marie sat up, sitting next to him. "Carl, a dairy farm?...Really? You are many things, but not a farmer…you're an artist…a designer..."

Carl interrupted her. "I know, Marie, but I can throw a hay bale, and milk a cow as good as anyone—just like I did after the war for a farmer near Eibenstock. Besides, this place will only be a temporary arrangement until I find work in New York." He stood up looking out the window. "What will it take to convince you that this is a good opportunity for us?"

Marie saw the hope in his eyes and couldn't help but be inspired by his enthusiasm.

"A washing machine and a running toilet."

Carl laughed loudly, while Marie put her finger to his lips. "Shhh, you'll wake the baby."

"I promise, before long, you will have both." He took her hand and drew her close again.

"Now that's the second promise you've made to me in a matter of minutes Carl." Marie said smiling at him.

"Yes, but you know I keep my promises." Carl kissed her on the cheek.

########

Months dwindled away as the paper work slowly came through. By October they had their passports. Every Sunday after church, Clemens, Carl, and Marie along with her brother Hans and Helene would gather at her parent's house. (Clemens had changed his membership to the Lutheran Church in Hartenstein to accommodate their meetings.) Her younger brother Gerhard would quiz them on the 31 questions that would be asked of them before they boarded the ship and the 29 questions that would be asked of them when they arrived at Ellis Island in New York.[3]

"Okay, Marie this one is for you. What is your final destination in America?"

"Oh that's easy," said Marie. "Buffalo, Minnesota."

"Hans," Gerhard continued, "What President freed the slaves?"

"Warren Harding?" Hans said while making a funny face—knowing it was probably a wrong answer."

Marie quickly added, "No, silly that's the name of the current president."

"You should know this by now Hans," Helene shook her head in disappointment.

"Carl, do you know what president freed the slaves?" repeated Gerhard.

"Hans," Carl continued. "An easy way to remember is to think of Abraham from the bible. He was another great man that God chose to be the Father of a great nation.[4] The president's name, Abraham Lincoln, is much easier to remember that way."

Hans gave him the thumbs up sign.

"Very good, Carl. That leaves Clemens. Your question is, 'What is America's national anthem called?'"

"Hmmm," Clemens closed his eyes to think.

Marie couldn't contain herself, "I know, I know!"

"Give Clemens a chance to answer, Marie," said Hans.

"It has to do with the flag…about the stars…The Star Spangled Banner!" yelled Clemens.

They continued on for several hours, laughing at times, but knowing the seriousness of what they were studying. Any false answer when they were at Ellis Island held the ability to have them deported and that was something neither of them wanted to experience.

#########

Since he was the one that started the venture, Carl was put in charge of organizing the trip. He worked hard to make sure everything was in order. Considering both ports—Bremerhaven and Hamburg for their departure—Hamburg won out. There was news of a newly built ship called the Thuringia. Her maiden voyage, the Hamburg—New York route, was scheduled for January 22, 1923.[5] This was the ship the men, and later Marie, Elisabeth, Lene, and Gertrud would take to America. To purchase their tickets for the January trip, and for their wives and children's later trip in May was no easy venture. Carl and Hans traveled together—Carl wanting the extra protection because of the amount of gold he carried. They walked to Zwickau where they caught the train to Hamburg.

It was several days journey with stops in between, before they finally arrived at the crowded port city. Hours were spent waiting in long lines with other people from many different nationalities. Purchasing their tickets, and with them safely tucked away inside his suit coat, Carl felt a tremendous amount of relief. He was glad to have their paperwork completed so they wouldn't have to wait at the port, days, weeks or even months as many other immigrants would have to do.[6] The ship's company provided all paying customers lodging at the 'Immigrant Hotel.' He was glad the company had this amenity available seeing they would be arriving a few days early.[7] They walked back to the train station, thankful the next train was leaving within minutes. Exhausted but with their mission complete, they claimed their seats, thankful everything had gone as planned without any diversions along the way.

########

Arriving in Zwickau, Carl made it a point to stop by Clara's bakery, giving her updates on Marie and the baby. She, of course, couldn't let them leave empty handed, so they watched as she loaded up a basket with the regular—lard sandwiches made with fresh baked Kriegsbrot bread, along with a container of beer.[8] Carl and Hans thanked her for her generosity. She made them promise they would stop by again when traveling back through on their way to America. With hugs and promises exchanged, Carl and Hans left Zwickau and made their way to Hartenstein.

########

November lead into December all too quickly. While the paper work was done and questions memorized, each of them still needed to have at least $25 cash to show the examiners before boarding the ship.[9] Not to mention anything else they could save to supplement their income until they found a job that paid a good wage. All of them did as much as they could to earn anything to put toward the trip to America. Marie gave guitar and voice lessons, Carl continued to do calligraphy—announcements for weddings and baptisms were popular. Clemens found odd jobs working at the sawmill, delivering coal, or farm work. Hans continued working for his father and Lene did alterations and needlework. Carl knew they still needed more money, but they would have to be satisfied with what they had saved. With only a month left there was not much time to earn a whole lot more.

As Christmas approached, Marie's emotions ebbed and flowed like the tides of the ocean—sometimes high, filled with anticipation and other times low when thinking of leaving much of what she cherished behind. Although many thoughts crossed her mind, fear wasn't one of them. She knew many women and children had made the journey—without their husbands and fathers—before her and many more would after her. It's how it was done. Elisabeth was a healthy baby and Lene and Gertrud would be with them too—this helped put her mind at ease. But for the peace in her heart, that came from God. Psalm 91 came to mind. *"He that dwelleth in the secret place of the most High shall abide under the shadow of the Almighty."* Yes, she knew they were well covered by His shadow.

Marie looked down at the box of Christmas ornaments at her feet. Most of them she had made herself. "How can I decide which ones to take with? Each one holds a memory," she thought as a tear slid down her face. Elisabeth touched her cheek and squealed. "You are so right my little angel." Marie brushed the tear away then spun around while holding Elisabeth in front of the familiar full length mirror. "We have much to celebrate—the birth of our Savior and the start of a new life in America."

Her attitude adjusted, Marie vowed from then on she would look on the sunny side of every aspect of this grand life adventure…or at least try…and she did.

"Marie!" Carl hollered from downstairs. "Time for devotions!"

"Coming" Marie hollered back.

Coming downstairs she saw Carl on the sofa with a bible opened on his lap. Next to him lay her lute—her favorite instrument. Mother sat in her chair next to the sofa holding her violin. Hans and Lene stood with their guitars next to the pump organ where her father sat. Gerhard held his trumpet by his side, standing next to Carl.

"How beautiful, how blessed, thank you, Lord," she thought, knowing this would be the last Christmas they would worship together as a family.

Helene had a blanket on the floor for Gertrud, Marie gently laid Elisabeth down next to her and placed a rattle in her hand. Picking up her lute from the couch she sat down next to Carl.

Carl read Luke 1 and Isaiah 9:6… *"For unto us a child is born, unto us a son is given: and the government shall be upon his shoulder: and his name shall be called Wonderful, Counsellor, The Mighty God, The Everlasting Father, The Prince of Peace."*

Good Christian Men, Rejoice was the first hymn. Marie struck the first chord on the lute and sang the first note for others to follow. Music meant so much to her and her family. She thought of the first night Carl joined them for family devotions. She knew immediately that her parents liked him because nothing was said as he loudly worshiped with never a note in tune. Her mother did say a whispered, "Oh my" under her breath afterwards, but only Marie had heard it. With father's back facing her, and mother's eyes closed—lost in the melody, Hans, Helene and Gerhard looked directly at her grinning ear to ear as if reading her thoughts. Their voices raised together, with Carl's the loudest, they worshiped with joy into the evening.

########

The time had come. Clemens had walked to church from Eibenstock the previous Sunday and stayed with them. Now it was Thursday, and time to make the journey again to Zwickau riding the train to Hamburg—they would be arriving a few days early to be on time for the Monday launch of the Thuringia.

Now that Hartenstein had a train station a mile outside of town, they were going to take the local train to Zwickau and then on to Hamburg. Carl decided to rent a horse and sleigh to take them to the local Stein Station. Each person was allowed to take only one suitcase with them on the journey. All of them found it hard choosing what to bring. The men talked among themselves deciding what tools would be most helpful and who would carry what—leaving out knives or anything that would be considered a weapon—wanting to avoid trouble with the authorities. Carl brought a few art supplies. The rest of the space was for clothes, food, and their Bibles. Marie would wait for Carl's letters before she made definite decisions on what to put in hers.

Small snowflakes fell from a grey sky landing on Marie's black hair. Carl looked down at her wanting to memorize the moment. Elisabeth squirmed in his arms, wrapped in a bundle of blankets.

"Here," Marie said, holding out her arms to take the baby. "I'll take her."

Before handing Elisabeth over, Carl reached out and pulled Marie close giving her a long passionate kiss. "I will be waiting for you. You have my heart…bring it back to me."

Reaching for Elisabeth and taking her into her arms, Marie said quietly, "Carl Rudolf you really are trying to make me cry, aren't you?" She smiled, looking over his shoulder at her brother Hans and Lene who were having the same exchange. Clemens watched both couples, giving an eye roll with an audible sigh to Gerhard who sat in the driver's seat.

Marie refused to cry in front of her brothers, but it was getting hard.

"I'll write you as soon as we arrive," I promise. He took her hand in both of his and kissed it. Letting go, he turned and stepped into the sleigh.

She stood with her parents and Lene and watched them, waving all the while, until they could no longer be seen through a flurry of snow.

After a few minutes of riding in the sleigh toward the Stein Station, Carl thought back to Christmas and the wonderful surprise their parents had given them. His family had made a special trip to spend Christmas Day with them in Hartenstein. At the afternoon meal both parents stood, and after making a toast, gave each of their children 25 American silver dollars for their trip to America. Fifty dollars for each couple was a lot of money—not to mention how they got American money. Carl was so thankful, he wept because he knew how hard his father worked to earn it. It was hard to say goodbye, he didn't know if he'd ever see them again here on earth, but he also knew that America was calling and he had to answer.

########

Hamburg was just as they remembered, even though it was much colder and covered in snow. He had kept the promise to Clara—being sure to stop in and say goodbye during a short layover in Zwickau while they waited for the train to proceed on to Hamburg. They were glad they did because her basket of blessing fed them during the two day train ride to the port city.

In Hamburg, they stood together in line waiting to register their arrival and possibly get a room at the 'Immigrant Hotel.' Having heard the accommodations weren't the greatest it didn't matter, all they needed were beds and a roof over their head for two nights. After registering with a clerk they were told that the Thuringia was on time and would be boarding early Monday morning. He gave directions and a pass to get a room at the hotel which wasn't too far from the docks.

When Monday came all three of them were bursting with excitement—no one had slept the night before. By the time they arrived to stand in line for their medical exam and baggage check—which included disinfection—the place was packed. While waiting to board the ship and cross over on the gang plank, the men met 2 women and 2 other young men who were just as excited as they were. Finally boarding—after passing the quiz of 31 questions—they all took in the view from the deck of the ship. It was a busy port with many large ships coming and going.   "A momentous occasion," thought Carl. He yelled at a passing deck hand. "Would you mind taking our picture?"

The deck hand obliged. Carl showed him what to look through and what button to push. It was a last second idea to set the life preservers in front of him and Clemens, but he thought it worked quite well when he saw the picture later. Thanking the deck hand, they headed down into steerage finding a place to bunk for their 10 day journey across the Atlantic. Following another deckhand they passed a small deck space, some heavy machinery, then went down a steep set of stairs into the lower decks. There were no windows and only sparse lighting. From what Carl could see the place was filled up already but he knew there were more people coming in behind them.[10]

"Quickly, follow me," said Carl as he made his way down a narrow hallway, climbing over luggage and children to find an empty sleeping compartment. Half way down they found one with 3 bunks with a single light bulb hanging from the ceiling.

"Perfect," said Hans.

"Top bunk!" yelled Clemens.

"It's all yours," said Carl.

"I'll take the middle, if that's alright with you, Carl."

"Makes no matter to me," said Carl.

After settling in, Hans pulled out his harmonica and started playing. People in the hallway stopped to listen and peaked into their tiny living space—there was no door. It was the melody of 'Silent Night' a favorite German hymn. Some quietly swayed, others softly sang, as they listened to the soothing sound. It had been quite a tumultuous day for everyone. After playing a few verses Hans stopped as the engines powered up indicating their departure.

"America! America!" the chant could be heard faintly then it grew louder along with the sound of the ships engines as it steamed out of the port of Hamburg.

########

They had been at sea 3 days when Carl had to get air. A migraine was making him sick and the smell of old food, sewage, and dirty bodies wasn't helping. He made his way through a large crowded room of people to the stairs. Stepping onto the deck, the brisk air made him step back a moment. He grabbed the railing with both hands and held on tight. It was a brilliant star-lit night. Carl didn't know it, but Clemens had followed him up. He was always concerned for his brother when he got a migraine—being afraid it might turn into a seizure or worse. He watched as Carl rubbed his head and expelled a large cloud of frigid air.

"Hey," Clemens said. "How are you feeling?"

"Better. Was just reminiscing about WWI and how this all happened," Carl said while tapping his head.

Clemens simply nodded, knowing better than to make conversation about something his brother never talked about.

"Do you miss her?" asked Clemens.

"Would you miss your right arm if someone cut it off? Maybe not that painful—but yeah a lot." Carl said trying to make light of his aching heart.

Clemens laughed. He was really enjoying this time with his brother and looking forward to the months ahead when they would work together on the dairy farm.

Talking for several more hours, the men eventually made their way back down the steep stairs into the fowl air of their confinement below. There were 3 things that made the next 7 days bearable. A piece of paper his mother had given him with encouraging Bible verses, Hans' harmonica, and the small framed picture of Marie he kept by his side at night. Without these 3 gifts from heaven he would have totally lost his mind. As Carl lay in the stench of steerage thankful for his small blessings, he couldn't see it yet, but his dark journey would soon be over. A marvelous light was beginning to dawn on the horizon.

########

January 31st, the Thuringia pulled into New York Harbor. Word spread quickly among those in steerage - groups of immigrants would be allowed on deck to see the Statue of Liberty for a few minutes as they pulled into the harbor. It was early morning—dark enough that the torch in her hand still glowed brightly. Carl, Hans, and Clemens stood with dreamy eyes as she passed before them. Clemens stood back and watched his brother thinking how proud he was of him. His planning and enthusiasm along with God's destiny for all their lives had brought them to this place. As he took it all in, he knew the moment of their arrival would be forever etched into his memory.

After docking in Manhattan and disembarking from the Thuringia, they were divided into groups of 30, all wearing a name tag with their manifest number on it. The 3 men, along with many other immigrants were taken by barges to Ellis Island. Here, after 3 to 5 hours of waiting in long lines to register, medical exams, and answering questions, they were free to step into their new country.[11]

Finding their baggage they went to the railroad ticket office to purchase their tickets and then got in line to take the ferry over to the train terminal in Jersey City.[12] Everything was fairly well marked and there were plenty of people to ask what to do if you weren't sure. Carl was thinking ahead of Marie and Lene and the children. So far he hadn't seen or experienced anything they couldn't handle. Thinking back on the trip over, he was encouraged when he saw how the women and children gathered together and supported one another. He would write Marie and tell of all that he experienced and what she could expect.

"Here she comes boys," Hans said as they watched their train pull into the station. The ring of the bell and the loud sound of the steam engine slowly moving past them drew them to their feet. As it came to a halt, a steward set a step down on the platform for those who needed help stepping up into the train. Getting in line they clambered on board and found their seats. Watching as the car slowly filled, Carl was amazed at the number of countries that were represented by the people who sat around him. "A melting pot," he remembered overhearing someone say. The blending of all these cultures into one country was a fascinating idea to him. That America would allow anyone to take part in her riches impressed him even more and made him want to become a citizen of such a free and open country. Now that his *Certificate of Arrival* had been filled out at Ellis Island, in 5 short years he would officially be a citizen.[13] Shortly after, Marie and Elisabeth would be citizens too. He missed them, and silently prayed for their safe journey across the Atlantic. God had blessed them so far and he knew His hand of providence would continue to hold and bless them into the future.

########

Arriving in Buffalo after 3 days of train travel was a relief—it was nice to stand on solid ground and not feel continuous movement under your feet. Almost to their final destination, the 3 of them felt like horses at the starting gate of a race. Anticipating the work ahead, and their new living arrangements, Hans and Clemens paced back and forth while Carl used the payphone. Pulling an old piece of folded paper from his pocket, he dialed the number Johann had sent him in one of his letters. "Hello, hello, Otto? This is Carl…Carl Tittel. We have arrived and are at the station…Yah, yah all of us have arrived safely. No, my wife and daughter will arrive this May along with Helene and Gertrud. Okay, we'll be looking for Johann within the hour. I will tell them. Thank you." Carl hung up the phone and looked at Hans and Clemens. "He said, 'Welcome to Buffalo and he looks forward to meeting us.'"

"Praise God from whom all blessings flow," Hans said while looking at his two friends.

"Looking forward to meeting us and not even knowing who we are is a pretty nice welcome, I'd say," said Clemens.

"Yes, he sounded genuinely pleased that we're here." Carl held out his arms, "Welcome to America!" All three of them embraced and patted each other on the back—a congratulation of sorts for having made such a safe and successful journey.

"It feels so good to see everything fall into place just as planned," thought Carl an hour later as they watched Johann pull up to the station. After loading up their suitcases, Carl and Hans climbed into the cab of an old pickup truck, while Clemens sat in back with their luggage. Along the way they exchanged the stories of their journey and greetings from back home.

As they drove up to the farm Carl's heart was bursting with hope - there were only two things missing to make his joy complete and they would be arriving in May.

All farmhands on Otto's Farm

########

Marie wept and clung to them for as long as Elisabeth could take being smushed between the three of them—Helene did the same while holding Gertrud. One part of her wanted to stay so badly but a larger part was excited for the journey and to see Carl again—four months was a long time to wait…she was ready to go and so was Helene.

Gerhard waited patiently for them. He would be taking them by wagon to Hartenstein's Stein Railroad. Her brother would travel along with them to Hamburg and see them safely onboard the Thuringia. She was grateful for his company in the first step of their journey to America.

"I will write to you, just as Carl was faithful to write me. Thank you for your love, your prayers and blessings. I will take them with me wherever I go and pass them on to Carl as well." Marie said through whispered tears.

"God bless you and keep you until we meet again," said her father.

"Know you are loved and cherished by one greater than us, and He walks with you," tears streaming down her face as her mother's hands gently held her face. "Be strong and courageous like Joshua…and you are, my dear one."

She embraced them again, burying her face into each of their necks to gather the fragrance of them into herself. She wanted to remember everything about them and all they had done for her.

Gerhard took Elisabeth from Marie, while her father helped her into the wagon. He then did the same for Helene and Gertrud. Marie turned and waved as she watched the two of them grow smaller and smaller as they drove down the road and round the bend until they disappeared from sight.

########

"How do I look?" asked Carl while slicking his hair back with his hand. "And pass the bacon will you?"

"You look the same as when you asked 2 minutes ago," said Clemens shaking his head grinning.
"She's just my sister, not the Queen of England," added Hans.

"Besides when you see her after a two day train ride your hair and clothes will be all mussed up anyway," Clemens looked at Carl pointing a sausage at him.

"You, my friend, are single for a reason," said Carl while pointing at him with a fork full of ham.

They laughed, each seeing the humor in the other's remarks. Neither one of them could believe their good fortune since they arrived at Franke's dairy farm. It was hard work taking care of 250 head of dairy cattle, but the food, the shelter, and even the small amount of pay made it worthwhile. All of them had bulked up since they had arrived in January—good food and hard work had changed all their physiques. Germany still had heavy rationing even after the war. Bread and meat—as least as Americans thought of them—were in short supply. While their clothes hung on them when they arrived they now filled them out much more—no longer having to make new notches in their belts.

Clemens held up a buttermilk biscuit with a slather of butter. "This is heaven," as he pointed to it with his knife. "I don't remember ever eating food so good in Germany—even before the war."

"That's just because you're hungry," Hans said as he picked up a ham steak, and slapped it onto his plate.

"Yes, you're right, I remember my mom's rye bread and Sauerbraten," retracted Clemens, "before the war," he added.

As Carl nodded his head in agreement, he looked up and saw Johann getting up from the table while pointing to his watch. "Gentlemen, we must excuse ourselves, our ride is leaving," said Carl as he nodded to Hans getting up from the table and tossing his napkin down on his plate.

It was Monday morning and they had a train to catch. Otto Franke had been so gracious to give them 5 days off from work—4 for travel and 1 to help their wives get acquainted with everything on the farm. It was without pay of course but both Carl and Hans didn't mind. All they could think of was seeing their wives and children again.

########

Marie stood at the train station on her tip toes trying to look over the heads of people. Elisabeth slept peacefully in her arms. She shifted the satchel on her back that held her lute—it was cumbersome, but she had to bring it—music was like air to her, she needed it to live.

"Do you think they misunderstood the day and time we would be arriving?" asked Helene. "Maybe we should look for a pay phone."

"No," said Marie. "Carl knew exactly the time and place. He will be here." "Carl, where are you…?" she thought worrisomely.

"Marie!"

Out of the cacophony of people and steam engines, she heard the most wonderful sound.

"Carl!" she put her hand to her mouth and tried to stop the sobs but she couldn't—being overtaken with emotion at seeing him. He ran to her, picking them both up in a smothering embrace of kisses. He took Elisabeth into his arms. "Oh to hold you again—I've missed you so much my angel. Look at Elisabeth—she's grown so much, Marie!" Carl said as a proud father.

"Almost 12 months to the day," said Marie. "She's not the only one who's grown. What have they been feeding you? You're built like an ox!" Marie looked over at Hans and Helene—she was pinching his bicep and laughing.

"I think you could carry both of us and the luggage to the train!" Helene said as Hans handed Gertrud back to her and picked up her suitcase and satchel.

"Wait till you see the meals they prepare for us. Each day is a banquet," said Hans.

Carl took Marie's hand. "You will love it here, Marie," he said as he grabbed her suitcase while carrying Elisabeth in the other. "We'll board the train and get our seats so you can rest. Then you must tell me everything about your crossing and Ellis Island."

########

After several days journey by rail, and long conversations catching up on all they had been through, they pulled into the Buffalo station. Carl called Otto who sent Johann to pick them up. When they arrived at the farm, Marie was impressed with it's size. They pulled into a gravel road that took them onto the property. They drove past pastures filled with black and white dairy cows, large barns, a bunkhouse—that Clemens called home, a large farm house, until finally coming to a stop in front of two small log cabins. The men jumped out of the back of the pickup. Hans carried the luggage, and Helene followed him carrying Gertrud into their new home. Carl helped Marie out of the pickup, taking Elisabeth from her. "This is it, home sweet home." Carl bowed with his free hand pointing towards the door.

Johann picked up Marie's suitcase and lute and set it by the door of the cabin. "Thank you, Johann. It was a pleasure meeting you." Marie held out her hand and he lightly shook it.

"Welcome to Buffalo, nice to have you, Lene, and the children here with us," replied Johann as he hopped back into the truck.

As he drove off, Marie turned and followed Carl and Elisabeth as they walked through the door of their new home. "Oh Carl, it's so much more than I thought. I was really expecting the worst."

"I knew you would like it. With a few of your special touches it will look even better." Carl set sleeping Elisabeth on the bed.

There were two windows—one by the door, the other over the kitchen sink. There wasn't really a kitchen, just one large room. The bed was in one corner with a sheet hanging from a rope that crossed the room to give some privacy. A potbelly stove stood in the middle, a sink with a hand pump was against the wall along with a small cooking stove next to it. A small table with two chairs, an ice box, and an old couch were the only furniture besides the bed.

"I'm so glad I brought the material you said to bring. First on the agenda are curtains." Marie said as she lifted the heavy suitcase and carried it into the cabin. Carl picked up the lute and shut the door behind him. She opened her suitcase to start unpacking.

"Wait," said Carl as he placed the lute on the couch. "You need to rest, Marie. Take a nap with Elisabeth, while I prepare you a magnificent supper."

"You've twisted my arm, Carl. I'm exhausted." Marie laid down next to Elisabeth and was sound asleep in minutes.

Carl did as he said and made a truly magnificent meal—just like Otto's wife and her daughters made for the working hands every morning. Marie could not believe the wealth of food on the table. They joined hands to pray over what God had so richly supplied.

"Carl, you were right," Marie said while savoring a bite of a buttermilk biscuit. "It is so much better here, than how we lived in Germany. We are so blessed."

########

For three years Carl worked hard for Otto on the dairy farm. After the first year, Clemens decided to join the U.S. Army in 1924. Soon after Clemens left, Hans—having saved enough—moved to downtown Buffalo and opened his own shoe factory. Buoyed by the success of his brother and brother-in-law—often he would purchase a New York Times newspaper looking hopefully through the want ads. Always disappointed at not finding a job description that encompassed his artistic talents, Carl never gave up.

"Must have knowledge of design and be able to work overtime and occasional weekends." Were the first words that jumped out at him from the want ad page.

"Marie! Marie!" Carl yelled as he threw open the door to their cabin.

"Daddy!" yelled 4 year old Elisabeth. Running up to him, Carl scooped her into his arms.

Marie turned from washing dishes at the sink. "What's all the excitement about?"

"Look, it's my job—I know it is."

Marie took the paper from him and read the job description. She sat down in the chair and looked up at Carl. "I believe this could be it, Carl," she said after reading through the entire ad.

"Let's pray and ask the Lord for his blessing upon it." Heads bowed at their humble table, they asked the Lord for favor and thanked him for all his provision, then ended with the Lord's Prayer. After praying, Marie got up and sat in Carl's lap putting her arms around his neck, she took a deep breath before beginning. "I have some more good news for you Mr. Tittel."

"Oh?" Carl raised his eyebrows.

"Yes. We will be having a special visitor arrive sometime in October."

"A visitor? Who could that be?" Carl asked innocently.

"That would be a baby," Marie giggled.

"Really?! A baby!" Carl jumped up and swung Marie around while Elisabeth laughed. After setting her down he raced for the door.

"Where are you going?" asked Marie.

"To tell everyone I'm having a baby! I mean you are. I mean we are." Flustered with happiness he ran to tell Otto, the other workers, and anyone who would listen to the good news.

########

It was the end of May, 1926. After mailing his resume and references to Arnold Constable & Company he was certain they would hire him as a window dresser.[15] Otto too had a good feeling and had congratulated him as if he had already been hired. A Christian man, he and his wife encouraged immigrants to step into better paying careers. Being of good character and a hard worker were the only requirements of getting an excellent reference from them.

Several weeks later a plain white envelope addressed to Mr. Carl Tittel arrived in the mail. Otto hand delivered it to Carl. "Well go ahead, open it." Otto said grinning ear-to-ear.

Marie and Elisabeth stood next to him as he slowly tore open the envelope. Carl read the letter aloud. "We are pleased to notify you that you qualify for the position of Window Dresser which we had listed in the New York Times. Please respond within 2 weeks of this notice letting us know a convenient time to hold your interview."

"Hallelujah!" yelled Marie.

"It's a miracle," said Carl.

"I knew it would be good news," said Otto.

Carl scheduled his interview for mid-June and again was grateful to Otto who gave him the week off to take the train there and back. He didn't want to count chickens before they were hatched, but all he could think of on the way there was the new home and a better way of living he could offer his wife and children.

After arriving at the station Carl caught a bus to 5th Avenue and 34th Street. He was amazed at the displays of wealth and opulence as he walked through the store to catch the elevator to the third floor. The interview went smoothly. Afterward, as he and the president's secretary left his office she asked him to wait before leaving. He thought he had done something wrong. Following her to her desk, he watched as she pulled out a folder with papers. "I'll need you to sign these before you leave," she said nonchalantly as she handed him the folder.

"What are these for?" asked Carl.

"These are saying you agree to the terms of hire—meaning hourly wage, hours per week, and company policies. Congratulations, Mr. Tittel you are now an Arnold Constable & Company employee. As you agreed in the interview – if you were hired — the starting date of your employment would be December 1, 1926. Since you have now been hired, we look forward to your arrival on that date. Here is a folder of available housing that you may be interested in, also train and bus routes from New York and New Jersey to the store." Very proficient and matter of fact she handed Carl the folder as she walked him to the elevator. "Welcome to Arnold Constable & Company," she said. Shaking his hand, she turned and walked away as the elevator doors opened.

Stepping through the open doors he waited for them to close before yelling "Thank you, God!" at the top of his lungs.

########

Arriving back at the farm, and after sharing the good news with everyone, Marie and Carl began to make plans for their new life. From the folder of information they were given, Carl found an apartment complex along with a phone number, in Dover, New Jersey. Marie's mother had written her, passing along information from their pastor. The Good Shepherd Lutheran church had been started in 1914 in Dover. It was a German church that held German speaking services. Many of the German immigrants that worked in the area attended there. Another good reason Dover, New Jersey sounded like a good place to raise the family.[15]

October 27, 1926, Herbert came into the world. The new little brother for Elisabeth was born in the bed of the small cabin. Uncle Hans and Helene were there to greet their new nephew. Another safe delivery for mother and child, Marie smiled at how wrong doctors could be and how much God had blessed them. She kissed the top of his head. "Welcome to the world, my little American."

Carl beamed, looking down at his wife and son. "We will christen him at the Good Shepherd Church in December."

Marie nodded in agreement while her eyes slowly closed for a much needed rest. Carl picked up Herbert who had been laying bundled in a blanket by her side. He was glad they had a month before moving so Marie could regain her strength for the trip.

########

Arriving in Dover the last week of November, they walked from the bus stop to their new home. Four stories high, with two apartments on each floor, theirs was on the 1st floor. Having reserved it a month in advance by phone, Carl had the first month's rent in his pocket. Thanks to the parting gifts from Otto and his wife, and Hans and Helene, they had plenty to buy all the food and furniture they needed. The landlord's apartment door was immediately to the left as you walked through the entrance. From what Carl could see, their apartment was on the same floor, but the door was at the end of the hall. Carl knocked on his door.

"Mr. Wessel, it's me, Carl."

Mr. Wessel opened his door and stepped out to greet them. As they walked down the hall to their apartment he looked Carl up and down.

"You wouldn't need a part time job, would ya?" Mr. Wessel asked Carl.

"I sure wouldn't mind one with a growing family." Carl said in quick response.

"Stop by and see me later and we'll talk." Mr. Wessel opened the door. Marie was the first to walk through.

"Wonderful, just wonderful," Marie walked into the kitchen and turned on the faucet. In the corner was a wringer washing machine. She walked into the bathroom and flushed the toilet. She came back and stood in front of Mr. Wessel and Carl. "It's every woman's dream."

"I guess she's a keeper," said Mr. Wessel handing Carl the key. "I best be goin'—don't forget to stop by and see me when you get a minute."

"You kept your promise," she said looking at Carl.

"Not quite my dear. The next washer and running toilet will be in your very own home."

"Now that's a promise I'll look forward to you keeping, Mr. Tittel."

The apartment came partially furnished. There was a couch in the living room, a double bed in their bedroom and single bed in the other. Marie got busy making a list of the essentials they needed. Carl took Mr. Wessel up on his offer of part time work. He took over feeding the large coal burning steam boiler in the basement. Every morning and evening before and after work he would check to make sure it was running properly and load more coal into it as needed.

Starting work in December, Carl had never felt so satisfied. To be doing something that God made you to do was very fulfilling—not to mention the great pay and work environment. He never would have dreamed as a young boy in Eibenstock, Germany that someday he'd be working on 5th Avenue in downtown Manhattan.

########

A year passed. Their savings grew and there was nothing they were in need of—except Marie. Her mother had written her saying how nice it would be to see the grandchildren. She knew they had more than enough money in the bank, but felt selfish to ask Carl for a vacation when he worked so hard. She prayed about it and wondered if she should even say anything when Carl broached the subject himself.

"Marie, you work so hard at making a nice home for me and the children. Would you want to take a vacation and go back to Germany for a visit? I know it would put your parent's minds at rest seeing how richly the Lord has blessed us."

Marie could hardly believe her ears. "Carl, you must be a mind reader! My mother has been writing me about how nice it would be to see the children," she threw her arms around his neck and kissed him.

"Then it is set," Carl said holding her by the waist. "No steerage this time either. I want you and the children to travel at least in a second class cabin. Let me save up a little more. It's always nice to have a cushion for emergencies. Now we're in December, 1927…how about early March, 1929. That gives me another year to save more money."

"And for that, I have no other choice but to make your favorite dish for supper."

"Sauerbraten and rye bread?"

"Of course my love," Marie said as she danced away to the kitchen humming a happy tune.

########

It was early February, 1928 when Marie knew for sure. She was excited, but with the baby due in July she still hoped they would still be able to go to Germany the following March. She placed her hands on her stomach feeling the little flutter of life within her. She heard Carl come home from work. Herbert was waking from his nap. Elisabeth, playing quietly in her room, yelled a greeting to her father. "Hi, daddy! Come and see what I made."

Carl ventured into Elisabeth's room to see her holding up a drawing of their family. "I think you may have your father's talent." Marie said from behind Carl.

"I think your mother's right," nodded Carl.

"Mommy's always right," Elisabeth said with her hands on her hips. They laughed together.

"How's my boy?" Carl reached for Herbert. Taking him from his mother's arms he sat on the sofa and told him about his day as if he understood every word. Elisabeth came out of her room and sat next to her dad on the couch.

"Well now is as good a time as any," thought Marie. "Attention family, I have an announcement," Marie stood in front of them with her hands folded in front of her…then paused.

"And the announcement is?..." asked Carl.

"I'm having a baby."

"Yippee!" yelled Elisabeth. "I want a sister to play with. Can you make it a girl, mommy?"

"No, Elisabeth, mommy can't make it a girl. We will take what God gives us. Boy or girl, they will be another wonderful addition to our family." Carl sat Herbert on the rug to play with some scattered toys. He went to Marie and wrapped her in a hug. "When are you due?"

"July."

"Have I told you lately how much I love you—how blessed I am that you are the mother of my children?"

"No, but I like hearing it so you can tell me gain."

"I love you, Marie. I am so blessed that you are the mother of my children."

"One more time," said Marie looking into his eyes.

"I love you, my angel," he said kissing her forehead. "I am so blessed," kissing her cheek. "That you are the mother," kissing her other cheek. "of my children," kissing her lips.

"Will we always be so blessed, Carl?" asked Marie with her eyes now closed soaking in the love that emanated from him.

"We may or may not be. But we will always remember the great things God has done for us."

########

Elisabeth got her wish. Christa was born that July in their little apartment in Dover, New Jersey. The delivery was long but Marie weathered it like a champion. She thought if all her pregnancies were like this she would have 10 more children—and she really hoped she would. Summer passed into fall and fall to winter. By the time Christmas came around Marie felt she was hardly ready. She was going to sing a solo with her lute Christmas Eve at church, but it was hard to find time to practice with the children. Elisabeth was learning how to play now too—teaching her was more important than practicing her own song. She would make sure all her children learned an instrument.

Carl came home early from work and helped get the children ready for the Christmas Eve service. Only several blocks away, it was a short walk for the family of five. He sat in the back row because of the children. Here they did not separate the sexes and Carl was glad for that. He enjoyed sitting with his family in church.

The service started with a beautiful organ piece. Then the choir sang. Then Carl remembered all over again how he first fell in love. Marie's voice carried from the balcony and flowed through the church along with the sweet accompaniment of her lute—the two made a beautiful pair. It was always intoxicating to him, to hear her sing. Even the children were quiet as they listened to their mother's voice.

Good Christian men, rejoice, with heart and soul and voice;
Now ye need not fear the grave: Peace! Peace! Jesus Christ was born to save!
Calls you one and calls you all, to gain His everlasting hall.
Christ was born to save! Christ was born to save!

After the service and their walk home, Carl sat by their Christmas tree lining up gifts for the children to open. Each one squealed in excitement as he handed them their gift. Christa was too young to understand, but her eyes grew big as she watched her siblings from her mother's lap. Saving the best for last he handed Marie an envelope.

"What's this?" Marie asked inquisitively.

Carl wouldn't say.

She opened the envelope and looked inside. There were 4 tickets for passage from New York to the port of Hamburg, Germany. "Carl…Thank you." Tears started to fill her eyes.

"Now, now. No tears. This is a time of celebration, remember?"

Marie laughed, "Yes, Carl, yes it is."

########

January 1929 came in fierce. Day after day, the freezing temperatures kept dropping while the inches of snow kept rising. Carl worked hard to keep the boiler fed. Marie remembered the morning it happened. It was still dark out. The children were still asleep. Then the apartment shook violently. She thought she could hear screams in the distance. For a moment she thought maybe they were at war. Then she heard Mr. Wilson's apartment door open and slam shut. She went to the door slowly opening it and looked down the hallway. She had a bad feeling in the pit of her stomach. She watched as Mrs. Wilson came through the front door of the apartment building. She yelled, running towards her with a grimace of pain across her face, "Marie there's been an explosion! I'll watch the children. You need to go to Carl now! He's out front. They're waiting for an ambulance." By then she had reached their door pulling Marie into the hall while she entered their apartment. Marie ran down the hallway, at least she tried to. Everything was in slow motion. Words jumbled in her head—explosion, Carl, ambulance…. Pushing through the entrance door of their apartment complex, she stood at the top of the stairs and looked down at a group of men gathered around a crumpled figure. There on the ground was a man with burnt clothing lying on a blanket. He was screaming her name. It was Carl. Mr. Wilson swiftly walked up to her before she reached Carl. "The boiler exploded. Men got him out of the basement when they heard his screams. He's burnt real bad. You may not want to…"

Marie pushed past him, kneeling in the snow by Carl's head. She grabbed one hand and held it tight. The other she placed on his head. She spoke loudly, "I'm here, Carl. I'm here! You must be strong!" His screams subsided at the sound of her voice.

From deep within her came reserves of strength she knew were from God, because everything in her wanted to collapse. "Marie, he said breathlessly…Marie…"

"I know my love, it will be alright, we will make it through this." Marie whispered into his ear.

As she watched Carl lose consciousness, she prayed a simple prayer, "God save him, God heal him." The ambulance sirens could be heard and soon the men came with a stretcher to take him to the local hospital.

########

January slipped into February. Carl was burned over 80% of his body. Having a split second to turn saved his face. Most of the burns were first and second degree on his arms and legs, his back took the worst. Third degree burns covered a large portion of it. Skin grafts needed to be applied that took forever to heal. Laying on his stomach Carl looked at Marie. He knew by the look on her face that her news wasn't good.

"Carl, our savings are gone. The rent, medical bills, and necessities have depleted it." Marie continued, "Arnold Constable & Company called giving their best wishes for your recovery but also stating that your services are no longer required." "There is some good news. We still have the tickets to Germany. We still have enough money to purchase one for you to come with us." Marie struggled to hold her composure. "Do you remember the promise you made me when we first spoke of coming to America?"

He couldn't answer. All he could think of was… a moment ago they were living a dream and in an instant hell itself engulfed them.

"It's time to keep that promise." Marie continued.

"I'm so sorry, Marie." He couldn't look at her as tears streamed down his face.

"Sorry for what? I've had the adventure of a lifetime and it's not over yet Mr. Tittel."

########

After a few more weeks of healing Carl left the hospital. Their apartment looked as it did on the day they first arrived. Their furniture and belongings were sold for money—they needed all they could gather for the trip back to Germany. The only indication they were ever there were a few cheery crayon marks left on the walls by Herbert. The pastor of their church had been over many times to pray and the Ladies Aid were ever faithful to bring meals to Marie and the children while Carl was in the hospital. Marie remembered writing her mother of the terrible news. Her response was swift as it was soothing. "My dearest daughter, prayer changes things, don't despair, God makes all things new. Carl's parents know too and all the churches in the area are praying for his healing. Our home is your home for as long as you need…"

Hans and Helene called, Clemens wrote to them too, along with Otto Franke and his wife and all the farmhands—everyone was praying for them. Marie thought of these things, bright flowers of blessings in this dark season of their life.

With only a few more days until their ship sailed, The Wessel's fed them and Mrs. Wessel helped Marie watch the children so Carl could rest. They continued to be good Samaritans by using a friend's car to take them to New York and see them safely onto their ship. Once aboard, the family of 5 watched silently as they passed the Statue of Liberty. "She's a pretty lady," said Elisabeth.

"Lord, let it be that someday our children will come back to her," Carl said as he held Marie's hand.

"Yes Carl, someday…someday they will come," Marie replied squeezing his hand in agreement.

1. In 1921, Congress passed the Temporary Quota Act, which set numerical restrictions on immigrant admissions, and in 1924, this was set at 150,000 per year, plus accompanying wives and children. Each country's quota was "a number which bears the same ratio to 150,000 as the number of inhabitants in the United States in 1920 having that national origin bears to the number of white inhabitants of the United States."Since there were more Americans of English and German origin in the United States than of Polish or Italian origin, England and Germany had larger immigration quotas than Poland and Italy.

    http://www.hoover.org/research/making-and-remaking-america-immigration-united-states

2. Authors Note: It was customary for many married immigrants that traveled to America to have their wives and children wait 3 or 4 months before crossing over. Some men settled into the job their sponsor had waiting for them, others looked for whatever was available. Also, they made sure they had a decent place to live—making sure everything was secure before having their families join them. Each sponsor had to supply a job, housing, along with food for the workers. The pay was very little, but it was a good starting point for many families entering the country.

3. After the 1893 U.S. immigration law went into effect, each passenger had to answer up to 31 questions (recorded on manifest lists) before boarding the ship. These questions included, among others: name, age, sex, marital status, occupation, nationality, ability to read or write, race, physical and mental health, last residence, and the name and address of the nearest relative or friend in the immigrant's country of origin. Immigrants were asked whether they had at least $25; whether they had ever been in prison, an almshouse, or an institution; or if they were polygamists or anarchists.

    http://www.oranger.com/ellis-island/immigration-journey
    New York City: A Cultural History By Eric Homberger – page 78

Through a translator the immigrants were asked their name and age. Were they able to understand? Immigrants were asked 29 questions, and the "wrong" answer could provide grounds for denial of permission to enter.

4. "And I will make of thee a great nation, and I will bless thee, and make thy name great; and thou shalt be a blessing…" Genesis 12:2 KJV

5. S/S Thuringia (4), Hamburg America Line. Launched august 12th, 1922. January 23, 1923 Maiden voyage Hamburg- New York.

    http://www.norwayheritage.com/p_ship.asp?sh=thur3

6. For many, simply getting to the port was the first major journey of their lives. They would travel by train, wagon, donkey or even by foot. Sometimes travelers would have to wait days, weeks and even months at the port, either for their paperwork to be completed or for their ship to arrive because train schedules were not coordinated with sailing dates.

    http://www.ohranger.com/ellis-island/immigration-journey

7. Assuming their paperwork was in order and tickets had been purchased, some provision was usually made for the care of the emigrants waiting for a ship. Steamship companies were required by the governments to watch over prospective passengers and, at most ports, the travelers were housed in private boardinghouses. Some port cities even boasted their own "emigrant hotels."

    ibid

8. Authors Note: The brewing and consuming of beer in Germany has been happening for 1,000's of years. Many times beer was considered safer to drink than the water. Breweries were often run by monks with the approval of the church. With its low cost and low alcohol content of 4% or lower, it was served at many church celebrations, and family meals. In times when food was scarce, beer was not. High in protein, carbohydrates and micronutrients it was a regular part of the everyday diet—even children were offered small portions to drink. Unlike American beer, German beer is served at room temperature.

9. Immigrants were asked whether they had at least $25; whether they had ever been in prison, an almshouse, or an institution; or if they were polygamists or anarchists.

http://www.ohranger.com/ellis-island/immigration-journey

10. Steerage passengers walked past the tiny deck space, squeezed past the ship's machinery and were directed down steep stairways into the enclosed lower decks. They were now in steerage, which was to be their prison for the rest of their ocean journey.

Ibid

11. It took 3 to 5 hours to go through the entire process at Ellis Island. https://quizlet.com/1964662/ellis-island-tour-test-flash-cards/

12. For immigrants traveling to cities or towns beyond New York City, the next stop was the railroad ticket office, where a dozen agents collectively sold as many as 25 tickets per minute on the busiest days. Immigrants could wait in areas marked for each independent railroad line in the ferry terminal. When it was reasonably near the time for their train's departure, they would be ferried on barges to the train terminals in Jersey City or Hoboken. Immigrants going to New England went on the ferry to Manhattan.http://www.ohranger.com/ellis-island/immigration-journey

13. Certificates of Arrival: This form confirmed the name of the immigrants when he arrived at the port of immigration, the date he arrived, on what ship (or other means of transportation), and perhaps the name of the shipping line. Again, this was to confirmed that the person applying for naturalization lawfully entered the United States and was admitted for permanent residence.

http://www.museumoffamilyhistory.com/erc-imm-coa.htm

14. 1950s American Style: A Reference Guide (soft cover) By Daniel Niemeyer, page 22. Arnold Constable & Company opened at Fifth Avenue and 34th Street in 1914. The flagship for this upscale department store, once the oldest in America, was built on the site of the Vanderbilt mansion. It served the 'carriage trade' of New York bringing the best French fashion to the Astors and Vanderbilts…
http://www.ushmm.org/wlc/en/article.php?ModuleId=10005206

15. The Good Shepherd Lutheran Church was organized in 1914. It was founded to serve the Germans who had migrated to Dover to work at the Guenther Hosiery Mills and Picatinny Arsenal. http://dovernjhistory.org/files/pages/doverchurches.htm

Chapter Three: Back to Germany

The journey across the Atlantic was proving to be quiet and uneventful—but it was only a lull before the storm that was brewing between Marie and Carl. Marie sat in a reclining chair on deck watching Elisabeth and Herbert play shuffle board, while Christa slept in her arms. "Carl's doing so much better. The salty sea air, good food, and rest has brought Him a healthy glow—one I haven't seen since before the accident," she thought to herself as she watched him resting next to her. She was grateful for the prayers of their family, friends, and church. Looking out across the ocean she thought how drastically their lives had changed in a matter of months. It was a miracle that he had survived the explosion of the boiler. She only wished his heart and spirit would heal as well as the wounds on his back. Morning and evening devotions that were once filled with hope and worship, were now just a routine of mumbled words followed by softly sung hymns. They had hardly spoken in days as she watched him wrestle with all that had just happened to them.

"The accident, losing my job, financial ruin…Why, God. Why?!" These thoughts grew in magnitude in the mind of Carl, the closer they drew to Germany. Laying on a deck chair next to Marie, he clenched his jaw, lost in hopelessness—not seeing the joy of the family that surrounded him. He felt a migraine beginning to build near his old war injury. He massaged his head with his hand. "...and if things aren't bad enough, what about when we get back to Germany? How am I going to support Marie and the..."

"Look, daddy, a seagull!" Elisabeth squealed loudly with excitement—pointing to one that had just landed on the ships railing not far from where they played.

"Shut up, child! Must you speak so loud!" Carl spoke in such an unfamiliar venomous tone that everyone stopped and stared at him—even baby Christa.

"Oh, daddy!" Elisabeth ran to Marie and cried on her shoulder. Herbert climbed up onto the end of his mother's lounge chair. Staring at his father with big eyes, he wondered how a bird could make someone so angry.

Carl turned and swung his legs over to one side of his chair. He now sat facing his family. He knew he loved them but right now everything was too much, the pain in his head, the loss of his livelihood, penniless, homeless, a family staring at him wondering what was wrong?... "I'm sorry, Elisabeth…if you'll excuse me. I need to rest." Carl said void of emotion as he stood up and made his way back to their cabin.

They all sat with their mouths agape as they watched him step through the door that led back into the ship. Tears abated, Elisabeth asked, "Mommy, why was daddy so angry with me?"

"Oh my dear child, your daddy wasn't angry with you. He has been through so much and is thinking about the future and worried about what will happen. When we worry and don't trust God all kinds of dark thoughts can come into our heart…fear, sadness, frustration, anger…and that's what you saw. So we have to encourage daddy to trust in the Lord. Do you remember the bible verse I taught you yesterday?"

"Yes!" said Elisabeth smiling again. "Proverbs 3:5-6. Trust in the Lord with all thine heart; and lean not unto thine own understanding. In all thy ways acknowledge him, and he shall direct thy paths."

"Very well done, Elisabeth." Marie said encouragingly. "Now let's pray for daddy."

That evening after the children were tucked into their bunks, Marie prayed before approaching her troubled husband. She sat on the bed next to him as he laid on his side. Turned away from her, staring at the wall of the cabin, Carl knew she was there but was in no mood to acknowledge her presence. She touched his arm. "Carl we need to talk… You're pushing us further and further away…I will not let you continue down such a dark path." With still no response, Marie kept on. "Do you remember what you said when I told you I was pregnant with Christa?"

Silence. "I asked you if we would always be so blessed." Silence. "You replied, 'We may or may not be. But we will always remember the great things God has done for us.'"

Carl slowly turned to face her. "I remember saying that, Marie…but there's a difference between saying it and actually living it out. I had everything a man could want—a good job, a good neighborhood to raise the children, plenty of money, my health for the most part…then God took it all away in an instant. Why?" Carl ended with anger in his voice. He pushed himself up into a sitting position adjusting pillows behind him to ease the pressure on his still healing back. His migraine gone, he thought by keeping quiet he could evade her questioning. Now when he heard his own words spoken back to him—he felt he had to respond…to explain himself.

Marie sat next to him with her Bible open on her lap. "I don't have all the answers, Carl, but I know where we can find them. Will you listen to what God has to say?"

"I'm all ears," Carl said sarcastically.

Ignoring his tone, Marie continued. "Let's see…some of the things that have happened to you remind me of another man in the Old Testament." Marie turned the pages to the chapter of Job.

"Yes, here it is. Job, in a matter of minutes—not months—he lost everything—livestock, friends, children, his health, to name a few. After this happened he said, '…Naked came I out of my mother's womb, and naked shall I return thither: the Lord gave, and the Lord hath taken away; blessed be the name of the Lord. Job 1:21.'"

Carl let out a long sigh.

Marie continued paging back to the New Testament. "1 Peter 1:6-7, Wherein ye greatly rejoice, though now for a season, if need be, ye are in heaviness through manifold temptations: That the trial of your faith, being much more precious than of gold that perisheth, though it be tried with fire, might be found unto praise and honour and glory at the appearing of Jesus Christ." "Here's another, 'And we know that all things work together for good to them that love God, to them who are called according to his purpose. Romans 8:28.'"

"Marie…" Carl tried to interrupt.

Marie pretended not to hear him. "And remember, Carl, the battle we fight, 'For we wrestle not against flesh and blood, but against principalities, against powers, against the rulers of the darkness of this world, against spiritual wickedness in high places. Ephesians 6:12'"

"Are you done?" Carl asked inquisitively.

"No, but you can speak now." Marie smiled looking up from her Bible with a bold stare.

Carl loved how she challenged him in his faith. The verses she read to him hit hard and convicted him of his anger toward God. "Marie, I know my sin of being angry with God and questioning His wisdom for what has happened to me—to us as a family… I still struggle with 'why?'" Carl said with his eyes closed and head bent down in remorse.

"I don't have an answer, but here is a verse that may help. 'O the depth of the riches both of the wisdom and knowledge of God! How unsearchable are his judgments, and his ways past finding out! For who hath known the mind of the Lord? Or who hath been his counsellor? Or who hath first given to him, and it shall be recompensed unto him again? For of him, and through him, and to him, are all things: to whom be glory for ever. Amen. Romans 11:33-36'"

Marie closed the Bible. "Carl, you see it's not about us making money, or children, having a house, the things of this life—although these are wonderful blessings—but it's God completing His work in us. In return we believe and trust in His word, fear and honor Him above all else and love Him because He first loved us." "'Why?' You ask," Marie added. My answer is 'Trust Him.'"

"Trust Him?" Carl responded.

"Yes. You can count on Him. He can't lie. His word is above His name it will never fail. And He likes it when we remind Him of it. He will never leave you or forsake you, He loves you, He wants the best for you. He died for you so you could have eternal life. This life is so short, Carl, the most important thing is to have faith and love and pass it on to your children and anyone else who will listen. Hardships have come into our lives, but we have so much to be thankful for." Marie's gaze drifted across the room to the sleeping children. She looked back at Carl who's eyes were filled with tears. "I know you know these things my dearest. I'm here to remind you of them. I pray the light and power of God's word has shed light on the lies of the enemy."

"It has my love, it has." Carl wept. "Forgive me."

"I already have. Let's go to the Father now in prayer and confess our sins together." They prayed then worshiped together with Marie's accompaniment on the lute. Softly so as not to wake the children, they sang a new hymn that had been introduced to them at their church in Dover, New Jersey. *Great is Thy Faithfulness* was based on Lamentations 3:22-23 and written in 1923.[1] Marie felt it was most appropriate for what they just walked through.

########

A few days later they stood on deck and watched as Germany loomed closer and closer on the horizon. It brought tears to both of them as they watched their motherland come into view.

"It's good to be home again," said Carl as he held Herbert bending to kiss Marie on the top of the head.

"Yes, Carl it feels very good," Marie said as she wrapped one arm around him while holding Christa with the other.

"Will grandma and grandpa be there to meet us?" asked Elisabeth.

"No, not in Hamburg, Elisabeth. We'll see them in Hartenstein—that's where we will be living for a while until we find a new home. Your mother's brother, Uncle Gerhard will pick us up in Zwickau and take us there. The train tracks are being repaired that lead to Hartenstein so your uncle with be picking us up by horse and wagon, then we will go to Hartenstein. The train ride to Zwickau with the children was exhausting. As they pulled into the station, Marie's heart leapt. Gerhard stood waiting for them on the platform. It felt so good to see someone familiar—especially family.

"Look children, there's uncle Gerhard!" Marie said pointing out the window.

Elisabeth jumped off her Father's lap to take a look. Herbert soon followed. There, on the platform, they saw a man waving. "Look mommy!"

squealed two and half year old Herbert. "He looks just like his picture, except a little skinnier," said Elisabeth.

"Come now, children," said Carl. "Each of you can carry a little something to help."

Stepping out of the train, they were greeted with bear hugs from Gerhard. He was careful to do as his mother told him and not hug Carl too hard. "And look at you, little princess," Gerhard said taking her hand in his and and spinning her around. "The last time I saw you, you were just a bundle of blankets in your mother's arms. My, how you've grown."

Baby Christa let out a happy gurgle as she watched her uncle play with her sister.

Letting go of Elisabeth, Gerhard squatted down to look at Herbert who was holding his father's hand. "What have we here? A son who's the spitting image of his father me thinks. Did you enjoy your trip across the ocean boy?"

Herbert shook his head no.

"Hmm," said Gerhard. "Would you like to see a large farm horse?"

Herbert shook his head yes, very vigorously.

"Well how about you come with me and we'll lead the way for the family," Gerhard said as he scooped him up with one arm and grabbed the largest of their bags with the other.

Herbert let out a joyful belt of squeals and giggles. Marie hadn't heard Herbert laugh in so long—it made her laugh too. She looked at Carl who was smiling back at her and laughing himself.

"Looks like our children have found a new friend," Carl said as he watched Elisabeth run after her uncle and brother.

"Poor Christa, left alone with mommy and daddy," Marie said as she made a sad face to the daughter she held in her arms. Christa cooed back.

"She'll be running after them soon enough. Right my little shatzi,[2]" Carl said as he tickled her under her chin.

"And you'll be the one chasing after her to see she doesn't get into trouble, I'm sure." Marie said, knowing Christa held a special place in his heart.

Carl winked at her agreeing.

Marie picked up a suitcase, then put the strap of the lute over her other shoulder. It reminded her of how she had crossed the Atlantic with Elisabeth—six short years ago. Carl gathered the rest of their belongings and followed Marie who followed Elisabeth who followed Gerhard through the busy station and out to their waiting horse and wagon.

After Gerhard introduced Herbert to the old draft horse that would be taking them back to Hartenstein, he handed him up to Carl. The three of them sat on the front bench with Herbert sitting between them. Marie, holding Christa, sat with Elisabeth in the bed of the wagon. It was mid-March, and while the temperature was cool it wasn't freezing— with the sun out it was almost warm.

"Can we take a moment and stop and see Clara at the bakery?" he asked Gerhard and Marie.

"Wouldn't feel right if we didn't," said Gerhard. "I'm sure she's heard of your return through the church grapevine."

"Yes, I can guarantee that," Marie said looking up at her husband. They both laughed.

"Besides, times have changed. People are calling it the 'Golden Age of Weimar.'[3] Food and jobs are more plentiful now. Clara is baking with wheat flour and even making desserts again. You came home at a good time," Gerhard said as he snapped the reins to move the old mare forward.

"Yum!" yelled Elisabeth. "I like desserts!"

"Then I guess it's unanimous, to Clara's bakery we go," Carl said as he tousled Herbert's hair.

Clara came rushing out the bakery door with two baskets of food along with 2 containers of beer. "My goodness look at you!" she said in amazement. "Blessed by the good Lord above you are," she said as she placed the baskets into the back of the wagon. "Look at you, my little liebling.4 Come give Clara a hug," she held her arms open for Elisabeth.

Marie nodded to her daughter, encouraging her to trust a woman she had never seen before.

Elisabeth hesitantly leaned over the side of the wagon and hugged Clara. She smelled so good. Like fresh baked bread and cookies. Elisabeth decided she liked her…a lot. Next was Christa. Marie handed their 9 month bundle of joy over to Clara.

"Such beautiful children, and all so healthy," Clara planted a kiss on one of her chubby cheeks before handing her back to Marie.

"And who might this be!?" Clara looked up at Herbert who now stood in his father's lap. Looking down at the largest woman he had ever seen, Herbert clung to his father uncertain of what to make of the situation. Carl removed his arm from around his neck, and slowly handed him down to Clara. Seeing his fear, she said, "Now, now, what have we here?" Pulling a large sugar cookie out of her apron, Herbert took it from her and began to eat the most delicious thing he had ever tasted in his young life.

"Hmmmm," a hum of satisfaction came out of his mouth while he ate.

Watching him take large bites with sugar and crumbs landing on his shirt, gave her the satisfaction that she was still a good baker. Children were always the best judges of her bakery items—always forthright and honest. Placing a peck of a kiss on top of his head she handed Herbert back up to Carl. Grabbing hold of Marie's and Carl's free hands - as they both held their children - Clara prayed over them…for their safe journey, their future, and the Lord's richest blessings upon them all. "Now off with you! It's getting late and you have a 2 hour ride to Hartenstein. Give your mother and father my love!" Clara yelled as the wagon moved forward down the street.

########

After an hour of travel they stopped to enjoy Clara's baskets of goodies. It was late in the afternoon. The children were tired from the long journey and slept peacefully, covered in blankets in the back of the wagon.

"It's so good to see things that you thought you'd never see again," Marie looked out over the mountains and valley below them. "That includes you, dear brother."

"I feel the same Marie—about Carl too and the children. I know it wasn't the best of circumstances that brought you back, but I'm so glad the good Lord did." Gerhard's eyes filled with tears. "We missed you."

"We missed everyone too, Gerhard—it took coaxing from Marie and a good word from the Lord to see the sunny side of the situation." Carl laughed while picking up Marie's hand and kissing it. "Now, we're ready— trusting that whatever He has in store will be the best for us."

########

Several hours later they pulled into Hartenstein. The town was quiet for the most part— a few people walking by, recognized them and welcomed them home. Most were inside preparing their evening meal. It was only Thursday—Sunday would bring the full barrage of hugs and a welcome home celebration.

As they pulled up to her parent's house, Marie was overwhelmed with emotion. Her father was first to come out the front door, then her mother. "Oh, pa," she said as tears of joy ran down her cheeks. Her father pulled out a handkerchief from his pocket, wiping them away just as he had done when she was little. It was such a comfort. Marie wondered if one ever outgrew the love and care of a parent. He reached out his arms to hold Christa as Marie passed her to him.

"Come, grandma, look at the pumpkin I've just found." Everyone laughed. Carl handed Herbert down to Anna. As she held him, Herbert looked at her wondering if she had a cookie hidden somewhere like Clara.

"Cookie?" asked Herbert.

"No. But I have something sweeter." She then proceeded to smother him in kisses before he squirmed out of her arms. They all laughed even harder than before.

"Now where is my princess?" Anna walked to the side of the wagon and lifted Elisabeth down. "You've grown so tall and are even more beautiful than I remember—just like your mother."

"And she can sing and play the lute too," added Marie.

"Oh my, I will look forward to hearing that during this evening's devotions," said Anna with genuine anticipation.

Carl jumped down from his wagon seat and scooped Herbert into his arms. They headed toward the front door. "How about if we check out your new room?" Elisabeth came alongside and went with them into the house.

Gerhard had already unloaded their luggage and was right behind Carl and the children with his arms full of suitcases. "Now give me my little one,⁵" Anna said while taking Christa from her husband. Marie's father, Paul, reached up to help his daughter down from the wagon. Once on solid ground Marie hugged him, then reached out to hold her mother's hand. She looked at them with sincerity, "I've missed you both so much."

Paul placed his hand on Marie's shoulder. She noticed that the crinkles near his eyes kept his tears from trickling over. "My dear daughter, we are so glad to have you and Carl and the children back with us. You have been through so much. Your mother and I are looking forward to helping you get back on your feet. Our home is your home for as long as you need it."

"Thank you, pa, thank you, ma," we are forever grateful.

########

The next Sunday friends and family came from the surrounding towns to welcome them back to Germany. It was a family reunion of sorts. Carl's married brothers and sisters introduced their spouses and his new nieces and nephews. When he first saw his mother and father outside the church before the service started, he almost didn't recognize them. It had only been 6 years, but somehow they had shrunk and become…old. He was now taller than they were. He embraced them both, one in each arm, and couldn't stop the tears from streaming down his face.

"My son, my son, how much we have prayed for you. How blessed we are that God has heard our prayers and brought you all safely home." Anna pulled her son toward her and kissed him on both his cheeks.

His father looked at him and smiled saying, "You look good, son, you look good," while patting him on the shoulder. "From what Marie wrote in her letters I thought the worst."

"No worries, pa. I'm pretty well healed up—the worst damage was to my back—no more lifting hay bales for me. But thank the Lord my hands are still good for artwork." Carl said while looking over their heads for someone.

"Marie, over here!" Carl yelled over the crowd that had formed in front of the church. Everyone wanted to hear the stories of their time in America and to see the children.

"Oh look at this bouquet of goodness, right from the Lord's hand," Anna reached to take Christa from Marie's arms.

"You must be Herbert, because you look just like your father," Emil said as he pinched Herbert's cheek. "And Elisabeth, my how you've grown - you're as pretty as your mother and I hear you have her talents too."

Elisabeth shook her head yes in response. The church bells started ringing, signifying the start of the service. "Come along everyone. Time to give thanks for all God's goodness," Carl said to those around him.

"Amen," added Marie.

########

Several weeks passed with a flurry of activity. Paul encouraged Carl to reapply for his government pension now that he was back in Germany and the economy was improving. Marie started giving piano, guitar, and voice lessons again. Looking up old clients, Carl did his best to find calligraphy and sign work. He traveled to nearby towns taking along a portfolio of his work. Many times not arriving home until late, Marie would always wait up for him. Somehow, though things seemed undeniably hopeless, there remained a burning flame of hope inside them both.

One night after returning from a particularly long and fruitless journey, Carl paused at the door of the house. He tilted his head back and looked up at the stars. "I trust you, God." Just like that, the weight of the world was lifted off his shoulders as he entered the house.

########

It was a bright sunny morning in July and Carl had decided to walk downtown to pick up the mail and a local paper. A few letters had arrived for Marie from the Ladies Aid in Dover, New Jersey.

"What's this?" Carl said out loud to a letter with his name on it. He stepped outside and tore open the envelope it looked very official. He read the letter…

Dear Mr. Tittel…Thank you for faithfully serving your country. A monthly stipend has been determined considering your years of service and war injury… please find a check for the amount of…Carl had to sit down. He was going to faint.

"Oh my God, Oh my God how Great thou art," was all he could manage to whisper. The check was for much more than he could have ever dreamed. More than enough for living expenses—they could now save for the future. Carl ran back to the house. Bursting in, he saw Marie standing by the kitchen table, her mother making breakfast, while her father was coming down the stairs.

"What's all the ruckus about?" Paul asked.

"That's just what I was about to say," added Marie.

Carl approached Marie and pulled a chair out from the table placing it behind her.

"Do you want me to sit?" she asked.

"Believe me you will want to after you read this," Carl said as he handed Marie the letter he had just opened.

Marie took it and began to read to herself. Her parents came close and stood by her. 'Dear Mr. Tittel…' she continued reading the short message then looked at the check. Marie screamed and plopped down into the chair.

"I told you, you would want to sit down." Carl said grinning at her.

Anna and Paul said together, "What is it? What is it?"

Marie held the letter in the air for them to see for themselves. "It's a miracle!" yelled Anna. "Thank God from whom all blessings flow," said Paul.

Marie held her head in her hands. "Lord, we are so thankful for your rich supply." Standing she looked Carl in the eyes and said, "I never had a doubt."

As she wrapped her arms around him he whispered in her ear, "I know my love, I know."

########

After a few days of searching they found an apartment complex not far from Marie's parent's house. The Schettler's had 4 boys around the same age as their children. Marie liked the idea of living near another mom—someone she could ask for advice and share recipes with.

Much like their apartment in America, it had two bedrooms, a living room, and a kitchen. Marie's parents were happy to bless them with the furniture that was in Marie's old room. Other friends pitched in, and before long they had a crib for Christa and two beds for Herbert and Elisabeth—a couch and a kitchen table with chairs soon followed.

"Well what do you think?" asked Carl. "City water, flushing toilets, a galvanized tub with a washboard...What more could a woman want?...well...maybe a washing machine...a sewing machine." "And you shall have them, someday soon," said Carl as he laid Christa down in her crib. "I promise, Mrs. Tittel you will have your machines."

Marie laughed as she hugged him from behind. They both looked down on the sleeping baby. "It's moments like these that I treasure and remember when the hard times come," Marie said quietly.

"I can only hope 'hard times' leave us alone for awhile," Carl turned and looked down at her. "But no matter what, I will always trust that God will carry us through to the end."

########

Summer passed by swiftly. September came with Elisabeth excited for her first day of school. "Look daddy, mommy made me a new dress for my first day." Elisabeth spun around in front of her father.

"You look like a princess," Carl said laying down the morning paper. "And mommy did a wonderful job of sewing it by hand." He looked up at Marie. "Is there anything you can't do?"

"Make rye bread like your mother."

Carl laughed. "But you come *pretty* close," he said teasingly.

Marie whipped him with a dish towel. As he jumped out of his seat and out of the way of another attack, Elisabeth joined him at the door. "Now out with you. Walk Elisabeth to school before the bell rings. She shouldn't be late on her first day."

########

September moved to October. In their morning and evening devotions they always remembered the miracle of Carl's pension and thanked the Lord for such a bountiful blessing. Having money saved in the bank made them feel secure, but they knew where *true* security came from and that was their faith in Jesus. They knew whatever storm would come, they had an anchor that would never fail.

As the end of October approached that anchor would be tested. Carl opened the morning paper. It was October 30, 1929, and the news wasn't good. Marie looked over at Carl while she was cooking and noticed his face turning white. "Carl are you okay," Marie said with concern. She went and sat down next to him.

"I'm okay but I fear that our country isn't." He showed Marie the headlines. *United States Stock Market Crashes*. "What does this mean, Carl?"

"It means that the 'Golden Age of Weimar' is over. It means we need to pray. Things may get pretty bad again with food and job shortages.[6]"

"What about your pension?" Marie said worriedly.

"That's another reason we need to pray." Carl took Marie's hand. "He has supplied our every need so far and watched over us as a family. He isn't going to stop now." Marie and Carl prayed with passion for their country, their children, their provisions, and their future.

Afterwards, Marie looked at her husband squinting her eyes trying to decide if it was a good time to say something. "I'm not sure this is a good time," she said slowly.

"A good time for what?" asked Carl.

"Well… with all the bad news, would you like some good news?" hinted Marie.

"I always like good news, Marie—what is it?"

"Well, it's not an *it*. It's a baby."

"A what!" Carl yelled.

"A B A B Y." Marie spelled out.

"Marie, that is the best news—in the middle of the worst news—a blessing. How good is God's timing."

Marie got up from her chair and sat in his lap. "You bless me with your loving attitude you know. Any other man would have had a nervous breakdown— hearing the stock market had crashed and his wife is pregnant the same day."

"Well it just so happens, that I have a wife who has taught me that no matter what happens, you can always trust that the maker of the universe has everything in His hand. That includes stock market crashes and babies, I believe."

"Carl Rudolph Tittel, I love you," she said as she kissed him on his forehead.

"I love you more, my angel," Carl said as he returned a kiss.

Marie stood up to finish cooking breakfast.

"So when are we due?" asked Carl.

"End of May. I'll make a special dinner tonight and we can tell the children afterwards."

"Oh, Elisabeth will be so happy. She loves babies. It will be great fun telling them," Carl said as he got up to get Christa out of her crib.

"Rise and shine children. It's time to face the day!"

########

With the slap on the bottom, the baby could be heard crying down the hall of their apartment building. Herbert raced back down to their apartment door along with 3 of the neighbor boys. He so hoped it was a brother so he could have someone like the Schettler boys to play with. Quietly opening the door he entered in leaving his friends behind.

"Is it a boy, daddy?" Herbert asked pulling on his father's pant leg to get his attention.

Marie's mother and father were there, along with Mrs. Schettler, the midwife, and their pastor's wife. "She's a beautiful baby girl and her name is Ruth," Carl said looking down into a disappointed face.

Herbert sighed. "Maybe next time it's a boy, daddy?"

"Yes…maybe next time, son."

Herbert ran back out to his friends waiting in the hallway. "It's a girl," Herbert said dejectedly.

"Awwww," the Schettler boys said together.

"But dad says maybe next time it will be a boy."

"Yeeeeah!" the Schettler boys shouted once again—now with Herbert joining them—as they celebrated the *someday* promise of the birth of another boy.

########

After Ruth's birth they needed a larger place to live. Carl's pension had continued to come in regularly every month even though the economy was suffering. So praying and stepping forward in faith they moved into a large duplex. This had 4 small bedrooms on the second floor, with a large kitchen and small formal and informal living room on the first floor. Moving was hard for Herbert. He missed the Schettler boys. Marie promised him she would take him over to visit once they were settled.

in the Fall On the other side of the duplex lived the Schott family. A nice couple—Mrs. Schott was expecting her first baby any day. Marie hoped they could strike up a friendship like they had with Mrs. Schettler.

########

Several years passed and Marie and Carl fell into the routine of caring for their children while looking for work to compensate their income. Marie now had her parent's piano so she continued to give music lessons while Carl watched the children. Not being able to work because of his physical injuries, he continued to do calligraphy and pen and ink drawings at home for local churches and families.

It was January, 1932, and Carl had been reading about a new man in politics and this man scared him. Maybe not the man himself, but his ideas, and not just his ideas but the way he captivated people and they became enraptured with his ideology. The German people were hungry for change and someone to blame for all their troubles. Adolf Hitler gave them answers that weren't right, but he made them seem so appealing—so many people were caught up in his charisma. A group of radical nationalists, Carl thought, if someone didn't stop them they would someday, very soon, step into power.[7]

"God have mercy on us if that ever happens," thought Carl. "The country's in enough mess without a lunatic running it."

In October, Marie was halfway to her goal of 10 children with the birth of Sigrid. While Herbert was greatly disappointed by the news, his sisters rejoiced at having a new girlfriend in their midst. Elisabeth was getting old enough to help with the chores of caring for the children and was a great help to Marie.

########

Hitler came into power in 1933. Marie and Carl listened to his fervent speeches on the radio at night and later discussed them. It was hard for them to believe that a leader of a country supported the idea of persecuting and demonizing an entire race of people—not to mention their fellow countrymen who supported him. Their faith taught them differently. All men were created equal— all men were made by God and were loved by Him. The Lutheran church they attended in Hartenstein thought the same. Their church did not succumb as other churches to preaching the ideals of

Hitler as truth from the pulpit. In 1934, as Hitler gained power, the Tittel family gained a new member. Paul-Gerhard was born on April 3rd. Although the pregnancy and delivery went smoothly, Marie felt an exhaustion she had never felt before with the other babies and her right side was tingling and numb right after the delivery. She forgot everything as soon as the midwife handed Paul-Gerhard to her. The moment she looked into his eyes she knew he was special. He was so little. She wanted to hold him and never let him go. He was her little liebling. Carl reached down to pick him up.

"What do you think, Carl?"

"I think he's about 6 pounds 10 ounces, and that Herbert will be very happy."

"No, silly. Look at him. You can see destiny, there's something special in this little boy."

"Hmmmm." Carl looked closer at the tiny bundle. Paul looked back. "I just see a little baby, Marie. I know that God has a special plan for each of us and that together we will pray for his destiny and hopefully *someday* see him step into it." Carl looked down at his sleeping wife. He quietly carried Paul to the rocker beside their bed. Gently rocking, he softly sang "Great is Thy Faithfulness" to his newborn son.

1. Great is Thy Faithfulness. Written by Thomas Obadiah Chisolm (1866-1960)

    Refrain:
    Great is Thy faithfulness!
    Great is Thy faithfulness!

Morning by morning new mercies I see.
All I have needed Thy hand hath provided;
Great is Thy faithfulness, Lord, unto me!

Great is Thy faithfulness, O God my Father;
There is no shadow of turning with Thee;
Thou changest not, Thy compassions, they fail not;
As Thou hast been, Thou forever will be.
Refrain:
Summer and winter and springtime and harvest,

Sun, moon and stars in their courses above

Join with all nature in manifold witness
To Thy great faithfulness, mercy and love.
Refrain:
Pardon for sin and a peace that indureth
Thine own dear presence to cheer and to guide;
Strength for today and bright hope for tomorrow,
Blessing all mine, with ten thousand beside!
Refrain:

http://www.sharefaith.com/guide/Chrisitan-Music/hymns-the-songs-and-the-stories/
great-is-thy-faithfullness-the-song-and-the-story.html

2. Schatzi - means treasure

3. The years 1924-29 are often described as the 'Golden Age of Weimar' because of their stability, economic security and improved living standards
http://alphahistory.com/weimarrepublic/golden-age-of-weimar/

4. Liebling - means darling

5. By the end of 1929 around 1.5 million Germans were out of work; within a year this figure had more than doubled By early 1933 unemployment in Germany had reached a staggering 6 million.

   http://alphahistory.com/weimarrepublic/great-depression/

6. The story of Nazi Germany has fascinated and appalled millions of people. The Nazis were a group of radical nationalists who came to power in Germany in 1933. Led by Adolf Hitler, they presented themselves as a new political option, but instead promised old ideas: authoritarianism, nationalism, military power and racial purity

   http://alphahistory.com/nazigermany/

Chapter Four: Life in the Duplex

August 2, 1934, only four months after the birth of Paul-Gerhard, Carl flipped open the daily newspaper and shook his head at the headlines: "President Paul L. von Hindenburg Dies, Adolf Hitler becomes Fuhrer."[1]

"The last time you looked like that, the New York stock exchange had fallen—and I told you I was pregnant." Marie poured more coffee into his cup as he looked at her with a raised eyebrow. "No, we are not expecting," she said with a smile. "Paul is only four months old, silly." She turned to yell up the stairs to the children. "Herbert, Christa, Ruth…come and get your breakfast!"

Marie looked over at the formal living room and watched as Elisabeth rocked Paul in his cradle with her foot while dressing Sigrid who sat on the couch. At twelve years old she had become an invaluable helper. Carl looked up at Marie, "The times we live in. I think I would worry myself to death if it weren't for my faith, and you and the children."

"That bad?" Marie said as she scooped scrambled eggs onto 5 more plates.

"Won't be long before another war, I'm sure of it. A man as hungry for power as Hitler—and with such radical beliefs…I fear for our country and the German people." Carl closed the paper and looked at Marie with concern.

"Sounds like we need an encouraging word Carl. What's the scripture for this morning's devotions?" Marie said as she placed a piece of toast on everyone's plate.

The children could be heard clamoring down the stairs. Elisabeth carried Sigrid over to the table and sat her in her high chair. Marie gathered Paul from his cradle as the rest of the family filled their seats.

"Psalm 121[2]—-"how appropriate," said Carl to himself. "Listen, children to what the Lord has to say." Carl read the psalm, along with the days reading, followed by prayer. Marie looked down at their bowed heads as she stood by the table holding Paul. She took in one of the rare moments of calm that a mother has. Looking at the beauty of the family that surrounded her, she thanked the Lord for giving her so much. She bent and kissed Paul's cheek. "My little liebling," she said softly as she looked down at his sweet face. Paul cooed and smiled. As the others prayed, she prayed a special prayer over his life and destiny. She knew the times they lived in were uncertain—but knew the most *certain* thing they could always depend on was the Word of God and His promises.

########

It was January, 1936, and it would prove to be a very eventful year for the Tittel family. Several years had passed and during this time they enjoyed the tranquility of their daily routine. Morning devotions, school, chores, homework, a combined music lesson and evening worship in the informal living room—this schedule filled their lives. There were family picnics and many church gatherings too—life seemed quiet and almost normal, except when Carl turned the radio on at night and they listened to a man whose speeches bordered on hysteria.

As Hitler grew in power, the tentacles of his reach finally touched the small town of Hartenstein. Marie and Carl noticed a difference in the text books the children brought home. All public schools now taught students love for Hitler, obedience to state authority, militarism, racism, and antisemitism.[3] Many nights were spent with their three oldest—Elisabeth,

Herbert, and Christa—discussing the word of God and then comparing it to Hitler's doctrine. They decided as a family—as they started to hear of the persecution of those who did not follow the regimes beliefs—to keep their personal faith amongst themselves. So the children grew up attending public school and Hitler youth,[4] but, within the confines of family and church, continued to grow in faith and in love with a Merciful Savior and not a crazed dictator as the Lord of their lives.

########

Early one morning there came a loud knock on the Tittel's door.

"I got it!" yelled Herbert as he ran down stairs.

"Not quite!" yelled Christa as she jumped up from her chair in the kitchen. Beating him by seconds she flung the door open just as Herbert ran to her side. They were both surprised to see their grandparents Anna and Paul. "Come in," said Christa.

"I'll get mom and dad," said Herbert seeing the serious looks on their faces, knowing it was probably not good news.

Christa took their coats and had them sit in the formal living room. "I'll put some coffee on, and be right back," she said as she went to hang up their coats and then to the kitchen to get the coffee started. Carl was already half way down the stairs when Herbert caught him.

"It's Oma and Opa,[5] they're in the living room waiting to speak with you and mom," Herbert said looking up at his father as he came down the stairs.

Carl turned and yelled up to Marie, "Marie, your parents are here and need to speak with us!"

"Be right down!"

It was Saturday, Elisabeth, Ruth, and Sigrid were in the informal living room practicing their lutes. They stopped when they heard the knock at the door and joined their grandparents. Elisabeth hugged them both before going to help Christa with the coffee. Sigrid climbed into her grandfather's lap, while Ruth squeezed between them to sit next to her grandmother. Herbert sat across from his grandfather on the piano bench—wondering what the reason was for their special visit.

A few moments later Marie joined them carrying Paul-Gerhard. She embraced them both then sat in a chair next to her mother. "So tell us what has happened to bring you out on such a cold day? Not that we don't enjoy your company," Marie said smiling.

Her mother's eyes started to fill with tears as she reached inside her purse to pull out a letter. "We just received this from Hans and Lene." Anna couldn't contain her emotions—she started to sob. The children watched wide eyed as Carl reached forward to give her his kerchief.

Paul took over telling the story. "They have lost everything. Very similar to what you both walked through…there was a fire."

Marie gasped.

"No one was hurt." Paul quickly continued. "But the shoe factory, their house, and belongings are all gone. They literally have only the clothes on their backs and what money they have saved in the bank."

"What are they going to do?" asked Carl.

"The same thing you and Marie did. Come home and start over."

Regaining her composure, Anna continued. "They will live with us until they can either rent or buy a home. I wanted to see the grandchildren, but not under such terrible circumstances…" Anna started crying again.

"Oh mother, be comforted. They will be fine. We are all here to help and encourage them. Look at how God carried us through such difficulties and blessed us with so much more than we had before."

"Yes…yes, you are right, Marie," Anna sighed in relief at her encouragement.

"Let us take time to pray for them and worship," said her father as he got up. Herbert moved from the piano bench to let his grandfather sit down, then ran to get his harmonica. The girls went to get their lutes and guitars.

The evening was filled with powerful prayers, moving worship, wonderful food, and smothered with love.

As the winter months faded so did the sadness and tragedy of the fire that took Hans' and Lenes' factory and home in America. March brought them home to Hartenstein and to a church welcome home celebration. Over a hundred people came to the little town to celebrate the homecoming of one of their own.

Hans quickly fell into his old routine of helping his father at the shoe factory. Marie's father was getting older and discussed passing the business onto him and Gerhard but Carl had no interest in it. He was more interested in getting a job at the local textile factory that would offer a better income. Lene took care of the family—they now had 5 children with another on the way. Soon they were settled in a house of their own. Marie thought it almost seemed like they had never left. The dream of living in America had slipped away from them like the morning mist on the mountains, evaporated by the warmth of the sun. It was a sight to see, but life was still beautiful without it. But having had a taste of what Lady Liberty offered she could only hope that it wouldn't be so elusive a dream for their children.

########

The month of April brought another knock at the door. This time it was Carl's family.

"Johanna, come in!" said Carl, surprised to see his younger sister accompanied by a handsome young man.

"Good to see you, dear brother," Johanna said as she embraced him. "I would like you to meet Renard."

"Welcome to our home, Renard," Carl shook his hand while leading them into the living room.

"Marie, come see who's here to visit!" Carl hollered upstairs. Marie could be heard coming swiftly down the stairs. The children were at school and she had just put Paul down for a nap.

"Johanna! How good to see you!" Marie said as she gave her a welcoming hug. "And who might this handsome young man be?" She held out her hand for Renard to shake it.

"Renard, this is my sister-in-law Marie." Johanna said as Marie and Renard shook hands.

"Would you like some coffee or tea?" Marie offered as they all sat down.

"Oh no thank you," said Johanna. "We must be leaving shortly to catch the train to Zwickau. You see…"

"Johanna, let me finish," interrupted Renard. "Carl, I've asked your sister to be my wife."

"Oh what wonderful news!" exclaimed Marie.

"Congratulations to both of you," said Carl.

"Thank you," they said unanimously. Renard continued, "That's why we're catching the train. You see, I'm from Leipzig and that's where we plan to be married. Johanna is going to live with my parents while I finish renovating the house we will live in. We're planning a September wedding…although I wish it were sooner." Renard reached for Johanna's hand and she took it, blushing slightly.

"I'm so happy for you, little sister, is there anything we can do for you?" said Carl looking at Marie.

"Yes—we know what it's like starting out with nothing," Marie chimed in.

"Actually, that's one of the reasons why we're here," Johanna said looking at the floor. What she was about to ask weighed heavily on her heart. If they couldn't help she didn't know of anyone else who could. She took a deep breath and continued, "You know that for the past fifteen years I have been living with mom and dad—helping take care of them. They are both well in their 70's now and need help with everyday tasks. When I think of leaving them…"

Carl could see the tears welling up in her eyes.

"Johanna, I understand," Carl said while she rested her head on Renard's shoulder.

"I've asked everyone else in the family—no one has the room or the resources to care of them. Father and Mother are just too old to be by themselves, let alone manage the daily affairs of a house. Is there anyway the two of you could take them in? I love them so much…I don't want to see them in a state facility.[6]"

Carl looked at Marie who had been looking at Johanna the whole time.

"Marie and I would have to discuss…"

"It would be an honor," said Marie, without even pausing to look at Carl.

"Marie…" said Carl, filled with compassion for his wife who already had a day filled with chores and children.

Marie looked at him with the strength and determination of a woman who had made up her mind. There was no arguing.

Carl continued, "…I… we will gladly accept the responsibility of caring for them. Thank you, Johanna for all that you've done already. I will make plans immediately to have them and their belongings moved here."

"Thank you both so much," Johanna stood up and hugged her brother and Marie. Renard shook their hands.

"Oh here," Marie said as she pulled Renard into her arms. You're family now and only hugs will do.

########

May was a month of transition, as the family adjusted to having their Oma and Opa living with them. Since Carl worked at home from a small desk in their bedroom, he would wake up early and help his parents dress and get ready for the day. Marie depended on Elisabeth to help get the girls and Paul ready, while she prepared breakfast for the family of ten. Elisabeth and Christa along with 6 year old Ruth would help set the table. Four-year-old Sigrid would play with Paul in the formal living room, to keep him out from underfoot—from the swirl of activities in the kitchen.

Herbert did the heavier chores of bringing in buckets of water from the well out back so they could brush their teeth and wash their faces. Each of the upstairs and downstairs bathrooms had a flushing toilet but no sink or bathtub with running water. A standing wash basin was used, with two buckets underneath—one for the used water and one for the fresh. Every morning and evening he emptied the buckets of used water into their garden in the backyard. Bath night meant double duty, filling and emptying the large galvanized bathtub with water. The coal bin in the kitchen needed constant refilling too, with so many mouths to feed, especially in the winter when the coal stove ran continually to heat the house.

Once Emil and Anna were readied for the day by Carl, they would each do a simple task. Although they had arthritic joints, Emil swept the downstairs floor and Anna, being less sure on her feet, folded clothes. Each member of the family had chores to do to help keep the household running.

Marie felt as if things were just beginning to settle down into a manageable routine, when she felt a familiar flutter. Sitting at the kitchen table while peeling potatoes, she set the knife down and held her stomach… and waited…there it was again. It was the confirmation she had been waiting for—having missed her last three menses. She smiled to herself. Oh, how she loved children. The joy of being a mother never left her heart. The thought of having another baby, even though she already had six, was just as exciting as the first one. "Now," she thought "how do I tell Carl we need a bigger house."

Carl received the news of another baby by sweeping Marie off her feet and then plopping down on the living room couch with her on his lap.

Marie laughed, "Carl Rudolf Tittel, the last time you did that was on our wedding day!"

"And what a day that was!" He tickled her and she laughed even more.

He looked down into her dark brown eyes. "I love you, my dear sweet angel. I thank my Lord for you always. Here, when I think I can't be blessed anymore, comes another gift straight from the Father's heart to us."

"I couldn't agree more, Carl. But, I've been thinking…with the birth of baby number seven…and the size of this house…."

Carl put his finger to her lips. "Don't say another word. I was going to show them to you at Christmas, but since it seems like a time to reveal wonderful surprises to each other, I have one of my own." Placing Marie on the couch, he ran upstairs and retrieved a large cardboard tube. Coming back down, he opened it and pulled out several large white papers spreading them out on the coffee table in front of her.

"Carl, what is it?"

"Look closer, Marie."

Marie looked at the structure drawn on the paper. She noticed other pages and lifted each one looking at the layout of each floor. "Carl, is this what I think it is? It looks like a house."

"Yes, Marie. A big house for a big family."

Marie jumped up from her seat. "Eeeeeeek! A new house! How?!"

"I've been saving for quite a while now. I still need another year to put more money away—construction should start in September of 1938. We will be able to move in, the spring of 1939."

Marie sat down and shook her head in disbelief. "Carl, this reminds me of the tickets you bought for me and the children to come back to Germany. You know what I'm thinking before I even say it."

"You know what they say…after you've lived together long enough you can finish each other's sentences and you even start to look like one another," Carl said with a wink.

"Well," said Marie grinning, "You had better start growing your hair longer because I definitely don't want to start looking like you."

They both laughed loudly.

Emil came out of their bedroom, or what used to be the informal living room, with Anna following him. "What's all the noise for?" Emil said with a smile.

"Sounds like good news to me," laughed Anna.

"A new baby coming in October with a new house shortly after," Marie put her arms around Carl's neck and hugged him.

"Tonight there will be a celebration," Marie said looking at Emil and Anna. "So be hungry."

"Does that mean rye bread with sauerbraten?" asked Carl.

Marie stood up and bent down to kiss him on the forehead. "What other meal could I make for such a good husband? And, with your mother here—the rye bread will be perfect."

"I will give you my secret recipe Marie so Carl will never taste the difference again," Anna said as she slowly made her way to the kitchen. "Lord knows it's time. I'm getting old and want to pass it on before He calls me home."

"The children will be ecstatic when they get home from school," said Emil.

"Mom, dad, don't let the cat out of the bag. Let's wait till after supper to tell them."

"Okay, mums the word!" yelled Anna from the kitchen.

Emil was right, the children were ecstatic. Herbert held Paul in his arms after supper and whispered into his ear, "The next baby will be another boy because there are already too many girls. Right Paul?"

"Yah!" was all the two-year-old could manage to say.

The girls were gathered around the blueprints on the coffee table. "Where will the house be built?" asked Elisabeth.

"Not too far from downtown – only a few blocks from Uncle Hans and Aunt Lene's house. It's part of a new housing development that sits on a steep hill overlooking the valley. We'll have city water—that means running toilets, with a bath tub and sink in the bathroom."

"Yeah!" the girls yelled together.

"No more hauling water," sighed Herbert.

Marie and Carl spent the rest of the evening answering their questions. Excited and full of anticipation as much as their children, they enjoyed hearing each of their thoughts on their soon to be, new home.

########

Several months passed. Everyone was looking forward to the first few weeks of August. The summer Olympic games were to be held in Berlin.[7] The Tittel family, along with other relatives and friends gathered in the evenings and on Saturday to listen to the broadcast of the live events. Carl opened up the windows in the living room so the people sitting outside their duplex could hear as well.

They had a house full. Hans and Lene came with their children along with Marie's brother Gerhard too. The children sounded like a herd of animals as they ran up and down the stairs. Marie chided them and told them they had to go outside to play or sit quietly and listen to the broadcast. Even the Schotts came to join them. Although Marie hadn't formed a friendship like she had with Mrs. Schettler, she was still a friendly person to visit with on special occasions. They mostly compared notes on their children. She had a girl born the same time as Ruth and then a boy the same time as Paul-Gerhard. Marie couldn't help but notice how much larger her son was compared to Paul. They were each two and half years old, but Siegfried looked 10 pounds heavier and at least 4 inches taller. "What a healthy boy you have," Marie remarked.

"His father says he's going to be a wrestler when he grows up," Louise replied. "Maybe, even in the Olympics someday."

"Now that would be something to see, Louise—and one never knows—it could happen."

Herbert came outside and sat on the steps next to them. "What kind of name is Louis Zamperini,[8]" asked Herbert.

"Italian I believe," Marie replied. "Why do you ask?"

"They announced him as one of the runners in the 5000 meter and I thought his name was fun to say—it sounds like a pasta…like tortellini," Herbert smiled, adding "I'm glad our last name is Tittel."

"I'm sure he likes his name too, Herbert. You never know, he may even be famous someday—after all, he made it to the Olympics. Who knows what God has planned for his life," Marie said as she pulled him close.

"I hope I get to do great things someday," Herbert said looking up at the sky.

"You will, son, you will," Marie said as she tousled his hair before he ran off with the other children. "And what of you, Paul-Gerhard? I already know that you will do great things too, my little liebling." Marie said as she pulled him into her lap and snuggled him close. Paul giggled as Marie tickled him under his chin.

Louise looked on, almost jealous of the outpouring of love and life that came from such tiny woman.

########

Several months later, in October, Magdalena joined the Tittel family. For Marie it was unlike her previous pregnancies. The birth took a tremendous toll on her body. She was very weak with periods of vertigo. Several weeks later, still barely able to leave her bed, Carl knew it was time for a talk. "Marie, it's time," Carl said as he sat by the side of the bed holding her hand. A tear slid down the side of Marie's face.

"Now, now," he said while wiping the tear away. "You know there are places not far away – havens of rest in the mountains. There you can regain your strength. Besides it's time you were pampered and waited on for once."

"Carl, my place is here with you and the children," Marie said pleadingly.

"Yes, it is, and it will be…after you've rested for several weeks."

"But…" Marie tried to interrupt.

"Marie, I'm not asking you to go – I'm telling you. We will be fine. I've already contacted your good friend Emma and her husband Frank. You know how much they love children - and how Emma has always wanted to come and help you with all your household duties. It'll be great having another man around too - with the same faith and political interests. It will be a tight squeeze, they will sleep in our bed and I'll sleep on the couch in the formal living room-but we'll make it work. I've planned it all out - they will be here while you are away."

Emma was a dear friend that Marie had known since childhood. While Emma and her parents had moved away to the Czech Republic a few years before her and Carl married, they had stayed in touch over the years by writing. Eventually she married her husband Frank Wolny and they settled in Sauerland. Lately she had written asking Marie if they could come for a long holiday. Carl asking them to come and help was actually what Emma had been wanting to do for quite awhile.

"When…?" Marie asked hoping for a few more days at home.

"Tomorrow. I've already made your reservation and will ride with you in the taxi to make sure you're properly settled. Elisabeth will help you pack your bags tonight. Emma and Frank will be here in the morning."

"In such a hurry to get rid of me?"

"No my love. I simply want you to be by my side when we hold our grandchildren." Carl said as he kissed her hand.

########

By January, 1937, Carl was beginning to relax again. Marie had returned home and although she hadn't regained her full strength she did what she could while everyone else did what she couldn't. For Carl, just seeing Marie back on her feet was enough. His life wasn't as bright without her by his side. After Magdalena's birth, he realized how much he depended on her. He couldn't imagine life without her and thought ahead of their senior years together. Hopefully, they would have time to share and reflect as his parents did now. He was mulling over these thoughts while going downstairs to help his mother and father get ready for the day. Opening the door to their room he said a loud, "Good morning, pa!" as he saw his father sitting on the side of his bed trying to pull up his pants.

"Here, let me help you with that," Carl said as he helped his father to a standing position and finished pulling up his pants and closing his belt.

"Thank you, son," said Emil.

"After all the years you helped me as a child, it's a joy to be able to serve you, pa," Carl said, reaching for a comb to smooth some stray hairs.

"I think your mother is sleeping in today, she's usually up before me." Emil said, nodding to the bed next to his.

Carl turned and went to his mother's bed. She was laying on her side, turned away from them. "Ma," Carl said as he slightly shook her blanketed body. As soon as he touched her he knew.

"Oh pa," Carl turned and looked into his father's eyes. Emil knew immediately what was wrong. Carl embraced his father and they wept for a while, before he went into the kitchen to tell Marie of his mother's passing.

#########

The following year, almost to the day, Carl's father passed away quietly the same way. Marie noticed what a toll their deaths had on her husband and wished there was something she could do or say to lighten his grief.

She saw the dark circles under his eyes from lack of sleep, his migraines seemed to come more frequently, and his temper grew short with her and the children. It felt as if a dark cloud had come over the house. It felt as if something were about to break—like the silence before a summer storm – and there was nothing she could do except wait for it to happen.

Both her and Carl had gotten up early. It was Monday morning, and the children weren't downstairs yet. She was cooking breakfast and had just poured him a fresh cup of coffee, when she heard his cup tip over on the table. "Carl, cup empty already?" she asked without turning to see what had happened. After no response, she turned to see his coffee spilled out before him, sitting with a blank stare on his face. His eyes were dilated, looking straight ahead at nothing. Marie set the fry pan off the stove.

"Carl!" she yelled standing in front of him. Then she noticed a small amount of drool coming from the side of his mouth. "Carl," she whispered. She was about to yell for Herbert and Elisabeth when he suddenly came to. He blinked his eyes and looked at her.

"Marie…what happened? You were standing by the stove, now you're in front of me."

Marie moved to stand by his side. She rubbed his back soothingly and said, "It's okay, Carl, I'm here." Marie was sure he had just had a blackout as a result from his war injury.

He reached for her and pulled her close. "Forgive me for being such an ogre."

"You've been under such stress lately, Carl, what is there to forgive, when I've already forgotten."

From then on, Marie could tell by his temper if a blackout was soon to happen. Sharing this with the children, they all made note to watch their father, especially if his moods became foul. His temper was usually a precursor to an episode, so they made sure he was seated or laying somewhere safe so he wouldn't be injured when he phased out.

########

Winter turned to spring. With the freshness of new life in the air everyone's spirits soared. It was the Easter holiday - Marie's favorite. She had been preparing for a while – planning the meal, making the children new outfits to wear for church and she even managed to have time to make one for herself. It had been years since they had taken a family portrait. So as Sunday morning came, bright and early, before church, she lined everyone up, including Carl, for inspection. "Okay, everyone looks clean and ready, looking their best." Marie said as she lifted Herbert's chin looking for a remnant of breakfast. "Carl, I would appreciate your keen eye —if you would arrange us on the front porch as to how we should sit." Louise has gladly agreed to be our photographer for today and is ready and waiting outside with the camera. Wanting to get a clear shot of all their faces, Carl thought to have the smaller children sit in front of everyone. He grabbed a blanket off the couch for them to sit on. He had Elisabeth sit next to them on the grass, hoping she could keep them occupied until the shutter clicked. After several pictures were taken, everyone sighed in relief. Taking a picture of a young family of nine was not easy—but somehow Louise managed to capture the perfect moment.

After the service and a light lunch, they took their usual Sunday stroll to take in the beauty of the Furst von Schoenburg forest and the Hartenstein and Schloss Stein castles. Marie would often bring a basket to gather mushrooms for the evening meal. As they walked, they would sing old folk songs or hymns accompanied by Herbert's harmonica. Besides church, it was the most enjoyable thing they did as a family.

########

Spring turned to summer and sadly, another family tragedy. Marie's mother Anna passed away in her sleep. This took a heavy toll on Marie's heart. Exhaustion overcame her after her mother's funeral. Although her father had moved in with her brother Gerhard and was only a few blocks away – there was nothing that could console her. Carl knew it was time to call in reinforcements again. After a quick phone call, Emma and Frank were on their way. The children cheered when they heard they were coming, having enjoyed their company during their previous visit.

After their arrival it didn't take long for Marie's strength to return and her spirit to lighten from the burden of grief she carried. Many walks were taken along the forested paths of Hartenstein with Emma and Frank singing along with them in their musical strolls. On one occasion Frank had them stop in a field of wild flowers to take a family picture. Marie insisted that Emma be in it too – and so she was.

After several weeks Marie was feeling much stronger. Emma and Frank knew it was time to head back home, so among tears of gratitude and promises to come back soon, they made their departure.

########

In the fall of 1938, just as Carl had promised the construction of their new house began. Often, they would walk as a family down to where it was being built and watch the men dig out the basement and pour concrete. Marie planned her garden. Paul-Gerhard loved animals and continually asked if they could have more than just chickens, ducks and rabbits. "How about a goat, mama?" he said pleadingly to his mother.

"Oh my kleiner, how you can pull the strings of my heart. But no, taking care of chickens, ducks and rabbits will be more than enough work for little boy." She patted him on the head, as she listened to the other children making their requests known. She loved all her children dearly but Paul-Gerhard held a special place in her heart. Maybe it had something to do with his size that made her want to always hold him close and protect him. Maybe that's why she made his name so long—to make up for what he lacked in stature. Whatever it was, Marie couldn't help but notice that it seemed as if the world came after him with a vengeance, which made her pray more fiercely for his strength and endurance to run his race well.

Just a few days before, she had broken up a fight between him and Herbert. While making super she watched as Paul played quietly in the living room with his toy soldiers and tanks. Suddenly, she heard Herbert yell, "I am the enemy and I will destroy you!" Before she could intervene, Herbert had stomped on much of Paul's toy soldiers breaking many of them.

"Herbert Tittel! You come here this instant!" Marie yelled as Herbert slunk his way to her with his head down. Paul's sobs could be heard in the background.

"Why? Why did you just break your brother's toys, Herbert?"

"I was just playing," he said quietly looking away from his mother.

"Playing? Paul-Gerhard is four and you are twelve. There is no need for such violent destructive behavior with one who is a quarter of your size and one-third your age. Look at me. Do you understand?"

"Yes, mama," Herbert said as he held out his hands. A thwack could be heard throughout the house that made every child flinch within hearing. Corporal punishment was not used often, but there were times that called for it, and Marie felt this was one of them. "Now go back and apologize to your brother."

Things settled down for a while, but several weeks later Carl told her of an incident that made them decide to take drastic action. It was a Saturday and Marie was out shopping when it happened, with Carl home alone with the children.

"I was standing at the back door watching Paul play with several of his neighborhood friends, when Siegfried Schott came over and joined them. After several minutes I heard Siegfried yelling at Paul, 'Titmouse, titmouse, you're as tiny as a titmouse!' Then before I could open the door he pushed Paul to the ground. I ran outside and told him to go home. Poor boy was shaken so badly he cried in my arms for several minutes. Marie, I'm concerned about Siegfried and his influence over Paul. He's always in trouble and if he isn't, he looks for it. Paul told me it's not the first time Siegfried has shoved him around. This boy is nothing but trouble. They are both supposed to start school next year and I'm really thinking we should hold him back a grade—otherwise he will beat him up and taunt him every day at school."

"I think you're right, Carl. I've been watching him and his shenanigans over the past year. Although he's only four, he's broken windows in other homes, stolen candy from the grocery, and hit, slapped, or punched just about every child in the neighborhood. Poor Louise, she has her hands full. We must pray for Siegfried, but yes, holding Paul back a year would give my heart peace."

The decision made, Carl and Marie both agreed Paul would not start kindergarten in the fall of 1939, but in the fall of 1940. Marie wasn't too concerned about other children teasing him for being held back. She knew because of his size he wouldn't look out of place.

########

The coming months were filled with the family preparing for the move to the big house. Christmas came, and while they didn't have money to spend on gifts for one another each one took the time to make something. The girls knitted scarves and mittens, Herbert made little jewelry boxes for the girls and his mom from leftover wood at the lumberyard. Carl helped Paul make a cross for his mother from two pieces of pine he found in the near-by woods. Marie made Carl a new shirt. Carl had drawn a scenic pen and ink sketch for Marie.

Christmas Eve was a choir of *oooohs* and *aaaaaaahs* as each person's gift was unwrapped and the workmanship enjoyed by all. About an hour later, there was a loud knock on the door. "Oh my, who could that be?" said Marie in mock surprise. Looking at Paul she asked, "Will you get the door please."

He ran to the front door and slowly opened it. "It's Santa Claus!" Paul almost screamed from excitement. All the children came running. Elisabeth and Herbert laughed loudly as they saw their uncle Gerhard dressed in a red suit with a white beard carrying a sack of goodies.

"Ho, Ho, Ho!" Gerhard belted out in front of the wide eyed children. He laid his large red bag down, then dumped everything that was in it onto the floor. The children squealed with delight as apples, walnuts, and hazelnuts poured out before them. A mass scramble for the treats ensued. Gerhard turned to leave, giving another "Ho, Ho, Ho!" while winking and waving goodbye to Carl and Marie.

Soon after, everyone prepared for the Christmas Eve service. All, except Carl and Magdalena had songs to sing and instruments to play. Paul stood next to his brother in the balcony. He watched him admiringly and listened to the beautiful clear tones of the horn he was playing. He loved his brother—even though they didn't get along at times—he looked up to him and wanted to be as big and strong as he was.

After the service, they walked home as a family, carrying their instruments, singing and humming the songs that were still fresh in their minds from the church service. Arriving home, they enjoyed a wonderful time of playing games, drinking spiced tea, along with Christmas cookies and cake that had been prepared the night before. Marie played her lute while everyone gathered around her to sing one of her favorite Christmas hymns—*Silent Night*.[9] She thought as she sang that her heart would burst with the joy that filled it. The celebration of Jesus birth—the greatest gift for all mankind—her family surrounding her, their new home only a few short months away… The lyrics brought her back to the present as she continued to sing…*Son of God love's pure light, Radiant beams from Thy holy face, With the dawn of redeeming grace…*

With the beginning of the New Year Marie knew that no matter what came their way—with the Father's love and the strength of His Spirit they could accomplish or overcome anything. She and her family would step forward boldly into the destiny that God had for them.

Jesus Lord, at Thy birth, Jesus Lord, at Thy birth.

Paul looked up at his mother and smiled as the final chords of the hymn faded, "I know why pa calls her an angel," he thought to himself. "She looks like one, sings like one, and loves like one…someday I'm going to marry an angel too."

1. With the death of German President Paul von Hindenburg, Chancellor Adolf Hitler becomes absolute dictator of Germany under the title of *Fuhrer,* or "Leader."

    http://www.history.com/this-day-in-history/hitler-becomes-fuhrer

2. Psalm 121 (KJV)

I will lift up mine eyes unto the hills, from whence cometh my help. My help cometh from the LORD, which made heaven and earth. He will not suffer thy foot to be moved: he that keepeth thee will not slumber. Behold, he that keepeth Israel shall neither slumber nor sleep. The LORD is thy keeper: the LORD is thy shade upon thy right hand. The sun shall not smite thee by day, nor the moon by night. The LORD shall preserve thee from all evil: he shall preserve thy soul. The LORD shall preserve thy going out and thy coming in from this time forth, and even for evermore.

3. German schools were in session year round with long holidays for Christmas, Easter, and summer.

    Schools played an important role in spreading Nazi ideas to German youth. While censors removed some books from the classroom, German educators introduced new textbooks that taught students love for Hitler, obedience to state authority, militarism, racism, and antisemitism.

    http://www.ushmm.org/wlc/en/article.php?ModuleId=10007820

4. Movements for youngsters were part of German culture and the Hitler Youth had been created in the 1920's. By 1933 its membership stood at 100,000. After Hitler came to power, all other youth movements were abolished and as a result the Hitler Youth grew quickly. In 1936, the figure stood at 4 million members. In 1936, it became all but compulsory to join the Hitler Youth. Youths could avoid doing any active service if they paid their subscription but this became all but impossible after 1939.

http://www.historylearningsite.co.uk/nazi-germany/hitler-youth-movement/

5. Oma and Opa—Grandma and Grandpa

6. Author's note: "During this time, taking elderly parents into your home instead of placing them into a state run facility was a choice that many Germans faced as their parents grew older. Only a few short years later it would be an even harder decision as Hitler instituted his euthanasia program to include, not only disabled children but adults who could no longer be part of the workforce."

In the spring and summer months of 1939, a number of planners—led by Philipp Bouhler, the director of Hitler's private chancellery, and Karl Brandt, Hitler's attending physician—began to organize a secret killing operation targeting disabled children.

Euthanasia planners quickly envisioned extending the killing program to adult disabled patients living in institutional settings. In the autumn of 1939, Adolf Hitler signed a secret authorization in order to protect participating physicians, medical staff, and administrators from prosecution; this authorization was backdated to September 1, 1939, to suggest that the effort was related to wartime measures.

http://www.ushmm.org/wlc/en/article.php?ModuleId=10005200

7. In 1931, the International Olympic Committee awarded the 1936 Summer Olympics to Berlin. The choice signaled Germany's return to the world community after its isolation in the aftermath of defeat in World War I. http://www.ushmm.org/wlc/en/article.php?ModuleId=10005680

8. Louis Zamperini – became the youngest distance runner to ever make the Olympic team. At age 19 he was still too inexperienced to mount a challenge for gold, but during a Berlin Olympiad held in the shadow of the burgeoning Nazi empire, he finished eighth in his race and won over the crowd by laying down one of the fastest final laps in the history of the event. Among the impressed spectators was none other than Adolf Hitler, who shook Zamperini's hand from his box and said, "Ah, you're the boy with the fast finish."

http://www.history.com/news/8-things-you-may-not-know-about-louis-zamperini

9. SILENT NIGHT

Silent night, holy night!
All is calm, all is bright.
Round yon Virgin, Mother and Child.
Holy infant so tender and mild,
Sleep in heavenly peace,
Sleep in heavenly peace

Silent night, holy night!
Shepherds quake at the sight.
Glories stream from heaven afar
Heavenly hosts sing Alleluia,
Christ the Savior is born!
Christ the Savior is born

Silent night, holy night!
Son of God love's pure light.
Radiant beams from Thy holy face
With the dawn of redeeming grace,
Jesus Lord, at Thy birth
Jesus Lord, at Thy birth

Chapter Five: The New House

"Spring will never come," a despondent Paul thought as he kneels on the living room couch looking out the window that sat behind it. It was the beginning of March and snow still covered the ground.

"Why so glum, my Kleiner?" Marie said as she stood behind him.

He turned around and sat facing his mother. "Mama the snow will never melt. We will never be able to move to our new home. Papa said we would move when the snow was gone, but it's not going away."

Marie looked down into the face of a very worried little boy. "So much like his father," she thought. "Paul," Marie said as she sat down next to him. "Snow or no snow, we will be in the new house in time for your birthday, April 3rd, I promise."

"That would be the best birthday present ever mama!" He threw his arms around his mother and hugged her.

Marie laughed as she held him enjoying his enthusiasm, and immediate change of heart. "Come now," she said as she got up and went to the piano. She sat down and patted the empty bench next to her, "Have a seat next to me my Liebling."

Paul stood on his tip toes and boosted himself onto the bench.

"I know the most appropriate hymn for this occasion," she said looking down at him by her side—*Fairest Lord Jesus*.[1] Do you remember the verses?

Paul shook his head, no. Although he did remember them, he much preferred to hear her sing. A song could always be heard in their house or an instrument playing a hymn or an old folk tune. "It's so much better than listening to the radio," he thought to himself.

"Let's worship, shall we?" She said looking at Paul who was shaking his head in a vigorous yes. "Join with me if you remember."

Marie began to play and sing:

Fairest Lord Jesus,
Ruler of all nature,
O thou of God and man the Son
Thee will I cherish, Thee will I honor,
Thou, my soul's glory, joy, and crown.

Paul listened and took in the beauty of the music and his mother's voice. Then as natural as a leaf budding forth from a tree, without hesitating, his small voice joined with hers for the second verse.

Fair are the meadows,
Fairer still the woodlands,
Robed in the blooming garb of spring:
Jesus is fairer, Jesus is purer,
Who makes the woeful heart to sing.

Elisabeth, Christa, and Ruth could be heard joining in from the kitchen for the third and fourth verses. Along with Carl's bold off-key voice bellowing loudly as he carried Magdalena down the stairs. Finally, from the upstairs bedroom, Herbert's horn could be heard as he played the melody. A rapturous sound, that turned all their hearts from the cold of winter toward a spring of new beginnings with many blessings soon to come.

########

Marie kept her promise. All the children gathered around Paul as he sat before his candlelit birthday cake. "Thank you, mama, thank you, papa it's the best birthday ever," Paul said just before he took a deep breath to blow out his candles.

"But you haven't even opened your gifts yet." Carl said as he placed a nicely wrapped box in front of him. Elisabeth removed the cake to start cutting slices. Everyone looked on with smiles and watched as he carefully unwrapped the first of several packages.

"It's huge!" Paul said as he pulled out a large wind-up tank from the box.

"Wind it up – let's see it go Paul!" Herbert yelled from the other end of the table.

Paul, usually not inclined to listen to anything his older brother had to say, put aside their differences and began to wind-up the mammoth beast. Holding it with both hands on top of the table, he waited until everyone moved their plates and silverware out of the way. Aiming for his brother, who sat seemingly miles away by the tank's perspective, Paul let go and watched while everyone gasped at the spectacle before them. The tank traveled at an unanticipated speed across the white field of the tablecloth with large sparks flying from its cannon. Its short burst of energy spent, it stopped just inches from where Herbert was sitting.

"I surrender! I surrender!" Herbert yelled with his hands in the air. Everyone laughed including Paul.

As Elisabeth placed slices of cake on everyone's plate, Marie gave him her gift. He could tell by the shape what it was. It didn't matter, he had been wanting a new one for a while seeing his old one had developed a crack in it. Paul removed the wrapping and ran his fingers over the shiny dark wood. It was a soprano recorder.

"Thank you mama it's beautiful," Paul said as he slipped out of his chair and hugged his mother. "I will play it every day."

"I know you will, my Schatzi."

"Frank and I have a gift for you too, Paul, but it's outside." Emma looked over at Marie and winked. They had already discussed what they wanted to buy him and their desire to bless their children on their birthdays since they had none of their own.

"After dessert Paul." Marie said as he started to walk toward the door.

Paul slunk back to his chair and hurriedly finished his cake. He waited patiently until he caught his father's eyes. "Paul, are you ready to go outside for your final gift?" His father asked.

"Yes, papa." He said as patiently as he could. "Couldn't they see how miserable it was to wait?" thought Paul. Emma, or Miss Wolny as Paul was asked to call her, got up first and headed for the foyer.

"Come, Paul," Emma said as she held out her hand. Paul gladly joined hands with her as they stepped outside. He liked Miss Wolny and her husband Frank. They seemed more like family than friends.

Once outside, Paul ran to a large package wrapped in plain brown paper leaning up against the backyard fence. Emma and Frank helped him unwrap it. Paul stood back and exclaimed, "A scooter, it's a scooter!"

Carl and Marie smiled at each other both enjoying Paul's excitement over his gift. "Can I take it out on the sidewalk and try it out?" he asked.

"Here, Paul I'll help you." Herbert said as he picked it up and carried it through the open gate to the sidewalk. They all watched as Herbert showed him the basics. "You put one foot on the scooter while holding onto the bars with your hands and push with your other foot." With that, Herbert took off with a shot and was soon a block away.

"Herbert, come back! Its my scooter!" Paul yelled at the top of his lungs.

Carl, seeing this had no effect on Herbert's joyride yelled, "Herbert Tittel!" Even at a distance one could see the effect of Carl's voice on his elder son as he immediately stopped and came back faster than when he left.

"Really, Herbert must you tease your little brother even on his birthday?" Marie let out an exasperated sigh. Herbert passed the scooter back to Paul swiftly while avoiding his father's gaze.

Marie stood near Emma and her husband Frank while they continued watching Paul learn to balance with the help of his sisters. It was quite a show and everyone had fun including Paul. "It is a little big for him," Emma said to Marie.

"Oh, he'll grow into it soon enough," she replied. She was so glad they came again to help her, not just with Paul's birthday party, but with their open house on Saturday - only 6 days away.

"My, how the children have grown since I was here last," Emma said as she nudged shoulders with Marie. "Herbert is only 13 but already looks full grown," she said nodding in his direction.

"Yes," sighed Marie. "Time's flown by. He graduates in June and then he'll be going to business college in September. I'm concerned about Hitler's new plan.[2] After his next two years of education he'll be required to do 6 months of labor—helping to build roads and bridges—then two years of mandatory military service. I continually pray that we won't be at war when that time comes." Marie sighed laying her head on her friends shoulder. "He will be the first to fly from the nest. We'll miss him tremendously. Until he leaves I plan to enjoy every day with him – even when he tries my last nerve by teasing his younger brother."

"Brothers will be brothers," Miss Wolny said as she laid her cheek against the top of Marie's head. "They have the bond of love and a shared faith that you brought them up in…as they grow older they will know this even more."

Paul watched his mother and Miss Wolny as they talked. He knew they were best friends because she made his mother smile. Her husband was quiet, but his father liked spending time with him. Paul would listen to them talk in soft voices late at night about a man named Hitler and all that was happening in Germany because of him. He would hear words like SS, Nazi, Jews, exterminate, and master race. All of which he knew little or nothing about. He was more excited about the new house and the garden and all the animals that would be living in it.

As Paul learned how to balance and push his scooter, everyone cheered. Then, as if on queue, a boy Paul's age came around the corner on a scooter too. He slid alongside Paul and held out his hand.

"I'm Klaus, welcome to the neighborhood. I live up the hill above you. Nice scooter by the way."

Paul grinned ear to ear as he shook Klaus's hand. "I'm Paul and this is my family," he said as he nodded in the direction of the small group of people that were now watching them.

"How 'bout if we get together sometime and play?" Klaus asked.

"That would be great," answered Paul.

With that, Klaus scooted away, then turned his head and hollered back, "See you tomorrow!" No sooner had Klaus rode off when Carl mentioned that he and Herbert needed to get to the hardware store before it closed to get supplies for the rabbit hutch and chicken coop. A carpenter was coming the next day to help assemble them. "Can I come too, papa?" asked Sigrid. "I can help carry the wood."

"That would be a big help, Sigrid," Carl replied.

Elisabeth stepped out onto the sidewalk giving her mother a kiss on the cheek. "Goodbye everyone, I'm off to work!"

"Goodbye, Elisabeth!" Christa, Ruth, Sigrid and Paul yelled back. While Magdalena waved from her mother's arms, they watched their sister hurrying off to work.

Elisabeth who was now 17, had gotten a job at one of the local textile factories. She still lived at home and helped her mother with the chores and children, but enjoyed having her own spending money and time away from household duties.

Carl, Herbert, and Sigrid hurried off with the wheelbarrow to get to the hardware before it closed.

After their departure, Frank took a group picture of his wife, Marie, Christa, Ruth, Magdalena, and Paul at the front of the house. It turned out well and Paul kept it to always remind himself of one of his favorite memories.

Saturday arrived quickly with much to do, but with Elisabeth's and Miss Wolny's help everything was washed, baked, and the yard made ready to seat guests for the festivities. Being a warm spring day, Marie knew that people would want to congregate outside instead of in a stuffy house.

"Paul-Gerhard, Magdalena!" Paul heard his mother call his name and came running to her side. Little Magdalena was not far behind.

"Yes, Mama." He replied out of breath.

"Here is the two quart container. Go to the pub with Magdalena and have them fill it. Here is some change. Keep it in your pocket, don't lose it, and hurry home!" It was a short walk to the pub. Paul didn't mind, he enjoyed being with his little sister. She reminded him a lot of his mother—a peaceful demeanor and quick to look on the sunny side of things. He could tell a lot about someone who was only four—because he knew a lot for being only five. After having the container filled and the lid put on securely, they headed home with each of them holding the handle and carrying it between them. Almost home, Paul felt the urge to satisfy a curiosity. He stopped, removed the lid of the container, and took a swallow of the warm, frothy drink. He shook his head and grimaced at the bittersweet taste. Magdalena looked at him with raised eyebrows and he offered her a taste too. She scrunched up her nose and said, "yuck!" Paul still didn't understand why adults liked such a fowl tasting liquid. Arriving back at the house, Paul saw that some relatives had already arrived and were sitting outside by a table in the garden. He and Magdalena hurried into the house and set the container of beer in the kitchen for Elisabeth to divide into glasses. Magdalena ran off to play. Paul stayed in the kitchen cautiously watching as his sister took the lid off the container. He wondered, "Would she notice that it wasn't quite full?"

Elisabeth observed his intense gaze. "Did you try some, Paul?"

Paul's mouth dropped open. He couldn't lie. Slowly he nodded his head "yes."

"Did Magdalena try some too?" she asked. Paul nodded his head again.

"Did you like it?" This time he shook his head "no."

"Did Magdalena like it?"

He felt his face flush. "She's just like mama, always knows what I'm doing even though she can't see me." He thought to himself while shaking his head "no" again.

"Paul-Gerhard every German drinks beer. When you get a little older you'll both appreciate the taste more, but for now I'd leave the drinking of it to the adults. Do you agree?" Paul shook his head yes again. "Now off with you. I've much to do in little time."

Paul stepped out of the kitchen with a sigh of relief. He was glad there was no one else around to hear *that* conversation. Walking through the informal living room, then through the formal living room, he looked across to the foyer where his uncle Gerhard had just entered. Running over to him, his uncle scooped him up into his arms. "How's my favorite nephew?" Gerhard asked as he tickled him.

Paul laughed, "much better now that I have a new scooter."

"You will have to show it to me after your mama and papa give me the grand tour of your new home."

More people came in behind them from outside. Paul and his uncle turned to listen as his father, with his mother by his side, began to explain the construction of their house.

"It was about three and a half years ago that I first surprised Marie with the blueprints of our new home. While it was always on my mind to have a house of our own someday, I was more excited to keep a promise to Marie that I made almost 17 years ago." Standing next to him, Marie looked up to Carl smiling, thinking he would make reference to their wedding vows. "My family and friends, welcome to one of the first houses in Hartenstein that has a running toilet, bathtub, sink, and washing machine." Marie elbowed Carl in his side. "I kept my promise, didn't I?" Carl said as everyone laughed. "Now, first we will show you the second floor," Carl said as he and Marie escorted them upstairs.

Here were 3 large bedrooms with a large bathroom. Everyone had to take a turn flushing the toilet. Paul watched as his Opa climbed into the bathtub and sat down smoking his pipe.

"A perfect fit dad," Marie said laughing with everyone else as they moved on down the hallway to see the bedrooms.

Paul didn't mind the sleeping arrangements. It was his hope that someday he would have his own room, but with 5 girls he already knew that the chance of that happening was pretty slim. For now he shared a room with Sigrid, Ruth, and Magdalena. He and Magdalena shared a bunk bed. Elisabeth and Christa shared a room, with his parents having their own room. Since Herbert was soon to leave, he slept in the informal living room on a pullout sofa bed. As they viewed his parent's bedroom, his Aunt Lillie, who was his mother's cousin, gasped as she saw every woman's dream sitting in the corner. "Marie...a peddle sewing machine?!"

"An early anniversary present from Carl." Marie blushed almost embarrassed at the abundance of blessings the Lord had poured upon them.

Lillie turned to look at her husband who stood behind her, "Our anniversary is coming soon."

Paul, along with several others, heard his whispered reply, "Lillie, I love you my lumpkin, but you'll be lucky to get a needle and thread on our income," He said as he wrapped his arms around her waist and kissed the back of her head.

The people around them chuckled as they moved down the hallway and to the stairs that led back to the first floor. Here they ventured into the kitchen, where oohs and aahs could be heard from every woman as they saw the latest conveniences laid out before them. A sink with running water, an icebox, a coal stove for cooking, and a large wood burning stove to heat the house in winter. At that moment Marie became the envy of every woman in the room. But in an instant she assuaged their jealousy by inviting them all to a weekly Monday morning coffee clutch where they could pray for and encourage one another. With such a giving heart she couldn't fathom keeping all that God had given her to herself.

Lastly, they led everyone downstairs to the basement. Paul knew this was his dad's pride and joy. After WWI it became mandatory that every new house have a bomb shelter in the basement. Passing through the room for coal storage and another which housed the washing machine (which every woman had to touch at least once), was a room with thick walls, a steel reinforced ceiling, and a heavy door. Here Carl shared with them the dimensions and specifications of the bomb shelter and how it could withstand almost a direct hit from light artillery. The men were impressed and ventured inside to sit on the thick benches that lined the walls. The women went back to the washing machine asking Marie many questions on how it worked and if it was truly better than a washboard and tub.

Finally, they exited the basement door into a scenic view. Here, they looked out over the valley where one could see the rooftops of other houses in the tiers below them. In the distance were the Ore Mountains (Erzgebirge). Gerhard set Paul down and they walked out into the garden. Marie pointed out the freshly planted apple and pear trees. Also, the watering system where the rain gutters emptied into a small cement trough which led to a large wooden barrel where a bucket could be used for watering the plants and trees.

Stepping away from the group, Paul showed his uncle the new scooter. He also introduced his egg laying chickens, holding each one up to him and telling him their name.

As everyone gathered around the table covered with a crisp white tablecloth, Paul and his uncle joined them. Elisabeth had brought out the glasses filled with beer— enough for everyone to have one. Marie's father cleared his throat as he prepared to say the toast and blessing.

Holding his glass high in the air with one hand, and with his pipe in the other he looked towards Carl and Marie and said:

With faith there is love
with love there is peace
with peace there is blessing
with blessing there is God
with God there is no need.

They raised their glasses and drank. Afterward, each took a turn in congratulating Carl and Marie on their new home. "Please feel free to come back inside and eat or bring your food and drink out here and enjoy the fresh air." Marie said for everyone to hear.

Some filtered back into the house, others stayed outside.

Paul noticed Frank with the camera. "Okay everyone, time to record the moment!" Frank yelled so all could hear. After getting their attention, he asked that everyone take a seat and face him. While they arranged themselves, Lillie's husband Carl serenaded them on his mandolin. When everyone was ready Frank took the picture.

Paul looked at the photograph later and wished his mother wouldn't have gone back into the house, because she wasn't in it. The picture showed from left to right: his Opa Loescher, Aunt Lillie, Uncle Gerhard, Sigrid, Christa, Ruth, Lillie's husband Carl, Gertrud (who had traveled across the Atlantic with Elisabeth as a baby), his papa, himself, and Magdalena.

A few days had passed. Miss Wolny and her husband returned to their home in the Sudetenland. Paul was sad to see them go.

They were a great help and lots of fun. He saw how much his mother relied on Elisabeth, and Christa, Ruth, and Sigrid too, for help with chores and other household duties. While she continued to cook, do light housework, and sew, she didn't have the strength to single-handedly do all the work for the family of nine. Although she relinquished many chores and activities, the one thing she could not let go of were the Sunday walks they took together as a family through the Furst von Schoenburg Forest that surrounded Hartenstein. Paul was glad for this. It was one of his favorite things to do with his mother.

########

Spring turned quickly to summer. Paul watched as Marie checked off another date on the calendar leaving only a few more days until the end of August and Herbert's departure. As his mother turned to face him he saw the sadness in her eyes. He jumped off his chair and hugged her aproned skirt. "I'm here mama. I'm not leaving." Paul said as he held her tight.

"Oh, my Shatzi," Marie bent down and drew him close. After a moment she gathered her composure, then stood up, patted him on the head and said, "What would I do without my Kleiner? Come along with me now and I'll teach you more about hunting mushrooms." Marie grabbed a basket that was hanging on the kitchen wall, and reached for Paul's hand. Walking through the informal dining room she leaned over Carl's shoulder and whispered in his ear, "Paul and I are going mushroom hunting. We'll be back in time for supper."

Without taking his eyes off his drawings he replied, "Okay my love, hurry home," turning to give her a quick peck on the cheek.

Passing the stairway that led upstairs, Elisabeth was on her way down with Magdalena. "Going mushroom hunting. We'll be home in time for you to get ready for work, Elisabeth. Thank you for keeping an eye on Magdalena." Marie said while passing through with Paul in tow.

"Try to find the stone mushrooms, they would go well with the chicken you're making for supper tonight."

"A wonderful idea Elisabeth. If we do I'll be sure to save you a portion in the icebox."

"Thank you mama!" Elisabeth said as Magdalena waved goodbye while she closed the door behind them.

"Over here Paul-Gerhard!" His mother yelled to him from farther down the path they had been walking on. Paul ran from where he was looking and found her not too far off the trail. "Look, a whole cluster of them right by this large rock. We are blessed—we will use some tonight with our supper."

His mother showed him how to pick them and place them gently into the basket. "They bruise easily so you must be gentle with them, Paul. The Latin name for this one is *boletes edulis.* We call them Steinpilz for stone mushroom because they are found near stones."

After gathering a nice cluster of them, they started looking for Aspen and Birch trees. Here, his mother said, they would find *leccinum scabrum* or the Birch mushroom as it was commonly known. They journeyed down the path and soon Paul saw a glimpse of white bark through the pines. They ventured through the evergreens until they came to a sunlit patch of birch trees. "Look at the bottom of the tree near the trunk, that's where they'll be."

"I found one!" Paul yelled as he held up a specimen for his mother's approval.

Marie took it in hand and carefully examined it. "You must be so very careful when hunting mushrooms, Paul. One wrong mushroom can make people very sick or even kill them. The wrong ones are very toxic, the edible ones very delicious, which is why people hunt them. This one, fortunately, *is* a Birch mushroom—look at the details in the cap and stem and study it carefully. Don't worry, I'll always come with you until I feel you're capable of hunting them on your own."

Finding only a few of the Birch mushrooms, Marie set her sights on another kind. "The next one we'll be looking for is easy to find and recognize. It's called the Maroon mushroom because of its deep reddish brown cap. You can find them under the evergreens. It's latin name is *suillus brevipes*."

After searching a large area there wasn't one to be found. Paul sighed, "Mama, it's disappointing not to find any."

"It's early in the season Paul, and we're not the only ones mushroom hunting. There are other women in town who know good spots to forage for them too. I will show you the best locations—the areas my mother showed me when I was a little girl. Be sure to keep them secret. Good mushrooms are worth good money to the right chef." Marie continued explaining the next type of mushroom they would be looking for seeing she had an attentive pupil. Even at his young age Paul loved the outdoors, especially the forested mountains and now learning about mushrooms with his mother held his attention.

"*Clavicorona pyxidata* is the latin word for the mushroom we call Ziegenpeter. This is a coral mushroom and it looks like the coral that you find in the ocean. Usually white or off-white in color the small stems remind me of a goat's beard. Some people call it the 'goat mushroom' too. It grows on the sides of rotten tree stumps and with its bright color is usually easy to find. I'll show you one of the secret places I was telling you about before—one that my mother showed me—where a lot of old tree stumps and rotten logs hold many Ziegenpeter."

Just as his mother said, after another ten minutes of hiking, they came to a clearing that held many old stumps and dead trees. Here on the sides of some old logs Paul was amazed to see such a strange looking mushroom. His eyes would never be the same now when he walked in the woods—he would always be looking for the Steinpilz, the Birkenpilz, the Maroon, and the Ziegenpeter.

As they made their way home Marie began to sing another one of her favorite hymns, "*Onward Christian Soldier.*"[3]

Onward, Christian soldiers, marching as to war,
with the cross of Jesus going on before.
Christ, the royal Master, leads against the foe;
forward into battle see his banners go!

Although he didn't know all the words to all the verses Paul knew the refrain:

Onward, Christian soldiers, marching as to war,
with the cross of Jesus going on before.

As Marie sang each verse with Paul joining in for the chorus, they marched forward down the trail back home. Neither were aware that someday soon real battles would be fought by real soldiers in their quiet town and local forests.

########

"Hey, little brother, hurry up. I have something for you!" Herbert yelled upstairs. Soon Paul's feet could be heard running down the wooden steps. He sped through the formal living room and into the informal living room where his older brother slept. With his pullout bed tucked away, Herbert sat on the couch which had been converted into his bed. Paul looked at his brother and threw his arms around his neck. "I will miss you, Herbert."

"Oh come on now, remember how much I tease you and you'll get over it." Herbert said in jest to cover the seriousness of the moment.

Paul stepped back and looked at Herbert with sore eyes.

"Alright come here." Herbert sighed as Paul threw his arms back around his neck again. "Happy?" Herbert asked as Paul stepped back again with a smile on his face shaking his head in agreement. "Now come here and sit down next to me. I have something I want to give you before I leave." Paul sat next to his brother on the couch. Herbert reached between his legs and pulled out a case from underneath him. Paul watched as he placed it in his lap and took out one of his favorite instruments - the brass horn.

"Paul, I know you want to play the horn, too. I've seen you watch me play and you can tell a lot by the way someone looks at you. I've already spoken to Uncle Gerhard and he's agreed to teach you how to play when you're old enough. In the meantime my horn needs a babysitter since I can't take it with me. Will you take good care of it until I come home at Christmas?"

Paul's eyes were so wide open you could see the whites all the way around. He thought he would explode. He loved the brass instruments and the sound they made. It always reminded him of heaven for some reason. He couldn't contain himself any longer. He threw his arms around his brother again.

"Okay, Okay, I take that as a yes!" Herbert laughed as he hugged his brother in return then put the horn back in its case. "I'm serious about you taking care of it for me. I expect it to be shined up and ready for me to play at Christmas okay?"

Paul nodded his head vigorously. Herbert stood and tousled Paul's hair, "Come on then, lets walk to the Stein station together."

Herbert and Paul joined everyone waiting outside. Before heading out for their mile long trek to the departing train, they all joined hands while Carl prayed a blessing over Herbert.

Later at the station, Marie watched while everyone gave Herbert their final goodbyes. She couldn't hold back the tears any longer. "My dear Herbert, may God watch over you and protect you. Keep the faith, be strong, study hard, and come back to me."

"Oh, Mom, Liepzig is only 2 hours away, you'd think I was going to America."

"And Christmas break is only 4 months away," added Carl trying to lighten Marie's heavy heart.

"I know my darling," Marie said as she held her hand to his cheek. "I will miss you. I know you will be in good hands – and I don't mean the school's – the Lord keep you till we see you again."

With that Herbert stepped into the train. Carl handed his two suitcases up to him. He watched from the window and waved as they all grew smaller and smaller in size with the trains departure.

########

The next day was Friday. Carl went to the mailbox to retrieve the daily post. When he opened the newspaper he read the date: *Friday, September 1, 1939* and then the headline: *Germany Invades Poland.*[4] He took a deep breath and slowly exhaled. The only thing he could think of was telling Marie that hopefully the battle would come to an end before their oldest son could be sent to war.

1. Fairest Lord Jesus,

    ruler of all nature,

    O thou of God and man the Son,

    Thee will I cherish, Thee will I honor,

    thou, my soul's glory, joy, and crown.

Fair are the meadows,

fairer still the woodlands,

robed in the blooming garb of spring:

Jesus is fairer, Jesus is purer

who makes the woeful heart to sing.

Fair is the sunshine,

fairer still the moonlight,

and all the twinkling starry host:

Jesus shines brighter, Jesus shines purer

than all the angels heaven can boast.

Beautiful Savior!

Lord of all the nations!

Son of God and Son of Man!

Glory and honor, praise, adoration,

now and forevermore be thine.

http://www.hymnary.org/text/fairest_lord_jesus_ruler_of_all_nature

2. German Education.
    http://countrystudies.us/germany/124.htm

3. http://www.hymnary.org/text/onward_christian_soldiers_marching_as

4. September 1, 1939
    https://www.pbs.org/thewar/at_war_timeline_1939.htm

Chapter Six: Boyhood Adventures

Paul woke to the sound of muffled sobs. Rubbing his eyes, he slowly sat up in bed, listening more intently for where the sound came from. He was sure it came from across the hall. That meant it could only be...

"Mama!" Paul thought to himself. Quickly he climbed down the small ladder from the top bunk and ran to the doorway. Across the hall he saw his father closing the bedroom door behind him, with a grim look on his face.

"Papa?" Paul asked with a worried voice.

"She'll be alright, Paul. Your mama needs to rest for awhile." Carl said as he picked up his concerned son and carried him downstairs. "How 'bout I make oatmeal with brown sugar and some toast. I'll tell you about our adventures in America and what your mother and I used to eat for breakfast in Buffalo, Minnesota."

"Yes, papa please do!"

Carl put fresh coal into the cooking stove. Heating didn't take long as the embers from the night before lit the fresh pellets. He took the bread from the bread box and sliced the entire loaf. After laying the slices in a fry pan coated with lard, he filled a large pot with water for the oatmeal - all the while sharing with Paul some of the most exciting moments in their journey to America.

Elisabeth entered the kitchen carrying Magdalena. Placing her sister in her chair next to Paul, she went to retrieve bowls, cups and silverware to set the table. Shortly after, Christa, Ruth, and Sigrid entered—still in their pajamas—having been woken by the delicious smell of frying bread and cooking oatmeal. While the oatmeal finished cooking, and with the children seated around the table, Carl continued sharing the story of living on the dairy farm in Buffalo, Minnesota. He expounded on the breakfast menu that was made for them almost every day. Of course the menu grew each time he retold it, but the children never tired of hearing it.

"It was all you could eat every morning." Carl spoke as they listened wide eyed. "Plates with large piles of pancakes, waffles, scrambled eggs, ham steak, bacon, and large sausages were set before us. The buttermilk biscuits were so light and fluffy they almost floated off the plate, with bowls of freshly churned butter and homemade jellies to spread on top."

Carl started scooping the oatmeal into each of their bowls, while Elisabeth distributed the slices of toast around the table. Setting the large empty pot into the sink he took his place at the table and continued. "There was always fresh coffee and large pitchers of fresh milk with the cream still floating on top. If that wasn't enough and you wanted something sweet- they had cinnamon rolls, apple dumplings, or other kinds of pies and cakes. I don't think your mother and I ever ate so well in our entire lives."

The children were all looking at him dreamily, each trying to visualize such a feast before them. "Now, shall we give thanks to the Lord for what we are about to receive?" All heads bowed, Carl prayed the blessing over the meal. Although not the enormous menu their father had just told them about, everyone enjoyed the story and the breakfast he had just given them. While Christa and Elisabeth cleared the table and did the dishes, Sigrid and Ruth took Magdalena into the informal living room to play. Paul watched his father as he finished reading the paper. "Papa, why was mama crying this morning?"

"Mama was crying because she was worrying way too much and not putting her trust in the Lord." Marie said quietly from behind Paul.

Paul turned around and yelled, "Mama!"

Sigrid, Ruth, and Magdalena joined her at the table along with Elisabeth and Christa. Carl was relieved to see the smile on her face again as the children gathered around her.

"Why so worried, mom?" asked Elisabeth.

"I was, but I'm not anymore. God gave me a wonderful verse to meditate on - Psalm 42:11. Why art thou cast down, O my soul? and why art thou disquieted within me? Hope thou in God: for I shall yet praise him, who is the health of my countenance, and my God."

"A great encouragement, Marie. You see children, our country is now at war," Carl said as he held up the front page of the paper for everyone to see. The bold headline could not be missed: *Germany Invades Poland* [1]. "We don't know what the future may bring but we know who loves us, protects us and supplies our every need…and that would be the good Lord, and that is what is most important."

"Not what the radio tells us, or the paper, or our worried hearts and minds, but what God tells us in His word is truly the only word to trust," finished Marie.

"Will Herbert have to go to war?" Elisabeth asked.

"That was my worry," said Marie, "but as the Lord watches over us he watches over Herbert too. He is too young to be drafted now—but it depends on how long the war lasts. We will pray for a swift end to it all… war is not good for anyone."

"But why is war not good, mama?" Paul asked innocently.

"Because people get hurt my Kleiner - many are injured severely like your father. Towns and cities are destroyed, many men die, and many people suffer…war is very sad, Paul. There is usually a victor at the end but at a very costly price."

########

Paul thought about what his mother said later that day as he and Klaus rode down the steep hillside beside his house on their scooters. It was an exhilarating ride and they built up quite a speed as they travelled down the hill. Before reaching the end of the slope, at a powerful velocity, they had to use their foot to break in order to make a sharp turn onto the dirt road behind the house. It was here—as Paul was thinking about war and death and how the only thing he ever saw die was the rabbit his father had killed last month for supper—that he forgot to break. He crashed through the neighbor's wooden fence that sat at the edge of the road. On impact, he sailed through the air along with his scooter and numerous chunks of wood. Klaus told him later that he flew like a rag doll, with arms and legs splayed in different directions. Paul didn't remember any of it - only landing with a thud that knocked the wind out of him. Laying still he heard his friend running down the hill toward him.

"Am I still alive?" Paul asked through squinted eyes.

"Of course, silly, you're still breathing aren't you?" Klaus replied. "Hurry on, get up, before the neighbors catch us."

Paul gingerly got to his feet making sure nothing hurt too terribly. They scurried back up the hill, Klaus picking up Paul's scooter along the way. Standing back on the dirt road they looked down at the carnage. Broken pieces of wood lay scattered intermittently throughout the yard. Thankfully, he had burst through between the fence poles.

"I never saw anyone fly before Paul. That was amazing."

"I'm glad you enjoyed it, Klaus because I won't be doing it again." They both laughed.

"You had better go home and get cleaned up. You have cuts everywhere," Klaus said looking him up and down.

Paul looked down at his scraped and bleeding legs. "Yah, you're right. No hiding from this one. I'll be spending the rest of the week fixing and painting a fence I guess."

"Let me know when you can play again!" yelled Klaus as he made his way back up the hill to his house.

Paul sauntered home walking alongside his scooter—grateful that just as himself—it had suffered only minor scratches. He knew what he was in for once he reached the house, but he smiled and thought, "That was one heck of a ride."

########

October came and showed it's brilliance in the trees of the Ore Mountains. Most of the people in the small town of Hartenstein were unaffected by the war so far. There was no lack or shortage of supplies, although rationing had begun in August.[2] Hitler continued his tyrannical speeches over the radio. At night Paul would play with his toy soldiers and watch as his parents leaned forward from their seats with concerned faces, listening intently to what the Fuehrer had to say.

As Germany continued to conquer more territories throughout Europe, Paul and Klaus conquered territory of their own. As curious five year old boys, they traveled further and further from their homes exploring the outer reaches of Hartenstein. Having heard stories from older siblings, the boys knew that the stone quarries were the best place for an adventure. Three had

 been dug not even a quarter mile from town. The stone was used to build the famous Hartenstein castles. The reason many tourists came to visit each year. It was just the right distance for the boys to travel on their scooters. Sitting on a hill northwest of the town square, it was a lot of work to get there, but worth the view.

"Come on, Klaus!" yelled Paul still out of breath.

Klaus came up behind him. "Wow, look how deep the hole is!" They laid their scooters down and ventured further to the edge looking down at a small pool of water at the bottom. They picked up stones and threw several into the pit watching them land with a large splash. Walking along the edge through evergreen and poplar trees, they carefully explored the perimeter until they could find a way to clamber down. Along the upper edge they could see that here and there, sections of stone had been cut away, leaving small caves that would make a perfect hideout. "Look over here," said Klaus as he moved a low hanging branch out of the way.

They both knelt down and slid over the edge onto a rock platform. Behind them was a large square black hole—where the rock had been cut centuries before—that lead into a shallow cave.

"You wouldn't have any matches with you, would you, Paul?" asked Klaus, hesitant to step forward into the dark opening.

"Why would I carry matches—I don't smoke," retorted Paul.

"But your grandpa does," added Klaus.

"Oh for Pete's sake!" Paul said with exasperation as he moved past Klaus and into the cave opening. Five feet inside it ended.

"Just the right size! Come on in, Klaus the weather's fine," Paul said as he felt the damp walls of stone in front of him. Once inside their eyes adjusted to the dark and they could see much better. After thoroughly investigating their small hideaway, they sat at the edge of the platform they had stood on earlier. While throwing pebbles into the small pond below, they watched the sunset quietly together. Paul broke the silent reverie. "Time to head home, Klaus, it's getting cold and almost time for supper."

Klaus nodded in reply. "I really like it here. We need to come back and explore the other quarries."

"Yah, Klaus, and the swimming hole too - that's just a little further from here—next summer for sure." The boys made their way home, each satisfied that they had discovered a great thing and that more adventures awaited them in the future.

########

Winter settled into the little town with a blizzard that left more than a foot of snow. The morning after the white deluge Paul woke to a winter wonderland. It was the beginning of December and everyone was already excited for the coming Christmas holiday. Herbert would be coming home for Christmas break. Paul looked forward to hearing him play his horn for the Christmas services. He and his sisters were practicing *Silent Night* on their recorders. Magdalena being only four was still too young to play an instrument but she could carry a tune and always sang along.

Paul looked out his bedroom window at the scenic sight. He jumped back as a snowball suddenly hit the glass in front of him. Looking down he saw Klaus waving and motioning for him to come out. Paul gave him the thumbs up sign as he watched him walk back up to the street in front of their house towing his sled behind him. Minutes later, running downstairs, he was about to throw on his coat and join his friend for a rapturous day of sledding when he heard his name.

"Paul-Gerhard!" His mother yelled from the kitchen. "Not one more step until you've eaten your breakfast."

He sighed. "Yes, mama, be right there!" Paul yelled back. He sailed into the kitchen and plopped into his seat next to his dad who was still reading the morning paper.

It was another leisurely Saturday morning of late breakfasts and casual routines unlike the weekdays when things were more regimented. Paul read the front of the paper out loud. "Olympic Games in Finland Cancelled."[3]

"Very good, Paul," Marie said as she placed a bowl of oatmeal in front of him with a small glass of milk. "Don't forget to say your prayers."

Paul bowed his head and silently thanked the Lord that his mother had taken the time and taught him to read so he could start school in the first grade come next fall. He looked forward to being in the same class with Klaus and his cousin Eberhard. Inhaling the oatmeal and chugging down his milk, Paul wiped his face with his sleeve then looked pleadingly at both his parents.

"Yes, you're excused, Paul." His mother said as she stood by Carl.

"Don't forget to feed the chickens and rabbits." His father said seriously as he folded the paper and laid it down on the table. "But most of all…(Paul waited patiently for him to finish his sentence)…have fun!" Marie and Carl laughed as they watched Paul jump up and run out of the kitchen.

Paul and Klaus worked most of the afternoon on the hill beside his house packing snow. Making a good ramp took time, but they both knew it would be worth the wait. Having completed their arduous task, they discussed who would go first. Klaus having concerns about the height of the ramp gave way to Paul's enthusiasm that everything would be fine. He knelt behind the sled to give an extra push just in case the steep incline didn't give enough momentum for Paul and the sled to clear the ramp. "Are you ready?!" yelled Klaus.

"Yes!" With Paul's reply, he shoved the sled forward with all his might. Starting slowly and then gradually gaining speed Klaus watched as his brave friend flew through the air after hitting the ramp just right. It was a perfect takeoff with lightening trajectory.

"Maybe I pushed too hard" Klaus thought. Paul landed the sled, hanging on tightly to the rope that controlled the steering. He pulled with all his might to the left to avoid the fence he and his father had just repaired the previous fall. He used the heel of his boots trying to slow down as he swerved into the adjacent neighbor's backyard. A wave of snow, from trying to break, sprayed out from each side of the sled. Heading directly for a small row of evergreens that had been neatly planted the summer before, there was nothing Paul could do except scream and hold on for dear life.

Klaus stood and watched from a perfect perspective at the top of the hill as Paul swerved to miss the neighbor's fence but hit another neighbor's small row of evergreens. Hitting the last tree in the row with the front of the sled it flew high into the air as it was swiftly decapitated. Running down the hill Klaus cried out, "Paul, Paul, you nailed it!"

"I nailed it alright," said Paul as he walked up the neighbor's backyard covered in snow. With the sled in tow behind him, he met Klaus on the plowed road. They looked down at the fallen tree. "I meant the landing," said Klaus.

"I know," Paul said as he shook his head. "I'm afraid if I tell ma and pa I smashed something again they won't let me play on the hill anymore. They both looked down again at the fallen tree.

"I have an idea," said Klaus. He dragged the tree back to it's stump. Around the stump he pushed a large mountain of snow.

"What are you doing?" asked Paul.

"You'll see," said Klaus. After finishing the mound, he picked up the freshly cut tree and jammed it down into the center where the stump was now buried. "There. Now, no one will know till spring that the evergreen was chopped down. We just have to be careful not to run anymore down."

"Klaus you are the best friend ever," Paul said as he swung his arm over his friend's shoulders. "Come on, now it's your turn!"

########

Several weeks later, just before Christmas, Herbert came home from school. Bursting through the door with his father behind him, Herbert let out, "Hey, everybody I'm home!"

Paul beat the girls downstairs. Carrying Herbert's case that housed his horn in one arm, he ran up to his brother and hugged him. Holding it up for him to see he said, "I took good care of it, Herbert, just as you asked."

"I knew you would Paul. I'm looking forward to practicing it for the Christmas Eve service."

Marie embraced her son then held his face in her hands. "And I'm looking forward to hearing it." Marie's eyes glittered with unshed tears as she embraced him again.

"Herbert!" Magdalena screamed as she came down the stairs.

Embracing his older three sisters first, he then lifted Magdalena up in his arms and kissed her on the cheek. "How's my Shatzi?"

"Good, I've been helping mama cook in the kitchen."

"I'm sure you've made something yummy. Shall we go see?"

"We made your favorite meal, and of course dad's too," said Elisabeth leading the way to the kitchen.

"Rye bread with Sauerbraten! Could life be any better?!" Herbert said with the joy of someone who had just spent months eating institutional food. Everyone laughed. It was good to have him back home again. Minutes later as they held hands in prayer, Paul watched as the candles on the advent wreath flickered washing all their faces with a warm glow. It was a memory he would cherish for a very long time.

########

Christmas Eve they walked as a family to their little church. Carl and Marie were glad their children were part of a congregation where the doctrine of Hitler was not preached-unlike the large state church which sat at the top of the hill above them. Carrying their instruments, Marie and the girls sang 'To Shepherds as They Watched by Night,[4]' the song they would sing together during the service. The stars sparkled bright and the song reminded Paul of the baby Jesus long ago who laid in a manger on such a night.

During the service, after playing 'Silent Night' on their recorders, Paul went down to sit next to his pa. Although Carl always sang off tune, which made Paul's ears itch, he remembered what his mother told him about his father's singing. "It's not the sound of the voice God hears, Paul-Gerhard, but the sound of the heart."

Herbert played a wonderful interlude on his horn while the offering was taken. After the sermon his mother and sisters sang the song he had heard them practice so often. He could even hear little Magdalena's voice. As his mother's solo began, he looked up at his father, who with eyes closed, listened intently to his mother's voice. Seeing such joy on his face, Paul thought he looked as if he were somewhere else entirely.

After the service, he ran outside with his cousins and threw snowballs. Hans' were always the biggest and fastest and of course stung the most. His Uncle Hans and Aunt Lene soon called them to start walking home. With eight children they had a busy night ahead.

Uncle Gerhard and his Opa Paul would be joining them for the Christmas Eve meal. They lived together in a four story apartment building that Gerhard had built. The shoe factory was on the first floor while apartments were on the other three. It was right across from the church so they had a short walk every Sunday.

Arriving home, with wonderful smells from the kitchen wafting through the air, the girls hurried to help set the table. The men filled their steins with beer from a small keg, and sat in the formal living room. Of course, the conversations were solely about politics and war. Paul - tired of hearing it - was glad when his mother gave the call for supper. After the meal, they gathered around the Christmas tree and exchanged gifts. Although crude in form, Paul was proud of the small animals he had carved from wood for everyone. Handmade scarves and mittens, sketches, and handmade clothes, were exchanged along with new slippers for everyone from Opa Paul and Uncle Gerhard.

That night, before sleep came upon him, Paul listened as his mother's voice softly filled the house. As she lay in her bed she sang the last verse of *Silent Night*. He smiled remembering walks through the woods with her. He then knew where his father was earlier as he listened to his mother's voice in church.

########

Soon after New Year's, Herbert left for school and the daily routine returned. Winter passed slowly with gray snowy days blurring together. Paul spent a lot of time with his cousins Hans, Waldemar and Eberhard playing chess and checkers. Their house was conveniently located only a few blocks away. They lived in a row of 6 duplexes. Behind where they sat was a steep empty field 3 or 4 blocks long. At the bottom of this was another road with houses. This was where the duplex sat-where the Schotts lived and where Paul was born. Behind this lay the forest where they often walked as a family in spring and summer and also where Paul and his mother had gathered mushrooms the previous fall. Nestled within this forest sat the castle

Hartenstein. Within the woods near the castle was a large rock. Here, as the months grew warmer, Paul, Klaus, and his cousins would play king of the hill. Hans being the oldest and the biggest would always

win. It was here that Klaus decided he didn't like playing with Hans and his brothers. The rock was a mammoth stone that stuck out from the side of the hill. Surrounded by evergreens at the top, it dropped slowly with 3 long steps of smooth granite until it abruptly stopped with a 4 foot drop at the end. The best plan of attack was to come from behind – to try and sneak up through the forest - then shove the ruling king off the top. This was exactly what Paul and Klaus decided to do. The taunts of his cousins could be heard echoing through the woods.

"Come on you big chickens!" Hans yelled.

"Balk, balk, balk," added Eberhard.

"Losers!" yelled Waldemar. Suddenly from behind them Paul and Klaus ran from the woods. Paul tackled Waldemar and Klaus pushed Hans from behind trying to topple him off the rock. Paul was successful in his endeavor - landing on top of a fallen Waldemar. Unbeknownst to Paul, Eberhard was right behind him jumping on top of him making a perfect sandwich. Klaus was not as successful. Hans simply moved a step away from Klaus's shove. Quickly turning around he grabbed Klaus by the seat of his pants and lifted him over his head. "Hans, nooooo!" yelled Paul who was sandwiched between Waldemar and Eberhard. If Hans heard him he didn't make it known. Flinging Klaus—with screams of protest coming from over his head—he threw him off the rock laughing maniacally. He watched with a grin as Klaus rolled down the granite stairs and disappeared over the edge.

"Hans! That was too rough!" Paul retaliated as he slid down the steps to his friend who lay at the bottom.

"Oh, you bunch of sissies!" yelled Hans as he and his brothers ran off into the woods.

"Klaus, Klaus can you hear me?" Paul said while shaking his friend.

Klaus opened his eyes and took a deep breath. Having the wind knocked out of him when he landed on his back was the worst injury - that and his pride. He sat up with the help of Paul. "I will never play with your cousins again, Paul."

"Can't say I don't blame you, Klaus. Hans was wrong to play so rough. I'm sorry." From then on Klaus no longer played with Paul when he was with his cousins.

########

It was the spring of 1940 and while rationing had begun the previous year, it took time for Paul to actually notice the difference in the meals his mother and sisters made. They had eggs from his chickens and meat from the rabbits when the rations weren't enough, but the thing he missed most was sugar. Sweet cakes, candy, and hot chocolate were things to be had only on special occasions now. The same with coffee and tea - something he heard his parents often wishing they had more of.

########

July's heat brought Paul and his cousins to the swimming hole not far from the stone quarries where he and Klaus had discovered their hideout. Covered with sweat and red faced by the time they arrived, there was no hesitation as each dove in after the other and swam to the surface into a back float. When the boys were younger, swimming was a family affair at the local pool where each learned to dive and swim. Now, what was once easily paid for could not be afforded anymore - simpler things, free of charge that offered the same pleasure took their place. Paul had never felt anything so refreshing. That was, until he felt a tug on his leg. Suddenly, he was totally submersed in water and being dragged even deeper. Opening his eyes underwater, he could barely make out the black swimsuit of Hans. Paul started seeing stars and was running out of air. Panicking, he raised his other foot and kicked at Hans's hand that was wrapped around his ankle. Hans let go and Paul shot to the surface. Coughing and sputtering while trying to inhale as much air as he could, he tried swimming to shore. Hans came up from behind, placing his hands on Paul's shoulders and pushed him under the water again. Paul had just enough time to gasp in a small amount of air. He could hear his cousins shouting before being submerged, "Hans knock it off!" Finally, just when Paul thought he was a dead man, Hans released his grip.

Coming to the surface Paul said through gasps and coughs "Don't ever do that again Hans!"

Hans laughed, "Just having some fun cuz. Lighten up."

Paul made it to shore, slipped on his shoes and grabbed his towel. Although he liked playing with his cousins, he knew how Klaus felt—he wouldn't be swimming with Hans any time soon.

On his walk home he thought about hunting down Klaus to see if he would want to see a flick later on. The movie house was only a few blocks from where they lived. Cheaper than the outdoor pool, sometimes their parents had enough spare change to let them see a matinee. Finding Klaus later at home, they walked down together to find out what was showing. *The Scoundrel* was up on the marquee and since it was a comedy, their parents gave them permission to see it, along with enough change to buy a small bag of popcorn. After the movie, during the walk home, Paul talked to Klaus about school and how excited he was to get started…except for one thing… and that one thing was Siegfried Schott.

########

September of 1940, the free world watched with fear and concern as Germany began its assault against London.⁵ Although unaware of Germany's attack, Paul was entering the first grade with fear and concern of his own. That would be whether an old bully would continue his tirade against him. "Come on, Paul!" yelled Eberhard.

"I'm coming!" Paul yelled back down the hall as he slowly walked toward the exit. He could hear the yelling and screaming of the children at play in the school yard. He had yet to catch a glimpse of Siegfried, but knew that his nemesis was lurking nearby. Stepping out onto the playground Paul was immediately confronted by him and several of his cronies. Paul brought his fists up in front of his face. Herbert had taught him a few boxing moves before he had left for school and he was ready to try them.

The next moment led Paul to drop his hands and look in disbelief. Siegfried and his gang abruptly turned around and walked away. A voice came from behind him. "I don't think he'll be giving you any more trouble," said Hans with a grin. Paul turned and looked at his cousins and friend.

"Nope, not with us around," said Waldemar.

"We got your back Paul," said Klaus.

"That's right!" said Eberhard.

"I thought they left because of my new boxing moves," Paul said with disappointment.

"Not a chance cuz, not a chance." Hans said laughing as he walked away.

"I thought you looked pretty strong," said Klaus. "Although you're about a foot shorter than Siegfried."

"Thanks, Klaus," Paul said with a slight grin.

After the playground incident, Paul hoped that Siegfried would leave him alone, and for the most part he did—except for the occasional shove and name calling—this was a great relief for Paul.

########

During the next year the war raged on with the German army approaching Moscow and the bombing of Pearl Harbor by Japan.[6] The Tittel family continued with the business of life - church, chores, school, work, and of course long walks in the forest. Listening to the news broadcasts and reading the daily post, kept them abreast of what was happening, at least what the Nazi propaganda would have them know.

The Christmas of 1941, Herbert came home with good news. After graduation in the spring of 1942, he would be returning home to apprentice at a small accounting firm in Hartenstein. Marie was overjoyed as was the rest of the family. Having him home to help with running the household and the extra income would be a blessing.

########

As the Battle of Midway[7] was fought, Herbert graduated from college and returned home to Hartenstein to start his first job. Being only a part-time apprentice though, was not enough to keep him from being conscripted into the Reichsarbeitsdienst[8] or National Labor Front. Both parents knew that he could be drafted at any time into the army while serving in the labor force. Marie seemed to take it in stride and rallied the family to pray over him before he left but Paul noticed how pale and frail she had become and worried about her.

Christa, because of receiving good grades in middle school, was given permission to attend a high school in Aue. Starting in the fall of 1942 she began taking the train to school every day.

Paul, having peaked an interest in wanting to play the piano, started to gather mushrooms to sell in order to pay for his lessons. The skill of mushroom hunting would come in very handy as the war continued. His Opa Paul, glad to hear of his interest in playing his favorite instrument, blessed Paul with his old piano. His Uncles Hans and Gerhard helped move it into their formal living room. Paul was so excited to have his own piano. He loved music as much as his mother and looked forward to playing it often.

########

Vicar Walter Hirschfeld was a vicar who came to the Tittel's church in the winter of 1942. After his vicarage he took a call in Saalfeld. This would become another important connection in the lives of Paul and Sigrid. A few years later they would see the Master's hand weaving relationships from their past into their future.

########

The Germans surrendered at Stalingrad[9], February 2, 1943. The outcome of the war had now turned in favor of the allies. Carl and Marie listened to Hitler's radio address the following day as he told the German people of the battles outcome. He could no longer hide the truth of such great losses. The stories of what was really happening in battle and to the Jewish people in concentration camps came flooding into the homes of the German people.

Although some chose not to believe, others did and saw the lies of Hitler exposed.

########

May 1943, brought Paul and his cousins – Hans, Waldemar, and Eberhard – along with his sisters - Sigrid, Ruth, and Magdalena - to confirmation class. Being a small church, and the children being close in age, made the pastor decide to group them together for teaching. Memorizing Bible verses were part of their studies, but what Paul liked best was memorizing the hymns. He and his sisters would sing them together on their walk home and this made learning them much easier. Marie made sure their picture was taken on confirmation Sunday.

Shortly after their confirmation in the later part of May, Marie received more sad news. Her brother Gerhard had been drafted into the German army. Her older brother Hans promised to take care of the business and their father while he was away. Marie promised him as a family they would pray for him often. Paul knew what a broken heart looked like, just by looking into his mother's eyes. It was a sad time for everyone.

At the train station her brother Hans, his wife Lene and their children along with the Tittel family bid farewell to Gerhard. He was headed for the western front, a small consolation was that it wasn't the eastern. Russia was a hornet's nest that had been struck. There was no mercy for Germans that were captured by them.

########

September was the start of a great school year for Paul as he started fourth grade. He met another good friend. His name was Dietrich, but he called him Dieter for short. Dieter loved music and he had two other friends that did too. Often they would get together and play as a quartet. Dieter and Max played the violin, Paul played the piano, and Godfried played the accordion. It was quite a group and they had a raucous good time together.

########

Their worst fears were confirmed in the letters they received from Herbert while he was working for the National Labor Front. October brought him home in a uniform. Like his uncle Gerhard, he had been drafted into the German army. Herbert was allowed to visit his family before heading to war. He was glad to have time to spend with his parents and siblings - telling them all with a wink that he had a giant guardian angel that would keep him safe - along with their prayers. Marie new it was coming, and so was prepared for the most part…still, she wept a river of tears.

As he got ready to leave, he gave his horn to Paul again to care for and promised him he would be back for it.

Paul saluted his brother as he took the case from him and Herbert returned the salute. As soon as his arm was lowered, Paul leaped into his arms, hugged him around the waist and cried.

"I promise, little brother. I'll be back before you know it," Herbert said with confidence.

"You promise?!" Paul said with a shaky breath from crying.

"Yes, I promise to return and tease you unmercifully for the rest of your life." Herbert reached under Paul's arms and began to tickle him until he laughed.

The family walked him to the train station and all of them cried as it pulled away. They had heard the horror stories from the eastern front – where Herbert's orders would take him – and knew the German army was failing and that the Russians were seeking revenge.

########

November 18th, the bombing of Berlin began. It was still hard for the Nazis and many German people to believe that they were losing the war. But for other Germans it was the hope they had longed for – the release from the tyranny of a madman.

########

Thanksgiving was only a week away and Marie was busy folding laundry at the kitchen table. Elisabeth had just brought up a basket from the basement where they sometimes hung clothes to dry in the winter. It was in the afternoon and Paul, Ruth, Sigrid, and Magdalena were soon to come home from school.

Elisabeth turned from the sink where she was doing dishes and saw the strangest thing as she looked at her mother. It was as if half her face had melted and her arm hung limp at her side. Then slowly like a large tree that had just been struck, she fell sideways out of her chair.

"Papa! Papa come quick!" Carl ran from the living room to the kitchen and knelt at Marie's side. Unable to speak she raised her good hand to his face. One side of her lips went up in a smile.

"My love, I'm here. I will never leave you," Carl said while cradling her head. Minutes later the ambulance came.

Paul and his sisters arrived from school in time to see their mother covered in wool blankets being loaded into the back of the ambulance with their father by her side. Elisabeth ran to them quickly comforting them and explaining all that had just happened. When Christa came home later in the evening she would do the same for her.

Paul loved his sister Elisabeth and looked to her as a mother. She had been there through most of his young life to help, comfort, love, and raise him when his own mother couldn't. He was glad that she was there for him, he needed her warm hugs and reassurance that everything would be okay… even if it wasn't.

########

A month later just before Christmas, Marie came home to a smother of hugs as Carl carried her over the threshold. "Reminds me of our wedding day," Marie said slowly and softly. "Only better, because the children are here."

Carl kissed her on the forehead and set her down on her feet. Elisabeth handed her the cane she needed to walk. Everyone watched her take her first steps and cheered. Her left arm was immobile but her left leg still had some strength and with a brace, made it possible for her to walk on flat surfaces.

Paul looked on as his mother walked across the living room floor to her new bed in the informal living room. Elisabeth would sleep there to help care for her.

He remembered an earlier conversation with Elisabeth. "Will mama ever play the lute again?" Paul asked as he held Elisabeth's hand while they walked to church the previous Sunday.

"No, Paul, mama will not play the lute again."

"Will mama ever sing again?" He asked – his eyes stinging with tears.

"No, Paul, mama will never sing again…at least not here, but someday, when we're in heaven we will hear her lovely voice again. I'm sure." Elisabeth stopped walking and looked down at Paul.

"Now listen here, Paul-Gerhard. There are many things mama will not be able to do anymore. But she can still do some of the most important ones—like loving us, praying for us, and encouraging us in the good word. Understood?" Elisabeth said smiling down at her little brother.

Paul shook his head yes. Although his heart ached for the mother he knew before the stroke, Elisabeth was right…he was just glad to have her home.

1. https://www.pbs.org/thewar/at_war_timeline_1939.htm

2. On 28th August 1939 the German people were surprised by the introduction of ration cards. Main food (meat, lard, coffee and sugar) were only to be obtained by using ration cards. From 25th September that year, bread and eggs were rationed as well.

   http://bills-bunker.de/171927.html

3. https://www.pbs.org/thewar/at_war_timeline_1939.htm

4. To shepherds as they watched by night
   Appeared a host of angels bright;
   Behold the tender Babe, they said,
   In yonder lowly manger laid.

   At Bethlehem, in David's town,
   As Micah did of old make known;
   'Tis Jesus Christ, your Lord and King,
   Who doth to all salvation bring.

   Oh, then rejoice that through His Son
   God is with sinners now at one;
   Made like yourselves of flesh and blood,
   Your Brother is the eternal God.

   What harm can sin and death then do?
   The true God now abides with you.
   Let hell and Satan rage and chafe,
   Christ is your Brother—ye are safe.

   Not one He will or can forsake
   Who Him his confidence doth make.
   Let all his wiles the Tempter try,
   You may his utmost powers defy.

   Ye shall and must at last prevail;
   God's own ye are, ye cannot fail.
   To God forever sing your praise
   With joy and patience all your days.

   http://www.cyberhymnal.org/htm/t/o/toshepat.htm

5. https://www.pbs.org/thewar/at_war_timeline_1940.htm

6. https://www.pbs.org/thewar/at_war_timeline_1941.htm

7. https://www.pbs.org/thewar/at_war_timeline_1942.htm

8. http://alphahistory.com/nazigermany/nazi-economic-recovery/

9. http://www.history.com/this-day-in-history/battle-of-stalingrad-ends

Chapter Seven: War Comes to Hartenstein

It started with a low rumbling sound that slowly grew louder, climbing in tone until it reached a screaming crescendo. Staying at the highest pitch for several minutes, it then slowly descended until it almost faded away, only to restart again. This continued until Paul thought it would never end. Holding the pillow over his head he tried to block out the 5 minute long, ear piercing wail of the air raid siren. He always thought that living a few blocks from the fire station was the greatest. The siren was always a clarion call for him, Klaus, his cousins, or any other child within hearing distance. Running down to see the fire trucks pull out of the station was the best, but now that they started blowing it several times a day he wished they lived on the other side of town.

Lifting the pillow from his head Paul looked over at his father who was sleeping soundly. Unbelievably, he had slept through the deafening howl. He thought it was most likely from having one of his seizures the night before. Whenever he phased out, exhaustion usually followed close behind. He thought back to several of his father's fits of rage over the years – the verbal violence was mostly directed at his mother—his father was not himself when these episodes came. But still, it hurt his heart to hear him say the things that he did. Elisabeth would sometimes step between them to try and turn his attention from his mother to her. Sometimes it worked and sometimes not. After several minutes of explosive anger he would collapse and come back to himself wondering what happened.

He studied his father's face. The wrinkles on his forehead, unshaven, and the dark circles under his eyes – he looked old. "How could someone who was so quiet and kind turn into something so... so much different?" Paul thought to himself.

Then he remembered a verse his mother had given him when he had asked her a similar question. He could still hear her saying it to him in the slow soft voice she spoke after her stroke. "And be ye kind one to another, tenderhearted, forgiving one another, even as God for Christ's sake hath forgiven you." Ephesians 4:32.

Paul forgave his pa, but it would take a long time for his screaming tirades to fade from his memory. Quietly, he slipped out of bed careful not to wake his father. Now that his mother and sister made their beds in the informal living room, the sleeping arrangements upstairs had changed. He slept where his mother used to sleep - alongside his father in a double bed. Christa and Ruth now shared a bedroom, with Sigrid and Magdalena sharing the other.

Quickly getting dressed, he hurried downstairs to do his chores. He could already hear Elisabeth in the kitchen. Bringing up coal from the basement would be his first priority. After dumping a fresh supply of it into the coal bin by the cook stove he headed outside to feed the chickens and rabbits. Gathering wood stacked by the house for the wood burning stove, he made a mental note that he would have to go to the nearby forest after school and restock it. Carrying in a large armful, Paul stacked up a small pile by the wood stove. Stirring the hot embers from the night before, he added several more logs until a good fire was blazing. Being early January the house was colder than the ice box, but the frigid air soon receded with the stoves heat quickly emanating throughout the house.

Elisabeth was making cream of wheat for breakfast and soon it was ready. "Paul, could you take mother's breakfast to her?" she asked, motioning to a tray that already held a bowl of warm cereal and a cup of hot tea.

Grabbing hold of the tray carefully he walked into the informal living room. "Good morning, mama," Paul said cheerfully as he set the tray on the table near where she was sitting. Elisabeth had already gotten her up. She sat at the table reading her Bible with a magnifying glass.

"Good morning, my Liebling," Marie said softly with a half-smile.

Paul set her bowl of cereal and tea before her. "I'm going to cut wood after school, mama. Father's not feeling well. I can handle the hand saw and wagon myself. The wagon was a small two wheeled cart that had two long bars extending forward. Standing in between these while towing the cart, one could haul quite a load.

"Yes, yes you can, Paul. You've grown into a strong young man," Marie said as she reached to cusp his cheek in her hand with her good arm. "Such a helper you are, my son. Work hard, study hard, seek God with all your heart and He will lead you into your destiny."

Paul smiled as he leaned forward to give her a hug. "I will mama, I will."

########

It was a dark cold winter and with it came the cold hearts of Hitler's SS. Paul, Klaus and his cousins watched one Saturday morning as a small caravan of trucks and cars drove through the town. They made their way to the Hartenstein castle.

Later, hidden behind trees near the rock they played on, the boys watched as they dragged the duke – Fuerst von Schoenburg, his now oldest son, prince Alexander, (3 older boys had died at Stalingrad and another in a Russian prison) his wife and their 7 other children out of the castle. The soldiers pointed their guns at the guest quarters and shoved them in that direction, obviously telling them this is where they would now be staying. For a moment Paul shut his eyes covering them with his hands, thinking the SS would shoot them in the back as they walked away. He peaked between his fingers as the moment passed and the duke and his family stepped into their new quarters, safely shutting the door behind them. The SS now had control of one of Hartenstein's most prized possessions and used it as their fortified center.

Walking back to their homes, the boys talked about the war knowing that the German army was failing. "Have you heard anything from Herbert, Paul?" Klaus asked.

"Only a note from the government saying that he was missing in action at the 2nd Battle of Kiev."[1] Paul hung his head low and looked straight ahead trying to hide his tear filled eyes. Minutes passed in silence without anyone saying a word. Only the crunch of snow underneath their feet could be heard.

"Mom says sometimes no news is good news. We haven't heard from Uncle Gerhard either. Pa says he's on the western front somewhere." Waldemar looked over at Paul and their eyes met in a moment of understanding.

"I wish the war was over," Eberhard said with longing.

"The way things are going it will be soon," Waldemar added. Just then they heard the sound of a truck engine coming up the hill behind them. The boys ran off the snow covered road into the cover of the thick pine forest that lined the thoroughfare.

As it passed, a spotlight was turned on by a soldier sitting on the passenger side. They drove by slowly while shining a light directly into the forest where they were hiding. Paul, Klaus and his cousins looked at each other wide eyed hiding behind the large trunks of old evergreens. They held their breath so the soldiers wouldn't see their exhale. It seemed like forever, but finally they moved on. Making their way out from behind the trees, they looked up the road at the receding tail lights and collectively sighed in relief. Having heard stories of the SS shooting people for just looking at them wrongly -   they did not want any kind of encounter with this formidable tentacle of Hitler.

Arriving home, Paul quietly closed the door behind him. Elisabeth came out from the kitchen with her hands on her hips. "Where have you been Paul-Gerhard? Out chasing German soldiers again? You had better be careful. I know I can't keep you cooped up in the house all winter, but don't go spying on the soldiers. They might mistake you for the Allied troops and shoot you by mistake. What would that do to mother and father? Come now and eat your breakfast before it gets cold." She turned and went back into the kitchen.

All Paul heard was, "Wha, wha, wha, wha…breakfast." He was hungry after their last excursion. He knew it was dangerous, but trying to keep him away from the soldiers, guns, and military trucks was like…trying to stop him from breathing. He had to have it or he would die. It was in his life's blood to explore and have adventures. Paul made his way to the kitchen and sat with his sisters and father. Elisabeth stood by her father's side.

"Mother is not feeling well this morning, let us keep her in prayer." Elisabeth said with her head bowed.

Carl prayed the blessing and included Marie in their morning prayer.

########

Spring brought more German troops into the area. It was March and the trains were packed with soldiers and refugees. The town too, was full of people from all walks of life, wandering through, looking for a safe haven, food and a place to rest. Some families in town had pity on the refugees and took them in - seeing the war must soon come to an end and surely things would be better then.

Opa Paul, Uncle Hans, and Aunt Lene, their children, Aunt Lillie, and Uncle Karl came to Paul's birthday party on April 3rd. It was a wonderful time. The air raid siren didn't sound once. Everyone that came contributed rations for Elisabeth to make a wonderful meal and a small cake for Paul. Gifts were given to him from all in attendance. He was most impressed with a new pair of paper shoes from his Opa. It was hard to believe they were made from paper. The technique that was used to make them, made them quite comfortable and long lasting. All quality materials went to the factories to support the war effort. New and inventive ways of making everyday products from less expensive material had become a part of everyday life.

########

Spring passed quickly into the heat of summer. July brought another tragedy to the Tittel family. Elisabeth woke to find that her mother had had another stroke and was now completely paralyzed on her left side. The ambulance came again to take her to the hospital, although there was not much they could do. A few days later she was wheeled into the house by Carl in her new wheelchair. Totally unable to walk, but still able to talk, the family counted their blessings. They could still hear their mother's voice.

########

It was early fall of 1944. Elisabeth, Paul, and his sisters sat on the floor before the radio. Carl sat in a chair by Marie's bed holding her right hand while they listened to the broadcast. The German army was in retreat. Along the eastern front the Russian Red Army had now crossed the German border and were looking for revenge from all that the German army had done to them. Millions of German civilians tried to outrun the oncoming carnage of an enraged nation that thirsted for German blood.

The speaker's voice came across loud and clear. He demanded that the German people stand their ground and fight to the death for their country. Boys under 16 and men 60 years and older were encouraged to enlist in the army and fight for the fatherland.

After the broadcast Carl and Marie prayed over their family. They were grateful that Paul was still too young to be drafted and that Carl, because of his previous war injury, was also exempt.

Marie suggested a time of worship was needed. The children ran to get their instruments and played many old hymns from memory - Paul and Magdalena on their recorders, along with Elisabeth and Christa on their guitars with Sigrid and Ruth on their mandolins. "What a beautiful sound they made as a family," Paul thought as he listened to the combination of voices and instruments. He could even hear his mother joining in, unable to sing but still able to speak the words of the powerful promises of God.

########

Christmas came with more troops coming and going through the small town. Studying was difficult for Paul. If it wasn't the air raid siren blasting through the walls of the school, it was a long caravan of trucks and troops coming through town. When Christmas came it was a great relief to the teachers as well as the students to be going home for a break.

"It's a quiet holiday...for the most part," thought Paul. The walk to church was special. They joined arm and arm as a family singing their favorite Christmas hymns.

Arriving at church Paul made his way to the balcony to play his trumpet with two other boys who played the horn and coronet. They had been practicing for several Sundays now and Paul thought they sounded pretty good.

He looked down and saw Magdalena sitting with her sisters in the front pew – old enough now to sit in front with the older women instead of in the back pews with the babies. His father was seated up front with his head bowed next to his Opa Paul. He remembered past Christmas's sitting with his pa while listening to his mother sing. He thought of Herbert and prayed, if he were still alive, that someday he would see him again. A tear slid down his cheek and he swiftly wiped it away.

It was time. They stood together, raised their instruments and began to play the song he last remembered his mother singing – 'To Shepherds as they Watched by Night.'[2]

After Christmas, on December 26th, Paul and his father spread the morning post out on the kitchen table to read about The Battle of the Bulge and the city of Bastogne, Belgium.[3] Here, a general for the allies named Patton, outsmarted the German forces - securing Bastogne, he pushed the German army back across the Rhine river.

"Soon, Paul the Americans will be here. We must make a plan and get ready to do all that we can to protect ourselves," Carl said as Paul nodded in agreement.

That evening the Tittel family sat together and discussed what they should do as the American army advanced toward Hartenstein. "We will move the beds to the basement, that way we will be right next to the bomb shelter if we need it," Carl said as they gathered around Marie's bed.

"I can prepare some dried food, and bread we could live on if we can't come upstairs to cook," added Elisabeth.

"We can help!" Christa, Ruth and Sigrid chimed in.

"Don't forget your Bibles and especially your instruments," Marie said looking at the children.

"I will take care of family heirlooms and any other valuables and hide them away," Carl looked down at Magdalena.

"Like my teddy bear?" Magdalena said as she held up her bear to her father.

"I think the teddy bear will be safest with you," Carl said as he scratched the top of the bears head. Magdalena laughed.

"Paul, there's a long iron bar we use to chip ice off the sidewalk. Be sure to bring it down to the basement. We'll use it to barricade the door if we need to.

"I'll get candles and extra blankets from upstairs," said Christa.

"I think that's it for now," Carl said as he stood up.

"Not yet, Carl. You know how we end every family meeting," Marie said smiling up at her husband.

Carl sat back down in his chair and looked admiringly at his beautiful wife. "Where would I be without her?" he thought. They prayed, thanking the Lord for bringing an end to the war and protecting them.

########

The air raid sirens never stopped. Day and night they blared out their warnings for everyone to stay inside and seek shelter from the approaching onslaught of terror.

It was February 13, 1945. Marie was dressed and in her wheelchair. The sound of the siren was muffled by the basement walls. Paul sat next to his mother and read from one of his school books. It was Tuesday, a school day, but all schools had been canceled until the fighting in their town came to an end.

Elisabeth and her father were upstairs making lunch. Hearing something strange, Paul stopped reading. It was a droning sound and it was growing louder.

"Paul open the door," Marie said, curious herself as to what it could be. Paul removed the bar and swung the door wide open. They could see the town spread out below, but as they lifted their eyes to the source of the sound they saw that the sky was almost entirely black.

"Paul, push me outside!" Marie said as loud as she could. The droning sounded like a plane engine only much louder.

Paul shook his head to clear it. He tried to understand what he was looking at – all he could think of was a flock of crows – it was something he had never seen before. Mesmerized by what he saw in the sky, he slowly pushed his mother through the door and then a few more feet out into the yard. They had shoveled an area around the basement door so Elisabeth could push Marie out for fresh air and sunshine when the fighting wasn't so fierce. They watched, captivated by the sight. Soon the rest of the family joined them. "Planes, look at all the planes, papa," Magdalena yelled pointing up to the sky. There seemed to be no end to the armada of planes. Hundreds upon hundreds of them flew overhead, heading northeast.

"Dresden, they're heading for Dresden," Marie said sadly.

Paul looked on in horror, thinking of all the young children that lived there. "What will happen to all the boys and girls my age?" he thought to himself.

"Mama, can we pray?" Paul asked, feeling weak and sick to his stomach for some reason.

"Yes my, Liebling," Marie said as she reached for his hand. They prayed for the children of Dresden. They prayed for the people who lived in the city. They prayed for the refugees who had come to Dresden from the east and Hungary - who had fled there for safety but soon would be incinerated.

In the early morning hours, before dawn, they went out and saw a fiery glow in the northeast. Seeing the brilliant red light in the distance, they realized it was not the sunrise they were watching, but the burning of a large city and all its occupants. Still, the planes continued their bombings, heading toward the burning ruins, blackening the sky above them.

As morning broke, they continued to watch the bombers pass overhead. Paul saw a dogfight breakout hundreds of feet in the air above them. "Mother, look!" Paul said as he pointed up to planes that were engaged in an air battle. The German fighters were trying to take out some of the Allied bombers. Surrounded by wings of allied fighter planes, it was almost impossible for the Germans to get near them. Their protective guardians would immediately engage any approaching enemy plane.

Watching the battle develop, several planes fell from the sky and crashed into the nearby Erzegebirge Mountain range that surrounded Hartenstein. They were too far away to see the insignia - whether they were German, American or British.

Later, after the bombings, Paul would find out that the four Shettler boys – that Herbert grew up with in the apartments – were pilots in the German Air Force. The day Marie and Paul watched the battle in the air over Hartenstein was the day all four were reported missing in action.

It brought comfort to their mother – the thought that maybe it was them that day flying over Hartenstein protecting the town from the bombs of the Allied planes.

Dresden was about 60 miles northeast of Hartenstein and was completely leveled – killing possibly over 500,000 people. The smaller town of Hanover - roughly 300 miles northwest of them - faired a little better and was only 80 percent destroyed. Although, 3,850 people died in Hanover, it could have been much worse. The town had prepared themselves by building hundreds of bomb shelters for the civilian population.

When the bombings were over, as a family, they thanked the Lord that none had fallen on their town. Not a person had been injured while the hundreds of planes flew overhead.

########

It was spring and the weather was warming. The American army was not far from them now. Coming in from the northwest, skirmishes could be heard as the Allied and German forces fought. Pamphlets had been dropped by the Americans commanding all civilian residents to have a white flag hung from a window or draped over their roof. This would ensure they would not be bombed by incoming aircraft - showing they were not sided with the enemy.

The SS, who still resided in town, warned the people that anyone showing the white flag of surrender would be shot. This had happened to several town leaders in other villages nearby. Hearing of this, Carl decided - since the American troops did not yet occupy the town - that when the air raid siren blew he would quickly throw a white sheet out the upstairs bedroom window that faced west. This was the direction from which the Allied army was coming and the direction from which the planes approached. As soon as the all clear sounded he would pull the sheet inside so the SS would not see it.

The duke and his family, still residing on the premises of Hartenstein castle, placed a large white sheet on the roof of the castle, staving off bombing attacks even though the SS resided inside. Unfortunately, the Germans caught sight of it and demanded that it be removed. Shortly after its removal, it became a target for the American fighter bombers.

Paul heard the air raid siren and then the approaching planes. He and Klaus were standing on the gravel road behind their house with their scooters. They stooped down as the low flying planes flew over them. Both knew exactly where they were headed. "The castle!" Paul shouted to Klaus as the roar of the planes passed.

Quickly they sped down the road. Within seconds, large explosions shook the earth making them both stop in their tracks. "Paul, it's not safe!" yelled Klaus over the air raid siren and explosions.

"I have to see. I have to know!" Paul continued down the road towards the castle.

A speeding SS car coming from the castle's direction flew by them. As they approached, they could see the fire and the pitch black smoke rising high into the sky. Ahead of them they saw the duke and his son, Prince Alexander, sitting in their horse drawn wagon. (In honor of his fallen sons, he and his oldest gathered the corpses of dead German soldiers and buried them in a mass grave in the town's cemetery.) While the duke watched the fire devouring all they owned, the rest of his family stood weeping near the wagon.

Paul looked up at him and listened as he spoke to the few people who had gathered to watch one of the 'pearls of the region' brought to ruin.

The duke stood up and spoke loudly for everyone to hear. "The Lord has given and the Lord has taken away. The name of the Lord shall be praised!" Sitting back down he gave his son the reins then jumped down to stand with his wife and children as they watched the burning of the ancient structure.

Paul and Klaus headed back up the road to their homes. The all clear had sounded. "We better hurry, our parents will wonder what happened to us." Klaus said as he hurriedly pushed his scooter up the hill.

"It was such a beautiful castle. I will always remember it's beauty," Paul said to his friend.

"One good thing came from it," Klaus said almost out of breath. "It flushed the SS out of town."

"Yah," said Paul laughing. "You could see their faces white with fear when they drove by us." Looking ahead Paul saw his family standing in the backyard waving for him to quickly come to safety.

"Later, gator," Klaus said as he ran up the hill next to Paul's house.

"Paul, that was much too dangerous. But I'm sure you already know that. We can't keep you chained at home like a dog. Please make better decisions about where you go - especially when the air raid sirens are blaring." Carl said looking at him sternly.

"We know we are at war and that you are young and fascinated with all that's happening around you, but it's very dangerous. Be so very careful." Marie held out her hand as he approached.

Paul leaned over and kissed her on the cheek. "It was the Hartenstein castle. It's completely destroyed. The Duke and his family are fine. The SS have left the area," he turned to look back down the road from which he just came. Thick, black smoke still billowed into the sky.

Magdalena who had been standing next to her father, turned and hugged his waist and sobbed. She cried for quite a while. It was her favorite castle and the one they would often walk by as a family during their Sunday strolls.

"Now, now little one," Carl patted her back. "It will be alright. No worries. We're all here and everyone's safe. Maybe someday they'll build a new castle."

Her father's words meant as comfort, had no effect…Magdalena cried even harder.

########

It was the end of March, and the 3rd day of fighting. The war continued around them – gun shots and machine gun fire could be heard in the distance. It had been a long day of cleaning and chores with the family trying to maintain some kind normality. After supper, Carl and Paul decided to sleep in the formal living room on the double mattress they had moved from the upstairs bedroom. It was close quarters in the basement and with the two of them sleeping upstairs it gave everyone more room to relax and get a good night's rest.

The shelling started in the middle of the night and grew louder. Paul remembered that it felt like the time he ran his scooter through the neighbor's fence landing on his back out of breath. One moment he was sleeping and the next he was in the air then hitting the floor with a thud. The explosion was so loud and strong the whole house shook. At the same time, windows could be heard shattering throughout the neighborhood. Carl cried out in the dark, "Paul, are you alright?"

From the other side of the bed, on the floor he answered. "I'm here, pa. I'm okay."

"Downstairs now!" yelled Carl.

"What do you think they hit?" asked Paul as they ran down the stairs.

"It was so close it must have been the movie house," his father yelled back over his shoulder.

Moments later, the huddled together family, listened and prayed for themselves, their neighbors, and the town of Hartenstein.

The American field artillery fired their cannons throughout the night – shells flew everywhere – but only a few buildings were hit. The movie house being one of them was totally destroyed. Another business that was bombed the same night was the coal delivery company. Like the movie house it had taken a direct hit. All the horses had been killed. The owner sent word by messenger throughout the town that fresh meat was available until it ran out. Having heard the news, Paul grabbed a knife from the kitchen and a leather satchel to put the meat in. He knew his father was not strong enough so he went in his place. No one had meat for a long time. Just the thought of it made his stomach churn. Running down the street, he started to notice others stepping out of their houses running in the same direction. Standing not 70 feet from what was once the coal delivery building, Paul watched as nearly 50 people moved in a writhing compact circle, screaming and growling at one another. The ones closest to the carcass pulled the entrails out and handed them back to the people behind them. He saw faces and hands covered in blood. Once more, having been raised close to nature, all he could compare it to were bees swarming over a broken honeycomb. He watched with his mouth slightly agape. Holding the knife tightly in his hand and his satchel in the other, people slowly walked past him wiping their faces with their coat sleeves. Gradually, everyone dispersed. Paul could hardly believe what he saw. There was nothing left, even the hooves were gone…only a bloody circle on the cobblestones remained.

"I'm too small. There was no way I could have fought through that crowd," Paul thought to himself trying to think up excuses to tell his family why he hadn't retrieved anything. Sighing in resignation, he was about to turn and go home, when a man came running up to him with 2 large chunks of bloody flesh. "Here you go, son," the man said smiling down at him.

Paul quickly opened his satchel while the man placed the meat inside. "Thank you," Paul whispered, almost unable to contain his excitement.

"I saw how you weren't able to come and get your own so I took a double portion. How 'bout if I see you and your costly merchandise safely home? There's still plenty of others hungry enough who wouldn't mind taking that off your hands. If you know what I mean."

Paul nodded his head and was grateful for the man's company. Upon arriving back at the house, he turned to thank him again for his kindness but he had simply disappeared.

Carl took the satchel from Paul pulling out the two large pieces of meat over the kitchen sink.

"Meat! Oh my goodness it's meat. Ma, pa what should I make?" Elisabeth turned and looked at both her parents.

"Something totally delicious I'm sure Elisabeth," Marie said encouragingly.

"Good job son," Carl said as he helped Elisabeth clean the two large sections of hind flesh.

"All I did was stand there," Paul rolled his eyes while sitting next to Magdalena at the kitchen table.

"Still, you went. That takes courage," Carl looked at him and smiled. "Because of your bravery we now have a delicious meal to look forward to."

"And because of God's rich supply and the man – whom I'm sure was a guardian angel He sent to see you safely home – we must thank Him for His goodness to us." Marie added.

An hour later they did exactly that before they enjoyed the best tasting meal Elisabeth ever made.

########

April 16, 1945, the first company of tanks moved into Hartenstein. They stationed themselves in the lower part of town called the Niederstadt. Paul and his family could hear the battle being fought during the day. There were casualties on both sides. The duke and his son were faithful to gather the German bodies and deliver them to the cemetery. By the end of April there were still small pockets of German army units residing in Hartenstein. Not far from where Paul lived, they built three machine gun nests embedded in the walls of three quarries. Even with the Russians taking Berlin on April

26th4, these men still thought they were winning the war and could hold the line against the advancing Allied army.

While these few remaining German troops were setting up their positions, Paul and Klaus were playing on the hill alongside the house. "I have a great idea, Klaus," Paul said as they came to a stop after racing down the hill on their scooters. "Let's check out the quarries. I've heard there are a few German units left in town and they've set up camp there."

"Paul, I don't know if that's a good idea," Klaus said shaking his head. "If we know the German soldiers are there, the Americans must know too."

"Ah, come on Klaus, we'll only stay for a minute…I promise." Paul crossed his heart and held up his right hand.

"Alright, it's a deal," Klaus started pushing his scooter up the path toward the quarries with Paul following close behind.

Minutes later the boys found themselves a few steps from one of the German machine gun nests. After parking their scooters under a nearby tree, they decided to crawl through the pines to the edge of the quarry. Paul held his finger to his lips as they approached the area where he and Klaus usually climbed down to their hideout. Klaus pointed down toward their cave. They could hear the voices of German soldiers. "They're in our cave!" Klaus whispered loudly.

Again Paul held his finger to his lips. The boys listened, their hearts pounding.

"Yah, can you believe the Russians have invaded Berlin," one German soldier said in disgust.

"No, I don't believe it. It's an Allied propaganda move. The German army will never be defeated. It's up to us to hold the enemy back. We can do it. We are in the best position to stop them and with a pile of ammunition too," another soldier responded.

"The Fuhrer would be pleased," a third soldier replied.

Paul and Klaus could hardly believe their ears. Paul motioned to Klaus to follow him. They slowly started crawling back to where they had parked their scooters. "What are they, stupid?" whispered Paul to Klaus. "We're only 15 miles to the Czech border. The war is over."

"Come on, let's get out of here," Klaus said as he picked up his scooter and started running back down the hill. Paul followed close behind. They didn't know why they ran, but only a few moments later, as they continued running down the road toward their homes, four fighter planes appeared out of nowhere. They bombed the quarries and Paul heard later that all the soldiers from all three quarries were killed.

Although he should have been afraid, he wasn't. To a young boy of eleven it was fascinating watching the war and the battles around him. On this particular day, he knew they had cut it close. He had actually felt the presence of God protecting them as they made their way back home. Still… he knew it wouldn't deter him from going out whenever he could to watch more of the war being fought in Hartenstein. There was something in him that he had to know and see. Why? Because someday, Paul knew, he would write a book and tell the stories of everything he saw.

########

After another four days of fighting, the bombing stopped. The American army made its way to the upper part of town, then pulled out again. Now, it was quiet. Paul had enough of quiet and enough of being cooped up in a stuffy room with seven other people. "Pa, can I at least open the door to let in some fresh air?" Paul asked as his father nodded. "Can I feed the chickens?" Paul said as he stood in the doorway.

Again his father nodded. He made his way outside to the garden. Here the air was fresh and he took in a lung full. Suddenly, he saw German soldiers headed downhill following their fence line. They were on the other side of the fence and in a hurry. He watched as they made it almost down to the gravel road. Out of nowhere, a shell landed on them. Paul was thrown to the ground as he watched dismembered body parts blown into the air. He scrambled to his feet, diving behind the small cement wall that held the gutter from the roof. A second later, he heard the impact of bullets hitting the wall he was crouched behind. The back yard was sprayed with machine gun fire. Paul turned and sat with his back against the wall his knees up tight against his chest. His heart was pounding loudly, but everything else was quiet. It was as if he were looking at a photograph. Nothing moved. He stared at the carnage before him. The demolished stockade fence combined with the broken and bloodied bodies – this had happened in an instant before his very eyes. He heard a slow creak as the basement door was opened and he dared to look over the wall. His dad had closed the door earlier after the first shell exploded. Now he opened it slowly, praying, hoping, that Paul was still alive. He saw him poke his head over the small cement wall and quickly motioned for him to come back into the bomb shelter. Paul leaped over the wall and ran into his father's arms. Carl quickly closed the door behind him. As a family, they wept and worshipped together grateful for another miracle from the One who saves.

#########

There were several more days of fighting then the guns grew silent. Paul and his family watched as more American troops moved into the center of the city. The German resistance had been for the most part extinguished.

Paul watched as Sherman tanks and armored personnel carriers were positioned throughout the town. He was overjoyed to see that one of these armed outposts was near their house. Paul, Klaus, and Eberhard would frequently go and visit the tank battalion that was stationed near them. This outpost consisted of two Sherman tanks, one ¾ ton truck, and a jeep.

The boys were captivated just to be able to stand near a real tank. Between the three of them they had chosen a favorite one. The tank crew took a liking to the boys and let them climb on top of and inside the tank. They couldn't get enough. It was a daily routine that all of them enjoyed.

Paul knew from his father's stories of the breakfasts they had eaten in America that Americans really liked eggs. He also noticed the abundance of chocolate, peanut butter, and cookies that the soldiers ate every day and came up with a plan. Bringing 3 eggs wrapped in a kerchief one morning, he offered them to a soldier while pointing to his candy bar in his pocket. Soon a wonderful bartering system took place – eggs in exchange for delectable delights that the boys had not had in years.

########

One morning they came to know the soldier who manned the jeep. Paul admired him for the large cigar that he smoked. They would watch him as he swirled it around in his mouth while going about his daily tasks. Later they found out he was from Texas.

During one of these conversations, the soldiers stood in their tracks as they watched a German tank battalion - that had been concealed in the forest on the other side of town - come out from cover. It only took a few moments for the American soldiers to be in gear and ready for battle.

"Y'all go home now and be safe," the Texan grinned as he drove off in front of the tanks and ¾ ton truck. The boys walked back to Paul's house where they had a perfect view of the unfolding battle. "I count 6 Sherman tanks!" Paul yelled as they watched the most incredible tank battle from front row seats.

"Whoa! Look at the blast from that tank cannon," Eberhard jumped into the air with excitement.

"This has to be the most fun I've had in my entire life," thought Paul. "Not considering human lives and property being destroyed." The boys watched and cheered after every shot was fired. They rooted for their new friends. It felt good to be on the winning side. It wasn't long before the battle was over, the Americans having outnumbered and out gunned the small company of Panzers.

########

The American army continued moving east. Paul watched as the army moved out and headed toward Raum – a nearby village. This is where the SS had gone after leaving Hartenstein. The village sustained heavy damage. The people had been evacuated so no civilians were lost, but Hitler's SS were completely annihilated.

########

May 7, 1945, Germany surrendered. [5] The Tittel family gathered around the radio to listen. The final demise of Hitler's third Reich was broadcast around the world.

Many Germans who loved peace, rejoiced at their freedom from their tyrannical leader. Others, still faithful to the Fuhrer, took his example and ended their own lives. There were many suicides in Germany that day, including the Burgermeister of Zwickau and his staff.

########

Prison camps were opened and prisoners set free. The atrocities of the third Reich were revealed and the horrors of the prison camps that held the Jewish people exposed.

Paul thought of all the families waiting for loved ones to return. He thought of his brother Herbert who was missing in action or was he in a prison camp? Would he be coming home soon? These thoughts crossed his mind as he and his sisters watched the parade of soldiers march through Hartenstein.

Thousands upon thousands of troops marched through their town. Each section holding the flag of the country they were from. First, the French army, then the British and so on. They were the soldiers who had been freed from German prison camps. Paul didn't know exactly where they came from, but he knew where they were going…home. Last in the long line of freed prisoners, came the defeated remainder of the German army. Some managed to break away from the marching parade and find refuge with compassionate families in town. Everyone had heard of General Eisenhower's orders – all German soldiers were to be turned over to the Russians – this meant almost certain death.

The Tittel family was one of the families that helped the escaped German soldiers to move past the checkpoints. After the German soldiers were seen safely out of town, Paul pondered his family's future.

Looking up at his father he asked, "Is the worst over, pa? Will things get better now that the war is over?"

"One can only hope and pray that things will improve, Paul," Carl said as he put his arm over his shoulder. "Remember what Jesus said, 'In the world ye shall have tribulation: but be of good cheer; I have overcome the world.'"

1. http://ww2db.com/battle_spec.php?battle_id=148
2. http://www.hymnary.org/text/to_shepherds_as_they_watched_by_night
3. http://www.history.com/this-day-in-history/patton-relieves-bastogne
4. https://www.pbs.org/thewar/at_war_timeline_1945.htm
5. ibid

Chapter Eight: The Russians

The overcoming Spirit of God was something the Tittel family would call on frequently in the years ahead. After the Yalta conference in February of 1945, they knew their country would soon be divided among the allies.[1] They prayed they would not be ruled by the Russians but providence would not have it.

The horror stories of the encroaching Red Army – pillaging towns, raping women and killing anyone who stood in their way – preceded their entry into Hartenstein. Although Paul had heard of these atrocities, this did not stop him from venturing downtown to watch their arrival.

Early one morning in May, he and Klaus made their way through backyards to the center of town.

"Over here, Paul!" Klaus said in a loud whisper as he motioned Paul to where he stood. Together, standing in front of a building not far from the town square, they watched the soldiers disembark from the back of trucks. Immediately Paul noticed a great difference between the American and Russian soldiers. While the Americans came with tanks, big guns, and well equipped men, the Russians arrived with just two trucks (American-made), a commanding officer and 18 soldiers. Their uniforms were tattered and worn from battle. "Look at the rags wrapped around their legs," Klaus pointed to two soldiers unloading some crates - noticing their legs from the knee down were covered in dirty rags. "They look horrible."

"They are horrible." Paul stated, remembering the stories he had heard from nearby towns. He noticed that each solider carried a grease gun - a gun that most of the allies used in the war. It functioned much better than the precisely made German guns that didn't work well on the battlefield –

always jamming because of the dirt. Paul thought, it was a time when precise German craftsmanship did not work for their advantage.

The boys watched until the Russian soldiers had moved all their supplies into the town hall. "Come on, let's get home. We don't want to overstay our welcome," Paul said pulling Klaus behind him as they went back the way they had come.

The Russians wasted no time in getting to work. The very next day word was sent out to the town's people. It spread quickly by posters and word of mouth - if they were in possession of any kind of German uniform they were to bring them to the town hall immediately. (All guns – whether part of a collection or used for hunting – had already been confiscated by the Americans and destroyed.)

Paul and Klaus made their way downtown again and watched as the Russian soldiers discarded their ragged uniforms into dirty piles. The soldiers laughed and pointed to each other as they put on crisp white shirts, shiny boots and the long tailored coats of the SS officers.

"It's like they've never seen real clothes before." Paul said as they looked on from a distance.

"Hey, you over there!" one soldier yelled in their direction, pointing his gun toward them.

The boys ran as fast as they could, needing no further motivation to vacate the area. Out of breath, having run the whole way home, they both agreed to be more discreet on any future excursions in spying on the Russians.

########

Several days passed. The town was on edge. People stayed hidden indoors. Everyone seemed to be holding their breath waiting for what the Russians would do next. Finally, the garrison of soldiers made their move.

Paul woke with a start after hearing the front door slam.

"Paul, come quickly!" Carl yelled to his son.

Paul jumped out of bed and flew into his clothes. Running down the stairs he hollered, "I'm here, pa!"

Carl met him at the bottom. "The Russians are searching house to house for anything suspicious. I've already hidden our family's valuables. We have to find a way to distract them from looking thoroughly throughout the house."

"What can we do?" Paul asked with a worried look.

"I have an idea. Go upstairs. In the bottom drawer of my dresser is a large Atlas – bring it to me."

Paul passed Sigrid and Ruth on the way up and yelled, "Hurry, ask pa what you can do – the Russians are coming!"

Carl walked swiftly into the informal living room where Elisabeth and Marie slept. Elisabeth was already up and in the kitchen preparing breakfast. Carl kneeled down at Marie's side and held her hand. "Our journey isn't over yet my love. I need you, Elisabeth, and the girls to pray while the Russians are here."

"He has preserved us so far. He will not fail us now." Marie said with confidence.

Carl kissed her on the forehead. "I knew I could count on you."

Paul came running to his father's side carrying a large book.

"Quickly. Set it on the kitchen table and open it to Russia."

Magdalena jumped. There was a loud pounding on the front door. The girls joined their mother and quietly began to pray.

"Coming!" yelled Carl, who was immediately joined by his son in the foyer. Paul nodded to his father as he opened the door.

"Welcome, welcome to my humble home," Carl said as the three soldiers pushed by him. "I have something you may want to see," he said as he led them into the kitchen and the large book that laid open on the table. "Have you ever seen an atlas?" The men looked down at the open book.

"Look," said one.

"It's Russia!" said the other.

"I've never seen a map before," another added.

Carl pulled out a chair and sat down. With Paul standing by his side, he began to point out major Russian cities. The three soldiers sat down and each found his hometown. Almost a half hour passed before one of them finally said, "We must be moving on to the next house." They left in a hurry.

Three more times the soldiers would visit their home. Three more times they were blessed with the miracle of them being more captivated by an atlas than in searching their house.

########

More troops continued to be brought into Hartenstein further expanding the size of the garrison. The Russians took over the town square including the Masonic Lodge and surrounding houses. As their numbers grew, so did the fear in the people's hearts.

Paul continued to go on forays with Klaus and his cousins. Stories were passed around about how dense some of the occupying soldiers were. One of Paul's neighbors was called in to show them how a toilet worked. Most of the soldiers had never seen one before. Come to find, the reason they asked for help was because they had placed potatoes in the water reservoir which was 4 feet above the toilet. After flushing the toilet they disappeared and they couldn't figure out why.

Another boy, who lived just down the road, had an old rusty bike. He had taught himself how to ride without using the handle bars. One day, while he was out riding not using the handle bars, a Russian soldier passed him riding a brand new bike. The soldier stopped him and asked if he would like to trade. The boy was more than willing. As he sped off, he turned to look at the solider fallen on the ground. Obviously, he thought the bike made it possible to ride without using the handle bars.

While these stories were humorous, and made Paul laugh, there were others that made him sick. He tried not to remember those. The ones he couldn't forget were the ones he saw himself.

########

It was August, and soldiers could be found everywhere throughout Hartenstein. The town square had become somewhat off limits to the German population - this didn't stop Paul and Eberhard from getting as close as they could to spy on the Russian soldiers.

Eberhard led the way – always scanning the area ahead for any sign of the occupying force. As they ran through back alleys, heading in the direction of the town square, they stopped as they heard the muffled cry of a woman.

"This way," whispered Eberhard.

Paul followed closely behind. They stood against the back of what was once a small grocery store. Stepping out to walk between buildings to get to the front, Eberhard froze in place. Paul pushed him to the side to see what made him stop so suddenly. The boys stood together and watched something no young boy should ever have to see. It took a moment for Paul to make sense of what he was seeing. Again, the only thing that came to mind was a farm scene - a female duck being followed by a row of drakes. Here, not ten yards ahead of them, in the alley, a young girl lay on her back. There was a man lying on top of her with at least eleven more waiting in line. Paul would always remember her face…it was the glazed look of someone who had already died.

Eberhard grabbed Paul by his collar and pulled him back behind the building. The soldiers preoccupied with their lust had not seen them. As they quickly retreated, both boys vomited what little they had eaten that day. Knowing they weren't followed, they sat down under a tree. Paul's face was flushed, he couldn't catch his breath. Tears streamed down his cheeks.

"We need to do something," Paul said in anguish.

"There is nothing we can do," Eberhard said in resignation as he sat down next to him. "Nothing but live…live to tell the story of what happened."

"Yes," Paul said as his breathing became more regular. "Yes, I will live and I will tell the story."

A little while later they quietly walked home together. In silence they parted ways - each contemplating the horror of what they had just seen.

########

September brought more travesty as the pillaging of Hartenstein began. There were several textile factories in town including the one where Elisabeth used to work. Paul watched one day as they pushed all the sewing machines out of the 2nd and 3rd floors of the factory. Crashing to the ground or into the backs of trucks breaking into pieces, the Russians obviously didn't want to sew, but wanted the metal for scrap. This happened to just about every piece of metal that wasn't nailed down. Train loads of crates filled with machinery parts were sent to Russia.

Metal wasn't the only thing that was shipped away. The Russian people were in the same shape as the Germans were after the war. Many were starving from lack of food. Any food harvested in land governed by the Red Army was immediately shipped to Russia. This left the people of Hartenstein in dire straits.

The garrison commandant was in charge of the food supply and was supposed to give everyone a week's ration. Unfortunately, what was supposed to be a week's worth of food lasted only a day. There were German caretakers in charge of negotiating with the commandant about food and work. He refused to listen. The result was that many of the people of Hartenstein slowly began to starve to death.

########

It was early in October, and for Paul and his family it would be a month of miracles. Through the darkness of being ruled by the Russian occupational forces, starvation and the fear of another home invasion at any moment, bright rays of light still sprang from the heavens declaring hope to battered souls.

Sigrid, Paul, Magdalena, and their cousins Eberhard and Waldemar attended a Wednesday afternoon confirmation class. As they were walking to church they passed the local mill, Sigrid noticed a movement of something off to the side of the road.

"Paul! Quick!" Sigrid yelled as she pointed to a cat running across the street carrying a paper bag in its mouth. Eberhard ran toward the cat. Paul ran toward where he thought it would run if it escaped Eberhard's grasp. Waldemar followed closely behind Eberhard. Seeing the boys swiftly approaching, the cat paused for a moment giving just enough time for Eberhard to dive at the brown bag it carried. It slipped through his arms just as he landed on the ground. Waldemar turned as the cat escaped and tried to grab the bag with one hand as he fell on top of Eberhard.

The girls screamed, "Paul!" While the cat was busy evading Eberhard and Waldemar, Paul speedily ran by and snatched the bag from it's mouth. The cat, defeated but unfazed, sauntered down the road in search of its next meal.

Laughing, they all sat on the street curb. Paul opened the bag pulling out a sandwich. It was thick sliced homemade white bread with bacon lard in the middle. To some it may not have been very appetizing, but to them it was manna from heaven.

"There are four sandwiches!" Paul exclaimed in a quiet whisper as he looked into the bag. They divided them among themselves, then bowed their heads and thanked the Lord for His bounteous supply.

Paul tried to savor each bite. But it was hard to eat slow on such an empty stomach. In a few moments it was gone.

Sigrid stood up and brushed the crumbs off her skirt.

"That was wonderful," said Magdalena looking up at her sister.

"That was a miracle," said Sigrid looking down at her smiling.

"I wish all miracles tasted that good," Eberhard added.

They all laughed again. Together, all of them sang "Praise God from Whom all Blessings Flow"[2] as they continued on to the church.

########

The second miracle came as an idea that popped into Paul's head.

Not far from town, there were small farms in the valley below. The larger farms were controlled by the Russians. Here, they knew every ounce of grain, pound of meat, and liter of milk that the farms produced. If the farm was ever found lacking or the books were off, the family was severely disciplined. On the other hand, the small farms were not so heavily monitored. Town's people would walk 5 to 10 miles outside of town with empty cups, paper bags, and satchels to beg for food from these farmers.

This is where Paul got the miracle idea that Elisabeth would later say, "Saved us from starving completely."

While walking along with an army of beggars toward one of these smaller farms, Paul was musing about the idea of bartering, or trade. He had been out to this particular farm before and noticed the 3 boys giving out food were around his age or a little older. "What would farm boys want in trade for food?" Paul pondered as he walked. "Toys? No, older boys would like more intellectual things." "Instruments? Yes, possibly, but I don't have any I can part with," he sighed. Then it came to him in an instant. "Stamps!" Paul almost stumbled at the thought.

Opa Paul had given him his collection several years ago and he had all but forgotten about it. Over 3,000 stamps, some close to 80 years old - each in its on wax paper envelope - sat in a box in the attic collecting dust.

"As good as gold," he surmised. "All that's left to seal the deal is an interested patron." Paul looked ahead of him in line and watched as the boys lined up with large bags of wheat that were to be given out a cup at a time – one per person. Paul held his satchel open for a cup of wheat. Looking at the boy he simply asked, "Do you collect stamps?"

Instead of the boy in front of him answering, his older brother interrupted, "Yes, as a matter of fact we do. What have you got?"

"A lot," said Paul emphatically. "Would you be willing to trade – food for stamps?"

"Yah, sure," all three spoke at once. "We must ask our father first, but he collects them too. He will most likely say yes."

Paul knew at that moment a miracle had just happened. Promising to return within the next several days, he took off at a fast trot. His feet barely touched the ground as he ran home. He knew they would have enough food through trading stamps to make it through the winter months ahead.

Later at home, after Paul told his story of the miracle of the stamps and trading them for food, they prayed and thanked the Lord again for His goodly provision.

########

The third but not the least of the miracles of October came as they sat down to enjoy a piano concert by Paul, played on Opa's old piano. He was becoming quite an accomplished player and everyone enjoyed listening and clapping at the end of every piece. Some he even wrote himself. Uncle Hans and Aunt Lene came along with all their children, Aunt Lilly, and Uncle Karl. Opa Paul was in attendance too, and curious to hear the sound of his old instrument being played again.

As if on cue, after Paul's final piece, there came a loud pounding at the front door. Everyone jumped or gasped – it was a time when a knocking at your door could possibly mean the end of your life.

"I'll get it," said Uncle Hans as he leaped from his seat before anyone could object , swiftly opening the door to a surprising guest.

Marie whispered softly, but everyone heard, "Gerhard."

The room exploded in joy. Tears, laughter, hugs, kisses – Gerhard was smothered by the love of his family. It was as if a new light of hope had been lit in everyone's heart.

They all commented on how good he looked – strong and healthy. "They must have been feeding you well in the prison camp," Hans said as he pinched his brother's side.

"As a matter of fact the British were quite accommodating," Gerhard replied. "Three square meals a day – breakfast, lunch, and dinner - I really couldn't complain. We were fed the same rations as the British servicemen."³

The room got steadily quiet. Gerhard took in their faces and figures for the first time. "You're all…you're all so thin." Gerhard said as he looked around the room. There was a long empty pause.

"Uncle Gerhard," Elisabeth broke the silence. "Under the Russian occupational force most of the food has been and still is being shipped out to Russia. There is not a lot of food here – at least not enough to live on – many have starved to death already. By a miracle Paul has been trading his stamp collection for grain and bread from a local farmer. Without it we would be dead by now."

"Carl's pension stopped after the fall of Germany – which made it hard for us at the end of the war. Other households may not have it quite as bad as we do. Some can find work at the local uranium mine or as common laborers, but we depend on the mercy of others and on Paul who is so thrifty at finding ways to bring food to the table." Marie smiled proudly at her son.

Gerhard slumped into the couch sitting next to Marie in her wheel chair. She placed her hand on his, "Dear brother, God brought you home for a reason – if not to join forces as a family - to weather through this ugly storm together and by the grace of God we will."

A resounding "Yes!" filled the room.

"Come now, it's time to celebrate your homecoming," Carl said as he held up a dusty bottle of wine – a rustic treasure he had hidden away years ago.

"Where on earth did you dig that up from?" asked Marie.

"A remembrance, from mom and dad's 50th wedding anniversary – I hid it well so the Russians wouldn't find it. I was saving it for a special celebration and today's the day!" While Carl leaned on the table to unscrew the cork, Elisabeth brought in glasses from the kitchen. Opa Paul gave the toast.

And now abideth faith, hope, charity, these three; but the greatest of these is charity.[4]

They clinked their glasses together and said, "To charity!"

"Speaking of charity or love as some would have it – I thought of you all often when I was away and have something for each of you in my duffle bag outside. They put us to work while I was a prisoner and even paid us a small stipend for our labor. I couldn't help but buy a few gifts while on my way out of the country." Gerhard made his way back out the front door returning with a large, oblong canvas bag. "I was going to wait until Christmas but now seems like the perfect moment."

Everyone watched as he unzipped the bag and started emptying its contents onto the coffee table in front of him. Chocolate, cheese, smoked sausages, scones, and tea were some of the food items, along with a doll for Magdalena and small pocket knives for the boys. Oohs and aahs could be heard from the children.

"Tea!" yelled Elisabeth.

"I think you best get the water boiling," Marie laughed.

Plates and silverware were passed around and everyone had a sample from each of the delectable delights Uncle Gerhard had brought home from Britain.

As their time together came to an end, Hans, Opa Paul, and Gerhard discussed the financial situation of the shoe factory and the apartment building Gerhard had built. They agreed Hans should keep everything under his name. With Gerhard's military service and political beliefs, there was a possibility the Russians might try to confiscate it. Gerhard and his father would need the little income it provided to survive.

It was not long before the merriment of Gerhard's return faded as the harsh reality of their living situation bore down upon them. The Christmas of 1946 was dismal. Frequently, funeral processions could be seen heading toward the cemetery on the other side of town. The very old and very young were many of the first to succumb to the ravages of starvation.

Christmas Eve was challenging for Elisabeth. With mostly bare cupboards and supplies limited, she found it difficult to make any kind of holiday meal. Still she managed to come up with a nice stew, a small cake, and a dozen cookies for the Christmas celebration – thanks to the help of Uncle Gerhard and Opa Paul. As usual, the two of them joined their family after the Christmas Eve service.

Everyone exchanged gifts. Paul made small hand carved animals again with the pocket knife Uncle Gerhard had given him. Elisabeth made mittens, Christa scarves, Ruth, Sigrid, and Magdalena made Christmas ornaments, while Carl drew another ink drawing of the countryside in spring for Marie. Uncle Gerhard handed out the new paper shoes they were now manufacturing at their factory. No one expected Marie to give anything, so when she motioned for Elisabeth to come near her everyone looked on with anticipation. Here, tucked under her lap robe she pulled out a small package wrapped in tissue paper.

Elisabeth sat down next to her and unwrapped it. She held up a beautiful red sash. "It's lovely, ma," Elisabeth said as she kissed her on the cheek.

"It's the sash I wore when I first met your father," Marie said as she looked lovingly at her husband. She took her daughter's hand and held it. "Someday, Elisabeth…someday God has someone for you, too. I just know it. These hard times won't last forever."

"I know, ma. I know," Elisabeth said with confidence as she wrapped the sash around her neck and tossed it over her shoulder. "This will surely catch someone's eye."

"It did for me when your mother wore it," Carl said while he winked at Marie.

They all laughed. Paul sat down at the piano, while the girls went and gathered their instruments as they prepared to sing some of their favorite hymns and folk songs.

Everything seemed as it should be, except for one thing. No one ever mentioned it - especially in front of Marie – and that was Herbert. There was no word yet if he was still alive. The last they heard was that he was in a Russian prison. The only time his name was said was during evening devotions when they prayed as a family. They hoped for a miracle and Marie believed with her whole heart that someday he would come home.

########

Good news came in February, 1946, just when the Tittel family was in desperate straits. Their cupboards were practically bare. The rations they received never seemed to be enough to stave off their continual hunger. Here is when Carl received a word from their pastor that a family in Wildbach was in need of a maid. Not only would they be paid a small wage, but they would also have access to left-over produce to do with as they pleased. Being only 5 miles away from Hartenstein, this would mean more food on their table.

Since they were already working on a plan to get Christa, Waldemar and Hans out of the country because of their American citizenship, Ruth was next in line and old enough to accept the position.

"I'd be glad to work for the family in Wildbach, pa," Ruth said smiling at breakfast the next day.

"Then it's settled," said Carl. "I'll notify pastor to tell them that you'll be there this Sunday after the service."

########

Paul's stamps and the occasional satchel of potatoes and carrots he retrieved from Ruth in Wildbach saw them through into the spring of 1946. When finally the stamps and extra produce from Ruth ran out, hunger began to be a part of their daily lives again. His stomach was continually growling and the pain was constant. It was a daily search to try to find anything edible to eat and hopefully bring home something for others.

It was early March, Paul and Eberhard were wandering in the woods to haul firewood. The snow had melted for the most part and little shoots of plants were starting to come up through the soil announcing an end to the long cold winter.

"Paul, I'm so hungry and weak," Eberhard said listlessly.

"Come," said Paul holding out his hand, "let's pray."

Not hesitating, Eberhard joined Paul on his knees in the middle of the woods. "Heavenly Father, we are so hungry, please give us food to eat to fill our bellies. Amen." As Paul finished praying they knelt in silence.

Eberhard sighed. "I don't think he heard us."

"You give up to easy. God always hears our prayers," Paul said as he stood up.

Eberhard stood next to Paul and brushed the pine needles from his knees. "Did you hear that?"

"Hear what?" Paul replied. They both looked up as they heard a cooing sound come from above them.

"Look!" said Paul pointing up to a branch about 20 feet above them.

"Oh my goodness! What is it?" yelled Eberhard.

"Quiet, you'll scare it away," whispered Paul. "I think it's the largest pigeon I've ever seen in my life."

"But the nearest farm is 4 miles away. How did it get here?" asked Eberhard.

"A better question is 'How did it fly here?' I've never seen anything so big." Paul said as he cupped his hand against his forehead to get a better look.

"Quick, grab some small stones, I think we can hit it – we're both pretty good shots." Paul began gathering stones in the loose soil around them. Eberhard did the same and between the two of them they hit the bird with a couple of shots. It fell from the tree and landed with a thud.

"It's the mother of all pigeons!" yelled Eberhard.

"It's a miracle, Eberhard. Let's thank the Lord," Paul said before he bellowed out, "Thank you Lord!"

Eberhard followed just as loud, "Thank you Lord!" Their voices echoed down the valley. They yelled several more times so thankful and excited to have been provided for by the Maker's hand.

After their loud praises, the boys brought the bird to Eberhard's house. Here his mother prepared it and made a large pot of soup. There was enough to feed everyone including a small pot for Paul to take home to his family.

########

The following month of April, Paul watched as his father grew even thinner. The dark circles under his eyes became more prominent. Both parents denied themselves food many an evening so Paul and his sisters could have more to eat. Carl's blackouts changed from outbursts of rage to small seizures. He would fall to the ground without a warning - his body twitching uncontrollably. Within minutes it would be over and they would help him to bed or to the couch to lay down and rest. Over time, with lack of any nourishment, the seizures worsened.

"Paul!" Elisabeth screamed early one morning as he was getting ready for school. He ran downstairs to the kitchen. There he found Elisabeth and Magdelena kneeling on the floor a few steps from their father. They dared not get closer.

Paul watched his father's body twist and contort while flying several feet into the air. This was a grand mal seizure. It was horrible to watch but they all wanted to be with him. "These may be his last moments," Paul thought somberly as he looked on with his sisters.

Gratefully, Marie was still sleeping soundly in the next room. Oblivious to the suffering of her husband, she was too weak to be woken by the sounds coming from the kitchen. After what may have been minutes, but seemed like hours, Carl's body began to relax and his breathing return to normal.

"Paul," Elisabeth said quietly. "Go and beg the neighbors for some food. Maybe if he gets some kind of nourishment it will help."

Paul ran to a nearby neighbor. A man of mercy came and brought a small amount of smoked beef, bread, and a potato. Elisabeth thanked him and promised if they ever had more than enough she would bless him back.

Later as their father lay on the living room couch, Elisabeth spoon fed him the small amount of soup she made. At first he refused – so she lied and told him they had all already eaten – then he ate. Soaking the bread in the broth she made it soft for him to swallow. He was like a hungry bird – too weak to feed himself.

Days later his strength returned with Elisabeth making sure he ate his small portion at every meal. His seizures quieted and were never as strong.

########

Paul was always thinking of ways to bring in more money and it wasn't always for food. There was one thing that meant more to him than the pain in his belly and that was music. He had to make enough to pay for his piano lessons.

It was the beginning of May and the air was still crisp at night and in the mornings. Paul knew that people still needed to heat their homes. He had already asked the local saw mill if he could have their sawdust. They agreed seeing that it would save them time from cleaning up the piles themselves.

Paul asked Magdalena to come along because the bags would be too heavy for him to lift and the cart too hard to push when it was loaded. Magdalena agreed to help for a small portion of his profit.

Walking to the mill, although it was four miles, went quickly. They sang along the way and sometimes visited with other people traveling in the same direction.

Upon arriving at the mill, Magdalena held the bags open while Paul filled them with a small shovel he had brought along. After an hour the three large bags were filled. Together they grunted and groaned as they tried to maneuver the heavy bags into the wagon. Finally succeeding, they made their way back onto the road and headed home. Paul pulled and steered while Magdalena pushed from behind.

It was hard exhausting work to push the wagon and it's weight. Having gone only several miles, Paul felt like collapsing. He could only imagine what Magdalena felt like. Looking up ahead he shook his head to clear it. He thought he saw Sigrid walking toward them, less than a block away.

"It's Sigrid! Magdalena, Sigrid has come to help us!" Paul yelled back to his sister.

Magdalena stopped pushing the wagon and ran to greet her sister. Paul could tell by her pale drawn face that something wasn't right.

As she approached, she laid a hand on each of their shoulders then bent down to look into their faces. "Mother has had a final stroke. She has gone home to be with the Lord."

People were passing them in either direction. To Paul it seemed as if they walked in slow motion. The noise of horse hooves hitting the gravel, along with people's voices faded away as he watched his sister's lips move again to say, "Mother has died."

Sigrid continued, "I need you both to hurry back home with your loaded wagon. Once you get there, wash and make yourselves presentable. We are having the viewing tonight and tomorrow will be the funeral."

There was no time for tears. They both simply nodded at their sisters directions. "I have to hurry back since there is much to do." She hugged them both then turned as quickly as she had come and disappeared into the crowd.

Paul looked down at his little sister, they embraced. They were too hungry and exhausted for any other emotion at the moment. Magdalena walked back behind the wagon and waited for Paul to pick up the bar before she began to push the wagon. As Paul began to pull, it felt as if the weight had doubled. He could hear Magdalena quietly crying from behind. He dared not look back to reveal the river of tears that streamed down his own face. With all his strength he pulled the wagon forward. Together they made the long trek home.

########

After Marie's death the house never seemed the same. Elisabeth moved her bedroom back upstairs since she now had a room of her own. The informal living room was turned back into a study of sorts for Carl and his drawings.

A picture of Marie was placed on top of the piano.

Sometimes, late at night, Paul would hear his father picking out a melody one note at a time. It was a melancholy tune, one that Paul would always remember. It was about a watch...at times he could hear some of the lyrics that his father sang.

"In my sorrows and joys,
In storm and rest -
Whatever happened in life,
It ticked the cadence for it.

It tolled at the coffin of my father
It tolled at the bier of my friend,
It tolled at the dawn of love,
It tolled at the altar of marriage.

It tolled at cradle of the child,
And, God willing, it will toll more often
If better days are coming
As my soul hopes..."[5]

Years later Paul would find the name of the song - it was simply called "The Watch."

########

Almost a month had passed since his mother had died. Paul couldn't decide which hurt worse – his stomach or his heart. He knew how to remedy the pain of one. After school he headed for their family garden where the fruit on the trees and the berries on the bushes weren't ripe yet, but he was determined to eat them. He was tired of the gnawing pain.

After eating all the green pears, apples, and berries he could find, he went to his Opa's garden and did the same. While consuming much of the fruit, a pain struck him in his stomach. He fell to the ground. Laying on his back, he then rolled to his side and threw up a brown, blackish syrup. It burned his throat and brought him more pain than what he had to begin with.

"Will this misery never end!?" Paul yelled while not caring who heard him. Hot tears slid down the side of his head into his hair. He lay where he was for a while, looking up at the blue sky above him and closing his eyes. Softly, he heard his mother's voice saying one of his favorite verses. 'Be of good courage, and he shall strengthen your heart, all ye that **hope** in the Lord.'[6] While the pain in his stomach continued, the pain in his heart dissipated.

"Thank you, Lord, thank you, ma," Paul said out loud to himself. He was grateful for all the verses his mother had made him memorize as a child – now seeing first hand, how they brought strength and comfort to his heart.

########

1946 was one of the hardest years for Paul to weather. With his mother's passing, and the pain of hunger almost always his constant companion, he thought things could not get any worse, but December 14th brought more sad news to the Tittel family. Paul woke to the sound of his father speaking with someone downstairs. He slipped quietly out of bed and sat at the top of the stairs to listen.

"I'm sorry to be the bearer of more bad news, Carl. When I woke this morning to go downstairs to start work, I noticed my father wasn't up yet. I went to his room and found that he had died in his sleep sometime during the night." Paul heard his uncle begin to cry.

"There, there, Gerhard." Paul could hear his father comforting his uncle.

Paul laid his head on his knees as he sat at the top of the stairs. "I don't think I can bear anymore sadness," he thought as he felt his heart begin to break all over again.

########

Christmas was hard, to say the least. As they gathered in the formal living room, Paul couldn't help but notice the weariness that appeared on everyone's face. As his father opened his Bible and read of Jesus' birth, the true meaning of Christmas came to him afresh, bringing with it the hope that only the Savior of the world could bring. Their hearts still ached for their loved ones, but they were strengthened in their faith by God's promises.

########

The spring of 1947, brought exciting news to the Tittel family as their mother's cousin Reinhold Loescher, took his coal truck loaded with people and successfully jammed it through at a northern border point. (Border control had not been developed yet). Ruth was one of the passengers. Their father had decided not to tell anyone – in fear of her life – until he had word she was safe in West Germany. Once there, with the help of the church, she found work on a farm near Rothenburg.

Also, during this time the plan for Christa, Waldemar, and Hans to leave the country became a reality. With papers in order, tickets purchased, and sponsors ready to receive them in America, the three made their way to Berlin. Once they arrived at the American Embassy they were swiftly put on an army truck and hidden under benches so the crossing guards would not see them. Safely arriving in Hamburg, before their ships departure, they wired their parents to let them know of their safe arrival.

########

At end of August, Sigrid received an invitation to become a housekeeper for a pastor in Saalfeld who once was a vicar at their church in Hartenstein. Sigrid, of course, accepted the position. Not long afterward, they walked her to the Stein Station and prayed for her safe journey. As he waved goodbye to another sister, Paul felt as if his family was slowly disintegrating… disappearing before his very eyes.

########

September brought Paul to his last year of middle school. Now entering the 8th grade, he looked forward to his studies and expanding his musical gifts. There was not much time for play. Advancement to higher grades came only to those with the highest scores. He spent long hours in books or practicing his instruments. Life had become a routine of studying, gathering wood for fuel, or scrounging for more food. Hunger was his constant companion.

########

The winter of 1947-1948 was one with some of the heaviest snow fall Paul had ever seen in his short thirteen years. He and Magdalena held the duty of keeping the house warm. Elisabeth did all the house chores, so it was up to them to keep the wood stove burning. Every family was allotted 200 pounds of coal briquettes for the winter. Unfortunately, these lasted only a few months.

"Paul, Magdalena, wake up! We need more wood!" Elisabeth yelled from the bottom of the stairs. Paul got up and ran to his window. It had started snowing the day before and he was curious to see how many inches they had gotten. He backed away from the ice glazed glass not believing what he saw…the snow was level with his window.

"It has to be over 9 feet!" Paul thought to himself. Their house stood at a steep angle on a hill. Outside Paul's window was a straight drop of 9 feet to the ground. Paul sank back on his bed. That meant he would have to shovel down to the basement door through 9 feet of snow to get to the sled so they could gather wood.

"It's impossible!" Paul yelled down at Elisabeth.

"You have to do it Paul, you and Magdalena together. You are the only ones." Somehow when Elisabeth spoke there was no other way around it – her word stood.

Although in different rooms Paul and Magdalena both sighed in unison. They put on extra pants and gloves because of the bitter cold. Paul climbed out his bedroom window and started digging down, down, down. He thought he would never hit the bottom, but eventually he did. Magdalena worked on making a tunnel out the front door to the street. By the time they finished it was noon and they needed a break. Elisabeth had a cup of warm water and a slice of wheat toast for lunch. Afterwards, they looked out the kitchen window to watch the horse drawn plow, plowing the road behind their house.

"Just in time. Come on Magdalena, let's get going," Paul said as they made their way downstairs to the laundry room and out the basement door.

They headed down the road that led past the ruins of Hartenstein castle. They met others along the way going on the same journey. Through word of mouth they found the location of the Forestry Department that was clearing out Norway Spruces. Here the men left the large branches behind – free for anyone to take and use as they would. It was an arduous journey for both children. The snow was deep, the hills were steep, and the cold was bitter.

After loading the sled as full as they could, they headed back. The sun was starting to set. Paul was cold, hungry, weak, and miserable. He collapsed on the road. Magdalena ran to his side.

"Paul, Paul!" she yelled as she shook him. "Paul, wake up, we need you! You can't die!" Magdalena cried.

Paul sat up hearing his sister's cries. "I'm not dying, I'm resting," Paul said, making light of the moment as he got back up and started pulling the sled.

"Don't ever do that again, Paul-Gerhard!" Magdalena yelled as she began pushing the sled from behind.

"Push harder, Magdalena! Push harder!" Paul yelled as they made the final few yards up the steep road to their house.

"I'm giving it all I got!" she retorted. The sled went over one last hump of snow before settling back in front of the basement door.

It was late in the evening, but they had done it.

"Another miracle," Paul thought as he and Magdalena stumbled exhausted into the house and upstairs to bed, both too tired to eat. "Tomorrow I'll cut up the branches so they fit into the woodstove," his last thought before drifting off into a deep sleep.

########

Because Paul continued to do so well in his studies, after graduation from 8th grade in the spring of 1948, he was given the opportunity to attend high school in Zwickau the following fall.

Over the last several years, he had grown in understanding the world around him. He had grown in faith and he also came to the conclusion that he did not want to be a part of - or live under - a communist regime. The seeds of freedom had been planted in him as a child by his mother and father. Now, at the age of fourteen, he was sure that as soon as he graduated from high school, he was going to escape East Germany and go to America.

1948 was also a year of elections for the GDR (German Democratic Republic). Under the supervision of the Soviets, several parties came forward. However, only the one backed by the soviets and the KGB would win. This was the SED or the Socialist Unity Party - they governed the German Democratic Republic or what would come to be known as East Germany. This new government had no use for those who did not fall in line with their ideological thinking. Christians were on their blacklist. The lives of most Germans living under the GDR went from bad to worse. The freedom hoped for by the people was shattered; food was still in short supply; rations were still handed out after five years; and many people were still dying from starvation.

Paul needed no further convincing. *Soon* he would discuss his plans with his father.

1. https://history.state.gov/milestones/1937-1945/yalta-conf

2. http://cyberhymnal.org/htm/p/r/praisegf.htm

3. http://www.radiomarconi.com/marconi/monumento/pow/pows.html

4. 1 Corinthians 13:12-13

5.

Die Uhr - The Watch
Lyrics: *Johann Gabriel Seidl (1804-1875)*
Tune: *Johann Karl Gottfried Loewe (1796 - 1869), 1830 op. 123 no. 3*

Ich trage, wo ich gehe,	Wherever I go,
Stets eine Uhr bei mir;	I always carry a watch with me.
Wieviel es geschlagen habe,	How often the bell has tolled
Genau seh ich an ihr.	I can see by it exactly.

Es ist ein großer Meister,	It is a great master
Der künstlich ihr Werk gefügt,	Who made its artificial works,
Wenngleich ihr Gang nicht immer	Although how it runs does not always
Dem törichten Wunsche genügt.	Satisfy my foolish wishes.
Ich wollte, sie wäre rascher	I wished it had run
Gegangen an manchem Tag;	faster on many a day;
Ich wollte, sie hätte manchmal	And sometimes I wished
Verzögert den raschen Schlag.	It had delayed its quick strike
In meinen Leiden und Freuden,	In my sorrows and joys,
In Sturm und in der Ruh,	In storm and rest -
Was immer geschah im Leben,	Whatever happened in life,
Sie pochte den Takt dazu.	It ticked the cadence for it.
Sie schlug am Sarge des Vaters,	It tolled at the coffin of my father
Sie schlug an des Freundes Bahr,	It tolled at the bier of my friend,
Sie schlug am Morgen der Liebe,	It tolled at the dawn of love,
Sie schlug am Traualtar.	It tolled at the altar of marriage.
Sie schlug an der Wiege des Kindes,	It tolled at cradle of the child,
Sie schlägt, will's Gott, noch oft,	And, God willing, it will toll more often
Wenn bessere Tage kommen,	If better days are coming
Wie meine Seele es hofft.	As my soul hopes.
Und ward sie auch einmal träger,	Sometimes when it ran slower
Und drohte zu stocken ihr Lauf,	And its works were nearly stopped,
So zog der Meister immer	The great master
Großmütig sie wieder auf.	Magnanimously wound it up again.
Doch stände sie einmal stille,	But if it would ever stop
Dann wär's um sie geschehn,	that would be the end of it
Kein andrer, als der sie fügte,	No other but he who made it
Bringt die Zerstörte zum Gehn.	Could ever make it run again.
Dann müßt ich zum Meister wandern,	Then I should journey to the master
Der wohnt am Ende wohl weit,	Living at the end so far
Wohl draußen, jenseits der Erde,	Beyond Earth
Wohl dort in der Ewigkeit!	Out there in Eternity.
Dann gäb ich sie ihm zurücke	Then I should give it back to him
Mit dankbar kindlichem Flehn:	With grateful and childlike supplication:
Sieh, Herr, ich hab nichts verdorben,	Look here, Lord, I didn't break it,
Sie blieb von selber stehn.	It stopped by itself.

6. Psalm 31:24

Chapter Nine: The Great Escape

Paul had promised himself that he would *soon* broach the topic of crossing the border into West Germany with his father. After a while, he discovered that the word "soon" could have many different meanings when concerning the length of time. What he originally thought would be days turned into years before he was ready to sit down and discuss his decision with his father.

There were several factors that caused Paul to put his plans on hold. The first was his education. He was just starting his first year of high school and had hopes of entering a university once he arrived in West Germany. This would not happen if he didn't graduate.

After obtaining a degree from a university in Germany, his hopes were that this would give him a good start in America. Of course, there were many "ifs" and it seemed like such a longtime to wait, but he felt it was a plan that would give him the most opportunities.

The second factor was money. Money was as scarce as food in the Tittel household. There were many expenses included in his high school education. Six days a week he took the train to the school in Zwickau, so he needed train fare. There were his books and labs, not to mention his beloved piano lessons. His education was free, but everything else added up to a considerable amount of money.

Being an entrepreneur, he was always thinking of ways to help support his family – like the stamps he sold to the farmer boys. While he continued to sell sawdust, he needed more than this to pay for his studies.

Providence always seemed to follow Paul, even though times were tough, God always made a way for him and his family. He had experienced many miracles throughout his life, but was always amazed at how God took a personal interest in his affairs.

Walking home from the train station in the early fall of 1948, Paul looked ahead and saw two elderly women out for an evening stroll. They were walking up the road from the ruins of Stein castle. As he approached them from behind he couldn't help but overhear their conversation.

"Helga, what I wouldn't give for some stone mushroom gravy to pour over my mashed potatoes."

"You and me both," said Mary. "I'd pay practically anything within reason of course for some fresh stone mushrooms."

They walked arm in arm. Paul recognized them as two of the wealthiest widows of Hartenstein. He knew others didn't have it as bad as he and his family and these women were some of the others. Their husbands had had good jobs and put away a lot of hard currency for their future. While not extremely wealthy, they had more than enough to get by during the hard times they lived in.

His heart leaped as he heard them mention stone mushrooms and especially what they would pay for some. "Excuse me," Paul said as he came from behind and walked beside them. "I couldn't help but overhear your conversation. You mentioned stone mushrooms. I know just where to find them. Would you be interested in purchasing some?"

Paul could barely contain his excitement. It was peak season for the stone mushroom. What were the odds of meeting these two women on his way home and catching their conversation? "Praise God from whom all blessings flow!" he thought to himself.

"Yes!" Helga said loudly.

"Yes, indeed," said Mary.

"Wonderful," added Paul. "Today is Friday…hmm." Paul thought for a moment. "I can have them to you tomorrow evening."

"You are a blessing," said Mary.

"No, believe me *you* are the blessing," said Paul smiling back at them.

They came to their street and turned to wave at Paul who continued up the road toward home.

Paul shared the miracle of the stone mushrooms and his new patrons with Elisabeth, Magdalena, and his father at supper. It cheered everyone to hear some good news. Now he would be picking mushrooms to sell and not just for them to eat.

"I'm proud of you, Paul," Carl said looking down at his son. "You are making a way for yourself," he said as he reflected on all of Paul's efforts to earn an income. "An education is important to get ahead in this life. I know you'll do well and I know your mother would be proud of you."

Paul beamed. Elisabeth and Magdalena also looked proudly at their brother. Elisabeth stood up with her hands on her hips and matter of factly said, "As mother would say, 'I do believe it's time for worship!'" They all laughed.

The children ran for their instruments - Paul his trumpet, Elisabeth her lute, and Magdalena her recorder. Quickly they returned to the formal living room. Carl had his song book open. Shall we start with "Now Thank We All Our God?"[1]

A resounding, "Yes!" was loudly spoken by all three.

The powerful words of the old hymn were carried loudly throughout the house in a boisterous off key melody by Carl. The children were old enough now to hear past his raucous tone enjoying the heart of worship in his voice.

The dishes could wait – nothing compared to worshipping together.

Later as he lay in bed, Paul's thoughts wandered to two others who were known to hunt the wild mushrooms as well. There were two older women in town he had stumbled upon several weeks ago. Unlike Mary and Helga whose husbands had left them well supplied, these widows lived like his family, day to day looking for anything to eat to stave off hunger. They were old and desperate.

"Desperate times make desperate people," thought Paul. A cold chill passed over him as he thought back to when he had last crossed paths with them.

########

His face flushed and his heart pounding from running, Paul rested his back against the trunk of a large pine. Tightly holding his basket of harvested mushrooms, he shook his head quickly not believing what he had just seen.

Only moments before he was kneeling near a group of birch trees harvesting a nice group of mushrooms known as Birkenpilz. He was deep in the woods, far past the Hartenstein castle. It was an area that his mother had shown him years ago and her mother before that. This was the best place to find the Birkenpilz. He heard a twig snap nearby and he looked in the direction of the sound thinking it might be a deer. There, to his surprise, not a stone's throw away were two elderly women watching him .

He smiled and waved. But they stood glaring at him. He noticed by their stance and stare that they were not friendly. He saw that they each held a basket for harvesting mushrooms and that one held a knife. Slowly she brought it up to her neck holding it inches away from her throat. Looking directly at him she slid it across her neck.

It only took Paul a heartbeat to get the message and turn and run. Light and little he ran like a chipmunk. He knew he could out run them. If they knew the prized area to find Birkenpilz, he knew they would be familiar with the woods. They would know the path of least resistance he would take. He paused to catch his breath by the large pine he was now leaning against. He waited for his breath to calm, listening for any sound besides the beating of his own heart in his ears.

Paul started to relax. Then a voice came out of the quiet that sounded merely a few feet from the other side of the tree he was leaning against. Being barely 4 feet and weighing 70 pounds, made him the perfect size to be hid from view behind the trunk of the tree.

"I'll kill him if I find him," said one.

"No one would know who dun it. Out here deep in the woods and all," said the other.

"Did you see how big the basket was he was carryin'? Thief! I know you can hear us!"

"He's taking our food right out of our mouths. The dirty little rat," the other woman said in a vicious tone.

"I say, if we catch'em we kill'em."

"Would make a nice stew, don't ya think?" the other woman looked at her friend for agreement.

"A little scrawny, but I think he'd do." They both laughed loudly, almost giddy at the thought of eating something other than wild greens and mushrooms.

Their voices trailed off until there was nothing but silence again. Paul slid down to a seated position, still holding his precious cargo. He waited what seemed like hours before he dared to make his way home. He knew he could never mention the encounter with the women to his father or Elisabeth. They needed the food and he needed the income too much. Next time he would go to another area of the woods. Now that he knew their intentions, he would be more aware of his surroundings and make sure his knife was freshly sharpened.

Paul rose early the next morning. He had to be up by 4 a.m. to make sure he had time to harvest and deliver the mushrooms to his new clients. He was cautious as he traveled the woods. There were several times that he came near to where the two women were working. Whenever this happened, he would throw a stone in the opposite direction of where he was to distract them. This gave him time to evacuate the area and find a safer location to harvest.

After several months, before the first freeze, Paul's clientele grew by 3 more families. He now had 5 households that ordered mushrooms from him. They paid him well and he always knew who to thank for supplying his every need.

########

The Christmas of 1948, brought glimmers of hope to the Tittel family. The first was a package from Christa sent from her new home in Buffalo, New York. Miraculously, it had made it through the border without being confiscated. It was a small package containing a little something for each of them and for Paul it was a quarter pound of coffee.

The other bit of good news had been heard throughout the year. The western allies were not giving up on Berlin. Even though the Russians had surrounded the city and closed every avenue to it, the British, French and American forces would not give up their portions. Needing food and other supplies to survive, the Americans dropped everything in by plane. The Berlin airlift[2] - as it was called - gave the Tittel family hope that they had not been forgotten and that a future of freedom for East Germany might still be a possibility.

Christmas Eve night, Paul lay in bed examining his small package of coffee. He thought about his family and was glad Christa had made it to America, Ruth to Rothenburg, West Germany to work as a farmhand, and Sigrid to Saalfeld, East Germany, to work as a housekeeper. It gave him peace of mind in knowing that they were in safe places away from the grip of communism and starvation. He prayed for Herbert, and like his mother knew that somehow, someday he would make it home.

########

It was New Year's day, 1949 and Paul was looking forward to the church service. He had been practicing his trumpet solo for quite a while and was hopeful it would turnout well. From the balcony he could see his father sitting in a pew near the front with Elisabeth and Magdalena sitting in the women's section on the other side.

After the sermon, the ushers moved forward with the offering plates. This was Paul's sign to begin his solo while the offering was gathered. The notes were clear and cheerful to ring in the New Year. He was caught up in the moment worshipping the Lord with his gift and breath when a muffled scream caught his ear. He looked back at the organist who simply shrugged his shoulders. Continuing to play, he saw the ushers looking back toward the narthex underneath where he sat. Several people stood up and turned to look back at what, Paul did not know.

He stopped playing when he saw his father turn and run down the center aisle passing beneath him. Paul laid his trumpet down on the bench and could hear people whispering loudly – others were crying. He heard the creaking of the steps as someone was slowly climbing the stairs to where he sat. He saw his head then his torso as he appeared above the balcony railing. Paul's mouth dropped open and from deep within him a cry came out that was at first the broken scream of a teenage boy, which gradually became wrapped in consonants and vowels. "Heerberrrrt!" He leaped over a pew in front of him and flew into his brother's arms. His father and sisters stood behind his brother, laughing and weeping at the same time.

"Now, now, dear brother. What's all the fuss? I told you I'd be back," Herbert said looking down at Paul. They all laughed together.

"It's a miracle. You're home, you're really home," Paul said hugging his brother again.

"We never gave up hope, Herbert, we've prayed for you every night. Mother knew you would make it back. She was right." Elisabeth said with tears still in her eyes.

"Welcome home, son, welcome home," Carl put his arm around his son's back and patted him heartily.

Magdalena stared at the tall man they called her brother. She barely remembered him, but looked forward to getting to know him again. After making their way downstairs and out the front door, they stood as a family with the pastor while everyone welcomed Herbert back home.

The first few days together as a family were spent recounting stories. Elisabeth shared the moment of their mother's passing which brought them all to tears again. Herbert told of his capture in the second battle of Kiev.[3]

They were cut off and surrounded by the Russians. Eight of his fellow soldiers from his battalion had survived the battle and two were uninjured. He had been struck by a small caliber bullet that had passed through his shoulder without striking any major arteries. While he was working on stopping the bleeding, he watched several Russian soldiers walk up to a wounded comrade and shoot him in the head. They were killing the wounded.

Quickly Herbert motioned to one of the soldiers that hadn't been wounded. "Pull the jacket off that dead soldier's body and give it to me. I must hide my wound."

Hurriedly, his friend pulled the jacket off the still warm body. He also tore the cotton shirt off the dead man's back. His friend put the cotton shirt over his wound and wrapped it with a shoelace into position. Herbert gingerly pulled the fresh coat over his shoulder just as the Russian soldiers headed in their direction.

With arms raised in surrender, they watched as they shot five more wounded soldiers in the head. Marching through the snow, Herbert knew there was only one thing he could do. He prayed. Six years later his prayers were answered when the Soviets finally decided to start letting some of their POWs return home. It was a miracle he was released when he was because many more soldiers were not let go until ten years or more after the war.[4]

########

A week passed by. While at first everyone thought Herbert looked in good shape for all that he had been through, his body quickly transformed into an emaciated figure before their very eyes. For some reason he had retained a huge amount of fluid. After a week it had drained out through urination. He stood before them now looking like the pictures they had seen of the Jews from Auschwitz.

Elisabeth made every effort to make hearty meals to help him recover. Aunt Lene, Uncle Hans, and his cousins did without and gave them milk from their goats every other day. A generous farmer from their congregation gave them eggs, along with the rations they were allotted, which helped Herbert regain some of his strength. Paul saw this first-hand as he watched him chop wood out his bedroom window one day in early March.

There were many reasons he was glad his brother was back home. Helping with chores was one of them, but he was also comforted in knowing his sisters wouldn't be alone with their sickly father. Even though he loved his brother and was glad to see him again, Paul's heart was still set on crossing the border and getting to America.

Paul had yet to mention to his father his intentions of leaving. There were reasons – his schooling and money - but the last and not the least important was transportation. Not being able to afford the train fare, he planned to bike to Saalfeld where his sister Sigrid lived. She worked as a housekeeper for Pastor Hirschfeld and his family. From Hartenstein this was a distance of over 130 miles. It was then another 150 miles that he would have to travel on foot to the border. Biking would be the easy part – it was building a bike that would be the challenge.

Here is where a new friend with many talents came to Paul's aid. He knew the moment they met on the train heading to Zwickau that God had brought him into his life. After a few morning conversations they found themselves having a lot in common. They had the same political views and shared the same faith to name a few. After much prayer and thoughtful consideration Paul decided in early April to confide in him about his plan to cross the border. He knew he was risking his life. Hans Joachim could be a Russian spy and that would end everything real quick. Still there was something in him that said, "You can trust him."

Walking home from the train station together, Paul began to share his plan of escape. Joachim, as he liked to be called, listened quietly as his new friend talked about America and his father and mother and how sick he was of not having enough food or enough money. If he stayed he knew he would most likely end up at the uranium mine dying an early death.

Paul took a deep breath, "Sooo, I'm going to cross the border and finish my education in West Germany, then go to America."

Paul waited for Joachim's reply.

"How can I help?" was all he said.

"Thank you, Joachim, I really need help. I need to build a bike before I can go anywhere and I don't have a clue where to find parts or how to build one," said Paul.

"Well, you've come to the right person. Do you have time to come over to my house? I've something to show you," Joachim said grinning.

"Sure, but not for long, Elisabeth will worry if I'm too late."

Joachim lived near the cemetery on the other side of town. As they approached his house, Paul followed him to a large shed in the back yard. Here Joachim pushed open a large rolling door. Stepping inside it took Paul a moment for his eyes to adjust to the darkness.

"Wow," was all Paul could manage to say.

Joachim laughed.

"How long did it take you to accumulate all of this?" Paul asked in wonder.

"Most of my life," Joachim said as he moved toward one of the tables loaded with machinery parts. "I think I kind of like to tinker with things."

"You think?" Paul said while laughing. He scanned the room seeing chains, belts, and ropes that hung from large hooks that were screwed into the ceiling. Wheels with spokes in many different sizes were hanging on the walls. Jars with nuts, bolts, and nails were neatly stored on shelves.

"When God answers prayers, sometimes it's with an exclamation point." Paul said looking at his friend.

This time Joachim laughed. "With God we can do anything Paul. We will have your bike built in no time at all."

They agreed to meet every Saturday until mushroom season in the fall. Hopefully it would be finished by then.

########

By September, the boys had found almost all the parts they needed to construct the bike. Many were discovered in Joachim's shed, while the body part and pedals were found in the junk yard not far from the cemetery. Since they could only meet one day a week, it took them much longer than Paul expected to find all the parts.

The last pieces were the tires and inner tubes. They would have to barter with someone who had access to them. Paul heard in a roundabout way that it was soon time for his uncle Carl, who was the husband of Lilly, Paul's mother's cousin, to receive a bonus. The government gave the miners bonuses in the form of everyday items for meeting more than their quota. A hammer, a cooking pan, and a jacket were some of the things his uncle received over the previous year, but what Paul remembered most were the bike tires and inner tubes.

He hatched a plan knowing his uncle's wife, Aunt Lilly, loved coffee on a Friday after school. He hid his quarter pound of coffee in his jacket and made his way to their house on the other side of town. Upon arriving, knowing his uncle was working at the mine, he asked if he could come in to discuss a small matter. Paul made his proposal asking if she might convince her husband to choose the tires and inner tubes the next time he was offered a bonus.

"Now Paul, you know I would love to do that for you, but we have to choose things that are practical and will help us weather the times we live in. I'm sure you understand."

Paul slowly reached into his pocket and pulled out a small paper bag and handed it to his aunt.

She looked at him strangely. Slowly, she unfolded the paper bag while her eyes grew double in size as they registered what was inside. Closing her eyes she inhaled through her nose. She couldn't remember the last time she had smelled fresh coffee. Folding the bag back up, she placed it on her lap. "I don't think there'll be problem in getting Carl to change his mind, Paul." Lilly looked at him smiling while she gently patted the paper bag in her lap.

"I didn't think so, Aunt Lilly. I really appreciate your help." Paul got up to leave and gave her a peck on the cheek before heading for home.

########

Weeks later, with no word yet from Aunt Lilly, Paul headed over to their house hoping for the best. It took several knocks before she came to the door. "Paul, oh Paul…it's good to see you." Lilly said in an uncomfortable tone.

Paul could tell already that the news wasn't good, so he didn't even bother to step into the foyer. "Have you any tires or inner tubes for me?" Paul asked, knowing what the answer would be.

"Oh, Paul, I tried to convince Carl to get them but he had his mind set on a coat…you know winter is almost here."

"I suppose you drank all the coffee." Paul asked with a sigh.

"Of course – that was gone within a week after you gave it to me." Lilly laughed. "You wouldn't have anymore, would you?"

Paul failed to see the humor. He was hoping to get it back to barter with someone else. His heart sank as he had just found out that a quarter pound of coffee was selling for $75.00 on the black market.

"Good day, Aunt Lilly." Paul turned abruptly and left her standing in the doorway with the door open.

########

It was early November and miraculously the Tittel's received another package from Christa. This time Paul received peanut butter and chocolate. It was harder this time to refrain from ingesting any of what she had sent him. Coffee was easy not to drink since he didn't like it, but peanut butter and chocolate? Paul listened to his stomach growling as he wrapped them in a paper bag and placed it his nap sack under his bed.

The next day after school, having arrived back in Hartenstein, Joachim agreed to walk with him to the uranium mine several miles past the train station. Once there, they waited for the shifts to change. With Joachim behind him, they patiently watched for the miners to come out of the meshed metal elevator doors.

Once the elevator reached the top, the door was lifted and a large group of men slowly made their way out to the road. "Sir...kind sir!" Paul said loudly as he ran after an older man, grabbing him by the sleeve of his coat. The man turned to face him. He was covered in dirt from head to toe. His face was blackened except where his mining helmet came down over his ears and forehead. Paul looked into his bright blue eyes and saw the weariness in them.

"How can I help you, boy," the man smiled and it changed his whole demeanor.

Paul relaxed and sighed inside feeling more at ease that the man wasn't upset that they had stopped him from heading home after a hard day's work. "I need help and was wondering if you would be interested in a barter?" Paul said raising his eyebrows with the question.

"I might. Depends on what you're offering and what you want."

Joachim stepped forward and opened Paul's nap sack. The miner looked down and saw the jar of peanut butter and several candy bars of chocolate. Food that some hadn't seen in years.

"And in return?" he asked.

"I need 2 bicycle tires and 2 inner tubes," Paul quickly replied.

"Meet me here same time in 2 weeks," the miner quickly replied.

"Deal." Paul held out his hand and the miner took it. The agreement was made. On the way home the boys could barely contain their excitement.

"Do you think he'll really come through?" Paul asked Joachim.

"Well, even if he doesn't. You didn't make the mistake of giving him the goods without receiving something in return."

"Yah, your right, Joachim. I learned a hard lesson with Aunt Lilly.

The miner came through just as he said. The boys made the exchange and headed back to town filled with excitement. They could hardly wait to finish assembling the bike. It seemed more a like a surgical operation.

"Screw driver," Joachim said while holding out his hand.

Paul slapped one into his palm.

"Wrench." Joachim held out his hand again.

Paul took the screw driver and slapped the wrench into his hand.

"Hammer."

Again Paul took the wrench from Joachim and replaced it with the hammer. Several hours later, Joachim stood the bike upright.

"Now, it definitely doesn't look store bought. And I don't think you'll have the problem of having someone wanting to steal it..."

"It's beautiful," Paul said interrupting his friend.

The wire basket that hung from the handle bars was bent. The seat, that had lost all its material covering and cushion, was now covered in a piece of sheep's wool wrapped with twine to keep it secure. The body was covered in rust, but still held its strength. The guards over the tires were scraped and dented, but fit perfectly into place.

"Beauty is definitely in the eye of the beholder," Joachim laughed. "We've one last thing to do."

"And what would that be?" Paul wondered seeing the bike as complete.

"The seat must be adjusted my friend. You're a bit on the short side at 4 feet so your feet won't reach the pedals."

"If you insist," Paul held the bike while Joachim lowered the seat.

"It's all yours," Joachim said as he watched Paul mount the bike and ride it out of the shed.

"It's incredible!" Paul said as he rode around in circles in Joachim's back yard. Paul raised his fist in the air, "To America!"

"To freedom!" yelled Joachim jumping into the air in excitement.

"Thank you, Lord!" Paul yelled as he came alongside Joachim. "And thank *you,* Hans Joachim," Paul said as he slipped off the bike and threw his arm over his friend's shoulder. "You know I never could have done it without you."

"Well, you could have, but I'm not quite sure you would have ended up with a bike."

Both boys laughed while they pushed it back into the shed keeping it hidden until Paul's departure.

########

While building his bike over the past nine months, Paul shared with Joachim the hardships of what he was experiencing at school. They took the same train to and from Zwickau – but attended different high schools. The train ride offered them both an opportunity to share about the day's events, but they had to watch what they talked about. Listening ears were everywhere. One wrong word could have devastating consequences if the wrong person heard you. Once they were alone in the shed, building his bike, Paul poured his heart out to Joachim. "I'm ready to go Joachim …this spring, once the weather is warmer, I plan to leave."

"Why so soon? What about finishing your education?" asked Joachim. "You still have two years of high school to finish."

"I know with my grades, I'll still be accepted into a trade school in West Germany," Paul said with confidence. "But that's the least of my concerns, Joachim. Because of my faith, I'm being continually harassed. I've refused to join the Free Democratic Youth, a copy of Hitler's Youth, and you know that if I stay I wouldn't have a chance of obtaining a higher education.[5] If school wasn't hard enough, my professors and fellow students make everything much more difficult."

"How? In what way?" Joachim asked with sincere concern.

"I'm continually asked a barrage of questions concerning communism and the German Democratic Republic. In math class, in science…in classes where the topic isn't communism, their political agenda is forced upon me. FDJ posters are taped to my locker and I'm continually told that my faith is a myth and the only road to success is that of being a communist."

"I know in my school I have felt some of the same things, Paul, but not to the degree that you're experiencing."

"Its hard, Joachim. I've been punched and shoved while on my way to class, called names because of my faith and they even assigned me the food detail knowing that I would never get to eat. I must serve everyone else first, then serve myself, but more often than not there is nothing left so I go hungry."

"Paul, I think it's time."

"Time for what?"

"It's time for you to talk with your father. It's time for you to go."

########

Everyone had gone to bed, or was about to. Carl was going through some papers that sat on the table in the informal living room. Paul mustered the courage to go and talk with his father. "Pa, can I speak with you?"

"I'm here son, have a seat."

Paul sat down across from him and took a deep breath. "I want to cross the border. I want to go to West Germany and then to America." Paul waited for his reply.

Carl looked down at the papers in front of him then looked up into his son's pleading eyes. "It's dangerous. They are reinforcing the border everyday with more soldiers, guard dogs, and fencing. You're still young, Paul. Can you at least finish your high school education?"

Paul replied with all the stories he had told Joachim. After he was finished, he watched as his father nodded his head. "I understand son. From what you've said…it's best for you to go before they come after you and take you to prison for your political and religious beliefs. You have my blessing to go. Remember to mention this to no one – not even to your brother or sisters."

"I've told Hans Joachim."

"Then tell no one else. If the wrong person hears of it, you will be shot."

"Yes, pa, I understand." Paul began to feel the weight of his decision.

"Now let me get a map. We must figure out the best route and hopefully find people along the way to help."

Carl agreed with Paul about his route. He would head west to Saalfeld and visit Sigrid. From there they knew that pastor Hirshfeld, who had once been a vicar at their church, would point him in the right direction. Paul watched as his father wrote out letters to pastor Hirshfeld and a friend from his school years who lived in Hannover, a city in West Germany. Prayerfully, these people would see him safely to his destination of Rothenburg where his sister Ruth lived.

########

While Christmas was a joy to celebrate, especially with his brother back home, Paul's mind was focused on spring and the great adventure that lay ahead of him.

The winter months seemed to never end. When his 16th birthday came on April 3, 1950, Paul could hardly believe that the time for him to escape East Germany was only a few months away. Joachim came for his birthday celebration. He brought the bike over with him. Paul acted surprised when he showed it to him and his family. His brother and sisters couldn't know his plan yet, not until the night before his departure.

########

It was Monday night, June 27th. Everyone was gathered around the table and had just finished eating. Elisabeth and Magdalena cleared the table to get ready for evening devotions. With everyone seated, Carl began to tell them about Paul's decision. "I have some news for everyone."

"I hope its good news, pa. I really like good news," Magdalena said cheerfully.

"Please don't say someone died again," begged Elisabeth.

"It must be good news – look at the grin on Paul's face – he already knows," said Herbert.

"You're right, it is about Paul," Carl said looking at his children. "It was a hard decision, but I've given him my permission to go."

"To go where?" Magdalena asked.

"Tomorrow morning I'm going to begin a two day journey by bike to Saalfeld to see our sister Sigrid and from there, somewhere north I will cross the border to West Germany. I want to eventually go to America, but the timing of that is in the Lord's hands."

"I can tell you're excited to be going," Elisabeth said. "To say, 'we will miss you,' just doesn't seem to say enough. Paul, my dear brother, just like Herbert, we will always be in prayer for you."

"If I had my full strength I would consider joining you," Herbert said emphatically.

"I will miss you, dear brother." A tear slid down Magdalena's cheek.

Paul stood up and went to his little sister's side to hug her. "The world is a small place, Magdalena. I will write and let you know of every adventure. I'm sure we will see each other again." Paul kissed the top of her head before sitting down again next to his father.

"Shall we begin?" Carl said as they joined hands and began to pray for Paul and his journey. Afterward they read Psalm 91 together.

Seeing that it was his last evening with his family, everyone gathered their instruments and soon the loud sound of praise and worship filled the house. Light broke through the somberness of the evening, and hope arose in their hearts once more.

"Don't be afraid for me, I know the Lord will keep me safe and that your prayers will always accompany me." These were Paul's last words to his family as he waved goodbye, pushing his bike up the hill toward the town square of Hartenstein.

He passed several Russian soldiers along the way. Almost to the outskirts of town, he found himself looking back to see if he was followed. Not that he was too concerned because many people traveled by bike to go on vacation, so there would be no reason for them to be suspicious.

He stopped for a moment and looked through his knapsack that sat nestled in the basket in front of him. Earlier that morning, Elisabeth had so kindly filled it with what little food they could spare. Inside were two flasks filled with water along with a few slices of bread, several small baked potatoes, a poncho, a blanket, an extra set of clothes, and a few family pictures. Paul took a gulp of water. He had to travel light since the bike was heavy and the mountain roads would be steep and hard to climb, so the less weight the better. How he wished he could have brought his trumpet.

"No time for regrets now," he thought to himself. "I have a hope and a future." He thought of Jeremiah 29:11 one of his mother's favorite verses:

For I know the thoughts that I think toward you, saith the LORD, thoughts of peace, and not of evil, to give you an expected end.

The first night of his journey Paul spent under a bridge. His legs ached from riding his bike and walking it up the long mountain roads. So far it had been uneventful and he was thankful for that. He began to sing and laughed as he heard his voice echo under the bridge. He sang *Praise to the Lord, the Almighty the King of Creation,* while he spread out his blanket and covered himself with his poncho. He felt safe and secure as he drifted off to sleep knowing the Lord was near him and watching over him.

The second night he saw an old, abandoned barn not far off the road. Leaving his bike outside, he climbed up to the hay loft and made his way to a large floor to ceiling window. Here, he could look out over a valley and see large mountain peaks in the distance. Sitting on his blanket munching the last of the bread and potatoes his sister had packed for him, he watched as the stars made a spectacular display. He was filled with such peace and hope while the stars looked as if they were at arm's length. Reaching up to pluck one of the sparkling gems from the sky, he pretended to place it into his shirt pocket. He never wanted to forget the moment and now he would always have the memory of the star to remind him.

The next morning after 25 miles of biking, Paul rode into the town Saalfeld. He knew the church and parsonage was located not far from the town square so he peddled faster as he saw the steeple not far ahead. Passing the church, he drove up onto the lawn of the parsonage. Paul pounded firmly on the door. He was a bit nervous, for not seeing his sister, and wondered how the pastor would receive him. His father had written pastor Hirschfeld telling him of his intentions but they had not heard back. He could reject him at the door not wanting to put his family at risk…the door suddenly swung open and Paul's fears were put to rest as he was engulfed in a huge bear hug.

"You must be Paul-Gerhard," a large man with spectacles said as he released him pulling him into the house for more hugs from his wife and children.

Sigrid was last in line and Paul was overwhelmed with emotion as she held him for a bit and smothered him with kisses on the top of his head. "It's so good to see you, Paul," Sigrid said as she held him by the shoulders looking him up and down. She pulled him close again and hugged him a final time before letting him go.

Paul wiped the tears from his cheeks. "You look good, Sigrid," he noticed she was now a healthy weight.

"You could look better, Paul. You're as little as a bird," Sigrid said as she scooped her little brother up into her arms, spun around and placed him back down.

Paul and Sigrid laughed together. At sixteen Paul only weighed 72 pounds – some due to his height of 4 feet but much due to malnutrition over the past several years.

"We will remedy that," said Mrs. Hirschfeld. "Sigrid, come, while the men talk we'll prepare a welcoming feast for your brother."

Sigrid planted another kiss on top of her brother's head before joining her in the kitchen. The children ran outside to play while Paul and Mr. Hirschfeld went into the living room to discuss plans for crossing the border.

"I'm sorry I couldn't respond to your father's letter. I was too concerned about the communists getting a hold of it and my life and family being threatened. I'm glad you made it safely here, Paul. I'll be sure to write your father and tell him." Mr. Hirschfeld stopped to load a pipe of tobacco. "Tell me, have you considered where you want to cross over?"

"I thought maybe 15 miles west of Saalfeld,"

"Paul, I receive a daily casualty report from that area of the border. There's no chance of crossing there anymore – it's too heavily guarded." He lit his pipe and after several long draws, he continued. "My Aunt Hulda lives on a small farm 150 miles north of here. I think you'd have a better chance crossing there. I know she could use the help too." Mr. Hirschfeld paused, "Are you sure you want to go through with this?"

Paul leaned forward and passionately told him of all that he and his family had suffered over the years – from the war to the Russian occupation of Hartenstein. He ended with how grateful their family was that he and his wife had taken Sigrid into their home giving her food and work to survive.

"I had no idea things were so bad, Paul. Sigrid has never shared a lot about her past and she has always been such a joy to my wife and children. I'm thankful to the Almighty for sparing us the horror of what you and family endured and that He gave you strength to survive and come this far. I see why you're so passionate to get to freedom."

Paul leaned back in his chair, relieved that he understood his quest and somehow he knew Mr. Hirschfeld would help him.

"Paul, you are welcome to stay as long as you want. I recommend that you rest up to prepare for the long journey ahead of you."

"Thank you, pastor, I will." They both stood and shook hands.

"Come now, I think I smell a wonderful dinner being prepared in your honor."

As they sat down to eat, Paul almost felt faint. Although not the size of the meals his father had talked about in America, there was more food on the table than he had seen in years. Steamed carrots, bread, butter, milk, with large plates of baked chicken and stuffing, reminding Paul of the days of Thanksgiving they had before the war when things were more plentiful. While Mr. Hirschfeld prayed, he pushed away the melancholy memories. After grace, Paul started filling his plate full of the goodness that was piled before him. Sigrid couldn't help but notice that the food was stacked so high that it was falling off and laying on the table.

"Paul," Sigrid said quietly leaning over to whisper in his ear. "There's plenty more where this came from. It's not like home. There's more to eat tomorrow and plenty to snack on, too."

Paul nodded his head and began to chew his food a little slower instead of just swallowing it whole.

########

The next few days were glorious. Sigrid gave Paul a bike tour of Saalfeld. Many times as they rode down small streets and alleys they broke into song together singing the hymns they had learned as children. The town sat in a tranquil setting surrounded by tree covered mountains Some houses had flower boxes adding to the quaintness of the old town. One would never know they were in East Germany except for the occasional East German army truck passing by.

After Paul's tour, they came back to a lunch prepared by Mrs. Hirschfeld. The pastor and his wife had given Sigrid several days off to be with Paul. They were a generous and kind family. Paul couldn't thank them enough for all that they had done for his sister and himself.

After another day of rest, Paul made the decision that it was time to go. The pastor and his family along with Sigrid by his side, prayed a blessing over him and especially for his protection. With hugs and well wishes from everyone he said his goodbyes and continued on his journey north toward Aunt Hulda's house.

It was an easy trek compared to what he had already travelled. The first 40 miles were up hill, but after that it was flat terrain. He made great time for the rest of the trip covering 140 miles in just 3 days.

Following the directions Mr. Hirschfeld gave him, he rode over many dirt roads that had wheat and rye fields on either side. He wondered how there could be such plenty when in Hartenstein many people begged for just a cup of wheat. Maybe it was for show for those on the other side to make it look like East Germany was a prosperous nation. Paul pondered these things as he pushed forward on his pedals feeling that every turn brought him closer to his destiny.

Paul had one more night to spend in the open before reaching Aunt Hulda's farm. The sun was just about to set. A rye field spread out before him. He walked his bike several yards into the rich unharvested field. Laying it down, he pulled out his blanket and poncho and made his bed.

The stars sparkled like diamonds. Paul remembered the one he placed in his pocket on one of his first nights away from home. He patted his chest pretending it was still there. This was another night he would never forget. He watched as several shooting stars shot across the sky above him. A song came to mind, and although it wasn't Christmas, he sang it anyway:

Silent Night, Holy Night
All is calm, all is bright,
Round yon virgin, mother and child
Holy infant so tender and mild
sleep in heavenly peace
sleep in heavenly peace

Paul rolled on his side and within a few breaths was soundly asleep.

He was awake at the crack of dawn. Repacking his knapsack with his blanket and poncho, he noticed how much lighter it felt when he swung it over his shoulder. Mrs. Hirschfeld had packed it full of food and he had consumed most of it. There were a few crusts of bread left which he swiftly consumed along with the last of his water. He had had several days of good meals in him and had become spoiled. He hoped Aunt Hulda (a name pastor Hirschfeld had asked he call her even though there was no relation) had breakfast waiting for him.

Paul could smell the bacon frying a mile away. Riding up directly to her front door he found her waiting for him outside.

"Was expecting you Paul. I've got a good breakfast for you before I give you the grand tour of the place." She held out her arms and Paul embraced her. Her eyes were a bright blue and her face crinkled into a smile around them. Her white hair was covered with a blue bandana and she wore an apron over her skirt. Paul noticed that her hands were calloused – those of a hard working woman.

Paul smiled back. He liked Aunt Hulda.

She climbed the steps to the door and held it open for him.

After she showed him his room and the bathroom, she told him to clean up and hurry down for breakfast.

Paul joined her in the kitchen. A nice table had been set for the two of them. She took his plate and started filling it with fried potatoes, eggs, bacon, and ham. Paul was again totally amazed at the quantity of food. As he took his plate he picked up a biscuit and slathered it with butter and jelly. He was hungry, but he remembered what Sigrid had told him about not piling his plate too full. Her words of *there's always more*, came to mind.

He took his place across the table from Aunt Hulda and slowly savored the food she had made for him.

As Paul ate, he pondered how she knew he was coming. She didn't have a phone. He remembered his father telling him of the way information passed from church to church – congregant to congregant – sometimes much faster than the sound over wires. He smiled knowing this was probably the way Aunt Hulda heard all her news.

After breakfast Paul was introduced to all the animals and the chores that went with them. This was one of his favorite things to do – caring for the animals.

After four days of helping Aunt Hulda on her farm, Paul found it was time to move on. It was a small community of local farmers and everyone knew everyone else's business. Paul listened from inside the house as a farmer stopped by on horseback to ask her who he was and what he was doing on her farm. She answered simply enough that he was a relative, come to help an old lady with chores and the care of the animals, but there was always the possibility the farmer was a spy. Paul couldn't bear the thought of Aunt Hulda getting into trouble because of him.

After he told her that it was time for him to go, she made him an offer. If he would stay she would give him the farm and all that came with it. She had no children and no one else to pass it on to. Paul knew her offer was sincere because she really needed help on the farm, but he had to turn it down, as he had to fulfill his goal of finishing his quest for freedom.

Early the next morning, Aunt Hulda made him another breakfast fit for a king. Paul ate as much as he could not knowing when he would have another one like it.

He parked his bike in her barn knowing that most people probably saw it as a dilapidated piece of junk, but to Paul it meant so much more. He patted the seat and thanked the Lord for keeping him safe thus far. The rest of his journey he would be hiking through rough terrain, fields and forests, nowhere a bike could travel.

Aunt Hulda came out of the house with his knapsack .

"I've filled your flasks with water and made several sandwiches loaded with bacon fat. You'll need the energy for what you're about to do."

Paul fell into her arms. She gave him a warm hug, then she prayed for him and his safe journey over the border.

Afterward, Paul threw his knapsack over his shoulder and walked westward turning to wave goodbye several times. Aunt Hulda continued to wave her handkerchief until Paul was out of sight.

########

The border was roughly 4 miles from Aunt Hulda's. It didn't take long for Paul to reach the 'death strip.' The name came from a short strip of land that separated the two countries where anyone trying to cross over was shot or taken to prison. Here he watched from the cover of the fir trees as guards and vehicles moved along the road that lined the border. There was a barren field on the other side of the road where he thought he spotted an area that he might be able to cross…

"Get up, boy! What are you doing here?" An East German solider grabbed him by the shirt collar pulling him up from where he had been hiding.

Paul didn't say a word as he was dragged by the soldier to a covered vehicle that was filled with men and women who had also been caught trying to cross over. The soldier picked him up and threw him into the back of the truck. They drove to a nearby house that was the border headquarters. Here the Russian and East German guards questioned them about their intentions and why they wanted to cross over into West Germany.

Paul had been thinking of what he was going to say as he watched the guards. A Russian and an East German soldier stood together as they asked one person at a time to step away from the line they stood in. They stated their name and age and were asked to briefly explain why they were trying to cross the border into West Germany. The East German guard took notes on a clip board while the Russian asked the questions and listened to the people's stories.

When it came his turn, Paul held his knapsack in front of him. He pulled out his family pictures and pointed to the one of Ruth.

"See," Paul said pointing to Ruth. "She is my sister and left for West Germany when it was still an open border. While she was working on a farm in Rothenburg, she was tragically hit by lightning. It has been over a year that she has been in the hospital trying to recover from burns. She needs someone from our family to be by her side to encourage her to get better."

The soldiers looked at each other for a moment. Paul held his breath.

Then they started laughing. "Boy, you had better come up with a better story than that when you stand before the magistrate." The East German guard said while tapping the clipboard on Paul's head.

Paul felt his face turning red. He looked to the ground embarrassed by the soldiers laughing at him.

They took him into the house, but instead of having him stay with the other captives on the first floor they put him in the attic. Here, Paul waited for several hours and still no one came. It was kind of scary being by himself in the attic. He had no idea what would happen or what they would do to him. So he did what Herbert did when he was captured by the Russians – he prayed.

Another half hour passed – finally, they came and took him down from his lofty cell. They put him back in line with the other men and women and marched them to the nearby town of Ellrich. In Ellrich there was a border prison, one side for men, the other side for women. Paul was shoved into a large holding cell with 30 other men who had been captured the same morning. They were told by the guards they would not be given food or water for 48 hours.

While waiting in the cell, Paul listened to the horrible stories of others who had tried to cross the border. One was of two men who were farm hands harvesting wheat near the border, but were still shot and killed because the guards didn't know if they were trying to escape. After listening to so many, he wondered if he should even try to cross over again.

Around 4 p.m. the same day, Paul was pulled out of prison. Before they took him out of the cell he gave away his bacon lard sandwiches to men who had not eaten in days. The soldiers took him out first, thinking he was a young boy because of his size and height. They brought him to stand before the magistrate. As Paul stood in front of the judge, he tried to keep his knees from shaking.

"Tell me son, why were you trying to escape East Germany?"

Paul repeated the same story he had told the border guards earlier.

The judge didn't laugh like they did. He looked at Paul over his glasses. "Young man, you should never try to escape again. I am sending you home with the Communist Youth Brigade."

Something rose up in Paul. He was on a mission and he knew God was on His side. He spoke loud and clear to the judge. "Sir, I do not need to travel with the Communist Youth Brigade. I came by bike and will go back by bike."

"Listen here, young man, if you ever try to do this again you will go to prison for several years and your father will have to pay a heavy fine!" the judge said in a loud voice.

"Yes, judge," was all Paul could manage to say.

"You're free to go."

Paul could hardly believe his ears. "Free to go?!" "Thank you Father!" Paul said as he ran away from the prison and out of town with great speed. It was getting late and the sun was starting to set. Doubts filled Paul's mind about trying to cross again. Echoes of the prisoner's stories came back to haunt him and also what the judge said… "years in prison and his father fined." Paul tossed it back and forth. "Should I? Shouldn't I.?" Then he heard a voice that came from all around him, "Go, you will make it."

########

He walked around the town's edge looking west. He was exhausted and hungry – everything in him wanted to stop and lay down. "Come on, keep going, you can make it," he said to himself reiterating the words he had heard earlier. He walked through a field and was heading up a hill when a man came over a small hill walking toward him with his back to the sun.

Paul couldn't make out his face and it seemed like the sun's rays outlined his figure.

"Could you tell me where West Germany is?" Paul said holding up his hand to shield his eyes from the setting sun.

The man simply turned and pointed to a mountain behind him that was considerably different from any other. This one had deciduous leafy trees instead of fir or pine. It was an easy landmark to follow.

"Thank you!" Paul said as he made his way over the rise of the hill and scanned the mountainous landmark in front of him. He knew why he had been caught the first time. He had headed straight west, right into the waiting arms of the border guards. This time he would hike along the lower part of the pine covered mountains that were parallel to the border – coming out – he hoped to be on the side of the mountain with deciduous trees. Here, once he got to the top he would be behind the border guards and safely on his way across the border.

He moved swiftly through the firs and evergreens staying hidden within the edge of the forest. His hope was that they would continue to look through their binoculars at the valley below and not the mountains beside them. The sun was almost set as he climbed the mountain the man had pointed out to him earlier. It was a steep climb. He was out of breath from exhaustion and anticipation of what lay ahead. As he neared the top, he saw several benches positioned to overlook the scenic valley below. There were 3 women sitting together on one of them enjoying the summer evening.

Paul thought, "Maybe, I've already crossed the border." He yelled over to them, "Is this West Germany?" The women didn't say a word but pointed down the hill to his left. One hundred yards away he watched as four border guards scrambled out of their foxhole. Running toward him with loaded rifles he could hear them yelling, "Stop where you are!" The women were yelling "Run!" Paul took a running leap and flew into the thick brush that stood between the benches and the forest.

Under the shrubbery, because of his tiny frame, he found there was space beneath for him to crawl away from the border guards. They couldn't follow him - being too big – they'd have to find another way. Once past the low lying bushes, he ran like a rabbit, quickly dodging tree limbs and rocky outcroppings. He paused thinking for a moment he might have outrun them. An explosion of bark next to his head told him otherwise.

He ran until there was nothing left in him. Seeing another bush up ahead, he dove underneath it. Crawling out the other side, he found that he was sitting on the edge of a shallow ravine that held a small brook at the bottom. He lay on his side trying to catch his breath. Swirls of gray mist enveloped him. Images from his family, scenes from the war, people dying of hunger passed through the shadows before him. Tears streamed down his face. He heard a guard dog in the distance. A final whisper fell from his lips as the black abyss of exhaustion enveloped him. "If this is it, I give up…so be it."

1. http://www.hymnary.org/text/now_thank_we_all_our_god

Now thank we all our God
with heart and hands and voices,
who wondrous things has done,
in whom his world rejoices;
who from our mothers' arms
has blessed us on our way
with countless gifts of love,
and still is ours today.

O may this bounteous God
through all our life be near us,
with ever joyful hearts
and blessed peace to cheer us,
to keep us in his grace,
and guide us when perplexed,
and free us from all ills
of this world in the next.

All praise and thanks to God
the Father now be given,
the Son and Spirit blest,
who reign in highest heaven
the one eternal God,
whom heaven and earth adore;
for thus it was, is now,
and shall be evermore.

2. http://www.history.com/topics/cold-war/berlin-airlift

3. http://ww2db.com/battle_spec.php?battle_id=148

4. http://www.history.com/news/history-lists/8-things-you-should-know-about-wwiis-eastern-front

   While the western Allies released their final World War II prisoners in 1948, many German POWs in the U.S.S.R. were kept under lock and key for several more years. Most were used as slave labor in copper or coal mines, and anywhere between 400,000 and one million eventually died while in Russian custody. Some 20,000 former soldiers were still in Soviet hands at the time of Stalin's death in 1953, and the last 10,000 didn't get their freedom until 1955 and 1956—a full decade after the war had ended.

5. http://www.spiegel.de/international/zeitgeist/scouting-for-communists-east-german-youth-organization-returns-a-509998.html

   For young people wanting to get ahead in communist East Germany, membership in the Free German Youth (FDJ *Freie Deutsche Jugend*) was a must.

Chapter Ten: Liberty

Paul watched his mother from behind as she did the dishes. He could hear the water gurgle as she placed each plate in a tub of water to rinse. It felt so good to see her. The sunlight trickled in through the lace curtains. He noticed the water sparkle as it dripped off the cup she was holding up for inspection. Having completed her task, she dried her hands on her apron, and turned to face him. Her smile was so beautiful and her eyes were full of so much love it made him feel warm inside.

"My liebling, it's not time for you to be home yet." she said in a soft gentle voice as she touched his cheek.

Paul smiled dreamily and watched as the outer edges of his vision turned gray and then to black. With a sharp intake of air he woke up. He could still hear the gurgling of water, but not from a kitchen sink, it came from the small brook below him. He sat up quickly. The night was as black as ink. He felt around him to make sure his knapsack was nearby. Feeling it next to his side he clutched it to his chest. All the memories he had left of his family were in it. His heart began to race as he remembered being shot at and the soldiers chasing him through the woods. He listened closely for any sound of his pursuers. A resounding quiet was his answer. He said a whispered prayer thanking the Lord for His protection.

"The border. I must cross the border." Paul thought as he slowly got up. He found his bearings…sort of…. He knew from looking at previous hand drawn maps of the border that his father had shown him that it weaved and flowed along mountain ranges and river valleys - it was far from being straight. Having crossed the first perimeter, where the soldiers almost ambushed him, he knew if he followed along the upper plateau then he would soon reach the second and final perimeter. He slowly followed the forest's edge on his right while on his left the small ravine turned into a marshy wetland. He continued on for a short while until he started to see a faint glow through the trees. It was about 100 yards from where he stood. He took cover in the forest and gradually made his way toward it.

Finally approaching a clearing, Paul crawled to the edge of the tree line. Here, right before him, was a large sign written in phosphorus paint, 'Border Do Not Cross, Penalty Severe.' Paul waited a while until he was finally satisfied that he could move without being seen and began to crawl toward the sign and the barbed wire fence that lay beyond. Making it to the fence, being slight of frame, he found a way to squeeze under the barbed wire. Having made it to the other side, he never looked back. He ran in the dark until he couldn't run anymore.

It wasn't long before he reached the West German border. He could see the border station from a ways off and there were large lights mounted on telephone poles illuminating a guard hut. The soldiers saw him coming from a distance and went to greet him. "Boy, how did you make it?" one of the guards asked.

"God helped me through," was Paul's firm answer.

After he told them his story, they took the time to give him directions through the countryside and to the next town so that he would not swerve back into East German territory. He was grateful for their help and was soon on his way.

After another 4 mile trek, he made it to the town of Walkenried. This was the first town after the border with a railroad station. He had several towns to go through by train in order to get to Ruth who now resided in Rothenburg. Knowing he didn't have enough West German marks to pay for the entire way by rail, he planned to hitchhike from the next town.

Approaching the brightly lit station he could see other travelers through the windows – some sleeping and others deep in conversation. He stepped through the doors into the waiting area and almost everyone looked his way to see who it was. He smiled and nodded in response to their stares. Paul saw that the paranoia from living in East Germany was still with them. Thoughts that anyone could be a spy and report you to the authorities would take time to fade. He inhaled deeply and closed his eyes for a moment. Freedom…he had finally made it.

He purchased a ticket to Nordheim – the next town in his journey north. Making his way to a bench, he sat near a group of men who were deep in conversation. He listened for several hours, right up until the train arrived. Each person had seen so much grief and tragedy. Stories of men, women and children murdered, shot, imprisoned and tortured by the Russians and the new East German regime. Paul was glad when the train came. He had heard enough, he had seen enough, and lived through enough. He wanted peace in his life again just as it was before the war. Walking to the back of the train car, he curled up into a ball on his seat. Resting his head on the window, using his knapsack as a pillow, he fell into an exhausted sleep.

The screeching of the train's brakes brought him out his slumber. He looked out the window and squinted at the bright sunlight. The town of Nordheim was bustling with activity.

Stepping off the train, Paul had an agenda. First was food and second, to find a way to Hanover City, which was close to where Ruth lived in Rothenburg. Across the street from the train station was a small fruit stand. He stood with his hands on his hips looking in disbelief. He had seen pictures of them before but had never seen them in real life, let alone tasted any. It was against his better judgement, but he couldn't stop himself. He used the last of his money to buy 3 pounds of bananas.

Sitting on the curb, he folded his hands and thanked the Lord for his safe journey and for the tropical fruit he was about to devour. After eating all 3 pounds of bananas, he thought it was the most delicious thing he had ever eaten. Having been satiated for the time, he felt renewed strength from his early morning snack. With a spring in his step, he followed the signs out of town to a major roadway and started hitchhiking.

Paul had been walking for over a mile before he realized he was walking in the wrong direction. He needed to go north and by the sign in front of him he was headed south. Before turning around he noticed a diner not far ahead. Diners meant truckers and truckers meant transportation – if one would be so generous to let him ride along. As he passed through the parking lot he noticed a truck that had a sign on its door saying it was from Hamburg, which was 80 miles north of Hannover City.

"Will God work my mistake into a blessing?" Paul thought as he opened the door to the diner. One of the Bible verses his mother taught him came to mind.

And we know that all things work together for good to them that love God, to them who are the called according to his purpose. Romans 8:28

It was bustling with activity. It didn't look like there was an empty seat in the place from what Paul could tell. He noticed two men at the end of the restaurant sitting in a booth. For some reason they looked like truckers. He approached them hoping they were the ones that owned the truck from Hamburg.

"Excuse me sirs, my name is Paul Tittel, I was wondering…" Paul paused as he gathered his courage. "Are you the drivers of the truck from Hamburg parked outside?"

Alfons looked up from his breakfast at a boy he thought could be no more than ten. Just a wisp of a lad that looked like he could use a good meal. He and his friend Audo were on their way back to Hamburg after making deliveries in the area.

"My name's Alfons and this is Audo," said Alfons as he shook Paul's hand with Audo doing the same. Alfons continued, "Yes, as a matter of fact it would be our truck," he said as he took a sip of his coffee.

"Why do you want to know?" asked Audo.

While the waitress came and left several times, Paul told the story of his family during the war and his determination afterward to cross the border.

"You've been through a lot for someone your age," Alfons said as he moved over and motioned for Paul to sit next to him.

Audo motioned for the waitress and ordered the supreme special breakfast for their new friend.

Minutes later Paul looked down at a plate of food from heaven. Eggs, sausages, and waffles covered in maple syrup lay before him and it smelled so wonderful that he almost forgot to pray. Bowing his head he thanked the Lord for the food, his safe journey, and for keeping His word of working all things for good, even his mistakes. He was never so glad that he started out in the wrong direction.

While he ate, between gulps of milk and food, Paul gave the men the details of his border crossing. They listened amazed that someone so young made it across without being hurt or killed.

"Must be like he said," thought Alfons. "God certainly helped him along."

Paul continued to share with them. He told of his need to see his sister Ruth in Rothenburg and how not being able to afford the train, he had taken to hitchhiking. After he finished eating, Alfons and Audo looked at each other and nodded.

"Paul" Alfons looked down at him smiling and said, "You're more than welcome to join us on our way back to Hamburg since Hannover City is right on the way."

"Really! That would be great!" Paul said as he got up from the booth and threw his knapsack over his shoulder.

########

Several hours later, after much conversation and the singing of favorite folk tunes, Paul pulled out a small piece of folded paper from his knapsack. It was the address of his father's childhood friend, one he had been confirmed with. Paul was grateful for the far reaching connections of fellow believers – church folk that opened their homes and hearts to help him on his journey.

Audo took the slip of paper from Paul, since Alfons was driving.

"This is just outside Hannover City," said Audo to Alfons. Alfons nodded.

If Paul didn't know better he thought they could read each other's minds the way they always nodded at each other without speaking.

"We'll take you right there, Paul," said Audo. "No worries."

Paul sighed with relief. He was glad for every mile he didn't have to walk. They drove through Hannover City and they would have taken him right to the doorstep of the house, if big rigs were allowed in residential neighborhoods.

Audo helped Paul down from the cab of the semi. "Take care, Paul. Safe journey!" said Alfons as he landed on the pavement in front of Audo.

"Here, kid. It's from both of us," Audo said as he handed Paul some German Marks.

Paul took the money and gave Audo a hug. "Thank you so much for your help."

"You just get safely to your sister and tell her Alfons and Audo wish her well," Audo said while climbing back into the truck.

"I will," said Paul. He stepped away from the truck. As they drove off Alfons honked his airhorn. Paul waved back in response.

Turning down the street, he watched the house numbers until he stood in front of the one that was on the paper his father had given him. Going up to the front door he rang the doorbell. Not sure of what to expect, Paul prayed that he would be a nice man like Alfons and Audo.

His prayer was answered by a large gregarious man who opened the door with a loud, "Paul, Paul Tittel! I've been waiting for you!" Theodor pulled Paul into his house with several pats on his back.

"My name is Theodor, Theodor Hummel. Your father and I go way back. I suppose he told you of our time together as children?" he asked Paul as he led him into the kitchen.

"Yes, just a bit, but not any details." Paul sat down at a kitchen table that was set for one.

"Oh, then while you eat I'll fill you in on the exciting parts. I took for granted you'd be hungry since it's past 1:00 already. I have some fresh pork and sauerkraut along with some dumplings, would you like some?" Theodor asked.

Paul nodded his head vigorously while Theodor took the pots out of the refrigerator and placed them on the stove to heat.

They visited while the food simmered. Paul shared of his journey and Theodor didn't disappoint in his stories about his father. Paul hadn't laughed in so long, he forgot how good it made him feel.

It wasn't long before lunch was ready. Theodor gave him an extra helping of everything. "Your wife is a good cook," Paul said while savoring every bite.

"Oh, I'm not married. I learned to cook from my mother and she could make a dumpling like no other."

"Yours are wonderful, I couldn't imagine anything, better Mr. Hummel."

"You can call me Theodor or Theo for short."

"Thank you for the meal, Theo," Paul said as he gulped down the last bite. "It was delicious."

"You're quite welcome, Paul. I am blessed to be a blessing and honored to help a good friend's son. The train leaves at 7:00 p.m. this evening for Rothenburg, so I highly recommend that you rest until 6:00. I'll wake you so you have time to get ready. It's only a 15 minute drive to the train station."

Theo showed Paul the bathroom and spare bedroom. As soon as he shut the door behind him, Paul laid on the freshly made bed and immediately fell asleep.

True to his word, Theo woke Paul at six o'clock. Paul took a long hot shower and it felt wonderful. It was the first time he'd had one since crossing the border. He put on his only other set of clean clothes, combed his hair, and smiled with a satisfied look in the mirror. He wanted to look his best when he saw his sister.

Arriving just in time, Theo saw him into the station and bought his ticket. Paul thanked him for his hospitality.

"God be with you, Paul, and I know from your stories that he already is. Remember I'm not that far from Rothenburg. If you ever need help you can call me at any time." Theo passed him a slip of paper with his phone number on it.

"How can I ever repay you?" Paul asked amazed at how kind and giving Theo had been to him. He thought of all the other people who had helped him throughout his journey. As their faces came to mind, the goodness of God overwhelmed him. Tears came to his eyes.

Theo saw the tears. "Dear, Paul, it's what we're here for – to help one another along. You would do the same if you had the opportunity. As a Christian, it's the joy of my heart to help those in need."

Paul nodded in agreement and gave Theo the biggest hug and climbed aboard the train. He gave a final wave goodbye before taking his seat. As the train departed, Paul took the time to say a prayer of thanks. He knew where all good things came from and took time to thank God for everyone He had put in his path.

########

Arriving in Rothenburg at 9 p.m., Paul was on pins and needles. He could hardly sit still in his seat waiting for the train to stop. He was anticipating seeing Ruth. He hurried off the train as quickly as the people in front of him would allow.

Using the money Alfons and Audo had given him, he took a taxi and went straight to the hospital. Now standing on the steps outside the building he looked up at the four stories of windows and wondered which one was Ruth's room.

Her doctor had written them of Ruth's tragic accident over a year ago. He blushed thinking back to how the Russian and German Soldiers didn't believe him when he told them what had happened to her. They were all shocked as a family when their father read them the letter from her doctor:

To: Mr. Carl Tittel,

I am sad to inform you that your daughter Ruth has been severely injured. The accident occurred at the farm where she was working as a hired hand. She was hit in the chest by lightning. While her burns are large and severe across her upper torso it is to my amazement that she is still alive at all.

We are treating her here at the Rothenburg General hospital. She will need many months of convalescence and care. The cost of her care is being taken care of by her employer.

If you would like to contact your daughter or have any questions about her care, please send mail via the return address. We will respond as quickly as possible.

Sincerely,

Dr. Walter Klein

Paul shook his head - that had been over a year ago. They had received a few letters telling of her progress and she did seem to be on the mend, but the doctor always said she had a way to go before she was fully recovered.

He climbed the stairs and opened the door to the odor of rubbing alcohol and cleaning fluids. He wrinkled up his nose – he didn't like the smell.

Making his way to the information desk he introduced himself. "My name is Paul Tittel, I'm here to see my sister Ruth. Could you tell me what room she's in?"

The receptionist looked at him over her spectacles, "You're Ruth's brother?"

"Yes," replied Paul.

She turned her back to him and he watched as she made several whispered phone calls.

Within moments, even though it was after 9 p.m., he was surrounded by hospital staff and doctors. Paul came to find Ruth was a patient celebrity. Not many people survive being hit by lightning and with the longevity of her stay everyone had become enamored with her gentle spirit and loving demeanor. She had become family to them.

Everyone was asking questions at once – it was a cacophony of sound. Paul stood looking up at them astounded that so many people knew his sister and now wanted to know him.

Finally one doctor's voice broke through the others. "Okay, everyone settle down. Let's give him some breathing room and give order to our questions. First, let me introduce myself, Paul. I'm Doctor Walter Klein, your sister's doctor."

Paul shook his hand and many others as he was introduced to the nurses who took care of Ruth and the chief surgeon who worked on her wounds. The janitor had even come to welcome him and laundry staff as well. After formal introductions, he began to answer their questions one at a time. He told them of his journey crossing the border and the many other stories he had heard from others.

"Well, it seems that Ruth isn't the only one who was blessed with a miracle," Dr. Klein said matter of factly. "The story of your journey has miracle written all over it." Everyone standing near him nodded in agreement.

"It's almost 10 o'clock, Paul. Seeing your sister now, would be too much of a shock for her system, she needs her rest. Are you hungry?"

"Starving," was Paul's immediate reply.

Dr. Klein pointed in the direction of a man wearing a white apron. "I'm on it!" The young man said as he swiftly exited the room.

"We need a place for him to sleep – any ideas?" Dr. Klein continued.

"I have a couch in my office," The chief surgeon volunteered.

"Sounds great. Would several of you nurses mind getting the linens to make his bed?" Dr. Klein raised his eyebrows toward two that were standing next to Paul.

"Right away," one replied as they both left in search of extra sheets and pillows.

"Is laundry here?" Dr. Klein asked while looking above heads trying to spot someone.

"Yes, here I am," a short woman with a bandana on her head stepped out from the group in front of Paul.

"I need you to show Paul where the shower is and wash his dirty clothes so he has something clean to wear tomorrow when he sees his sister."

"Right away, Doctor," replied the laundry woman.

"Alright, the party is over for now. Paul, follow her, get a shower, a good meal, and plenty of rest. We'll join you tomorrow afternoon at your sister's bedside as she receives the great surprise of your visit." The crowd quickly dispersed.

Paul followed the laundry lady up to the second floor. She pointed out the office where the nurses were making his bed and showed him the showers. Paul gave her his dirty clothes from his knapsack. She then waited while he undressed behind a curtain in the shower room for him to give her the clothes he was wearing.

Again, just as he had at Theo's house, Paul enjoyed a long and luxurious hot shower. Wrapping a towel around himself, he walked across the hallway to the chief surgeon's office. "Wow," Paul said to himself as he looked down at his neatly folded clothes on top of a nicely made bed of clean white sheets and fresh pillows. On the desk was a tray heaped with good food and a tall glass of milk.

Later, as he lay nestled between the sheets, he pondered the difference between living in East Germany and West Germany. 'It's the difference between heaven and hell, between light and dark, and life and death,' Paul thought looking back at his life after the war in Hartenstein and comparing it to life in West Germany. There was such a wide gap between how the two countries functioned even though at heart they were the same Germany. He surmised it was the ruling authority over them that made the difference.

Freedom. Now that he had a taste of it, he wanted more and this made him think of America and his dream of living there someday. "Someday," he thought. "Someday I will get there, but for now I need to be with Ruth and finish my education. Through the grace of God it will come."

########

Early the next morning it was the same as the night before. Paul showered and dressed and by the time he came back to the office, his bed was made and a tray of food sat on the desk. After eating his breakfast, the chief surgeon stopped by. Paul had his feet on the desk and was perusing a medical book he had taken off one of the bookshelves that surrounded him. He quickly removed his feet from the desk and jumped up - the book spilling to the floor.

"Sorry I didn't mean to scare you, Paul. Make yourself at home and don't worry about using my office. I only use it for naps anyway. There are other places here in the hospital where I can put my feet up if I need to. It's yours for as long as you're here. See you this afternoon." He left as quickly as he arrived.

Paul slumped back into the chair and picked the book off the floor. He shook his head, amazed again by the generosity of complete strangers.

Early that afternoon the nurses came to get him to take him to Ruth's room. Paul was giddy with excitement. He knew it would be a great surprise for her.

The nurses left him outside in the hallway while they joined the doctors and other staff who were already standing around Ruth's bed. Paul could hear their conversation from where he stood in the hallway.

"Ruth, we have a very big surprise for you today," said Dr. Klein.

"What is it? What could it be?" Ruth said excitedly.

"You can come in now," Dr. Klein said as everyone looked to the doorway.

Paul could see the whites of Ruth's eyes as he entered the room.

"Paul! Is it really you?!" Ruth yelled at her brother.

"I hope so," Paul approached her bed and gave her a kiss on the forehead.

Ruth gently put her arms around Paul's shoulders. He was careful not to embrace her too hard, noticing the bandages wrapped around her chest.

"Now let me pinch you and make sure you're real," Ruth said as she pinched his arm.

"Ow!" Paul yelled and everyone laughed.

Soon after, the doctors and nurses left the room to give them some time alone. Over the next several hours they each shared the past year of their lives. "God has surely been good to us, Paul. You know what mother would say."

"Time for worship!" Paul said loudly. They laughed as they agreed on the hymn to sing. Together, with two part harmony they sang one of their favorites – 'Praise to the Lord the Almighty.'[1]

At the nurse's station, they smiled as the beautiful sound of their worship drifted down the hallway and into the rooms of other patients.

########

From then on, for the next two weeks, Paul visited with his sister daily. During their days together he met her employers, Mr. and Mrs. Holston, who always stopped by to see how she was doing. He also met her pastor and some of the women from her church.

Paul finally took the time to write his father, sisters and brother to let them know he had safely crossed the border and that Ruth was doing well.

At the end of two weeks, Dr. Klein pronounced her well enough to leave the hospital. It was no surprise to Paul as he had seen how her countenance had changed and how the walks they took grew longer as her strength increased.

Arrangements had been made for both of them. A widowed woman from Ruth's church lived alone and offered Ruth to live with her in Boeterson while she continued convalescing. Ruth's former employers, the Holston's - offered Paul a place to stay at their farm until he found another employer.

The hospital gave them a great send off. Ruth was handed flowers as everyone lined up to give them both farewell hugs and best wishes.

If he had a choice, Paul would never have chosen the lifestyle of a farmhand, but circumstances warranted it. While he was at the Holston's farm, he slept in the barn, being that the 4 bedroom house was already full with their children, the maid, and another farmhand. They kept him as long as they could. After several weeks they found another farmer nearby that needed help so he moved on.

The Toelke's farm was larger than the Holston's farm. It rested in a valley in the town of Huepperhoefen near Boeterson. Paul was glad for this because Ruth lived only 2 miles away and they were able to attend the same Lutheran church that was only 8 miles away in a nearby town called Sottrum.

Although he lacked bodily strength and still weighed under 100 pounds from his years of malnourishment, the Toelke's took him on as a hired hand. Here, Paul quickly learned the importance of living beings. The knecht or farmhand, as he was called, had his place among the animals. To the owners, Mr. and Mrs. Toelke, a cow or a horse were every bit as valuable as their knechts.

The house where the owners and their children lived was attached to the barn where the animals slept. The knecht and maid each had their own room inside the stable that was well sealed and insulated. Paul slept on a mattress filled with straw. He was hoping for a room by himself, unfortunately in the evening he had to share it with others. Little feet could be felt scurrying across his face at night. As several months passed and the owner took a liking to him, Paul could have said something but he already knew he wouldn't be there for long.

His days consisted of waking at 5 a.m. and chopping wood for the stove in the house so the maid could make breakfast. Before eating the large morning meal, he would feed the horses, cows, chickens and sheep. After breakfast, it was his job to hitch the horses to the wagons and plows then leading them to different areas on the farm. As July lead to August and then September, the harvesting of corn, rye, wheat, hay, and potatoes took up most of his days. Hauling the large bags of corn to the mill to be ground was one of his hardest tasks. Mr. Toelke had to help him with this. Gradually, from all the heavy labor, Paul grew in strength and stature.

########

Often at night after falling exhausted into bed, Paul would cry into his pillow. He missed his family, he missed the songs, the worship, prayers, faith and love they had shared together. Not that the Toelke's were mean to him since they even gave him an old bike so he could go to church each

Sunday and visit with Ruth. It was being with people that loved you and accepted you with all your faults and weaknesses. Yes, he had that with his church family, but he missed the physicality of a home and family. It took time, but eventually his homesickness and the ache in his heart passed.

The farm work was hard and very tiring, but not without fun. At the end of the day as the animals got to know him, they became less skittish and relaxed enough for Paul to enjoy their company. The young lambs would often come near and jump and play around him. Often he would go horseback riding with Lore – the owner's daughter. Mr. Toelke was an ardent horse lover and often went to horse shows in the city of Celle. His daughter worked with the horses to get them ready for show. One afternoon Lore asked Paul if he would take a picture of her with two of the horses which he did.

Work on the farm was also dangerous. The harvesting machinery was very powerful. Paul heard many stories of men getting limbs ripped off or losing their lives to one of them. He always tried to be careful no matter what he was doing. Danger was around every corner and he had to be continually on his toes, avoiding horse hooves, dropped axes, mill machinery, and angry cows.

Unfortunately, as much as he tried to be careful, one day Paul made the mistake of jumping out a barn trap door into what he thought was an empty spot on the ground below. He landed on a piece of wood that had nails in it that went right through his foot. Limping to the house, Mrs. Toelke took him inside, looked at it, cleaned it up and bandaged it. For Paul this was a sure sign that the knecht life was not for him. Later, after supper, this feeling was confirmed when the Toelke's asked him into their formal living room for a talk.

"Paul have a seat," Mr. Toelke motioned toward a large couch that sat across from where he was sitting. Mrs. Toelke sat next to him in a similar chair. She held a handkerchief in her hand. Paul noticed that she was twisting it nervously around her fingers.

"This doesn't look good," thought Paul.

"Paul, let me get right to the point. Do you like working here?" Mr. Toelke asked leaning forward and looking him square in the eye.

"I'm glad to have a job and grateful that you took me on to work on your farm." Paul said honestly.

"Let me rephrase the question. If you could, would you rather be doing something else?" Mr. Toelke raised his eyebrows with the question.

"It's not that we want to get rid of you, Paul," Mrs. Toelke chimed in. "We want you to be happy and if there's anything we can do to help you find that 'something else' we're here to help you."

Paul sighed an inward sigh of relief and thanked the Lord again for putting people in his path that genuinely were looking out for his best interest. He gathered his thoughts and answered, "Yes, as a matter of fact, I've been thinking about an apprenticeship in electronics. I also have a dream of going to America someday."

"That settles it then," Mr. Toelke said standing up. "Tomorrow I'll look up the names of electrical firms in Rothenburg that have apprenticeships. As for going to America, you'll have to make the trip to Hamburg to the American Consulate and apply for your immigration visa there. I've heard it takes several years for the application process, but in that time you can work on your schooling."

Paul stood up and shook Mr. Toelke's hand thanking him. Mrs. Toelke came alongside Paul and pushed his bangs away from his eyes in a motherly way.

"You're a hard worker Paul Tittel, and a fine young man. In all your ways acknowledge the Lord and he'll make your paths strait."

########

Several weeks passed while Paul's foot mended. Mrs. Toelke kept an eye on it for infection. It healed nicely. Mr. Toelke gave him the name of an electrical company and a recommendation from him speaking of his character and good work ethic.

Paul knew that getting into the apprenticeship program wouldn't be easy. He was three years older than the other students. Most boys entered an apprenticeship program right out of middle school. He had almost graduated from high school before he left Hartenstein to cross the border. But his age ended up being of no consequence. Although it took several months, by the spring of 1951 - with the prayers of his church family and Mr. Toelke's reference Paul was accepted into a three year program.

The Toelke's sent him off to his new home in the small village of Boeterson. Here the pastor of his church found an elderly couple, Mr. and Mrs. Miesner, that needed help with daily chores. For a little rent and labor Paul had a nice place to stay with daily meals.

########

It was mid-July and Paul was enjoying his classes and making new friends. Everything was going just as he had planned. He had no worries and felt that the only way his life could be better was if he could be in America.

Coming home from school, he didn't think anything of it when Mrs. Miesner handed him a letter from his sister Elisabeth. "Supper's in 20 minutes!" She yelled to him as he ran up the stairs.

Opening the door to his room, he flopped onto his bed and opened the letter. After reading a few lines it felt like someone had just punched him in his stomach.

Dearest Paul,

I'm sorry to write you of this. How I wish I could be there in person to tell you and wrap you both in my arms. Our dear father has passed away this date of July 10, 1951. Be comforted in knowing that he died peacefully in his sleep.

I know that both of you will be unable to come because of the border. By the time you get this the funeral will be over and our father will be days in the grave. Do not worry over this. We know your love and your prayers are with us – as ours are with you.

Paul, share this letter with Ruth and let her know of our love and prayers.

Herbert, Magdalena, and I will worship at his funeral together as if you were with us. We know our Redeemer lives, what comfort this sweet sentence gives.

God bless you and keep you always in His care,

Elisabeth, Herbert and Magdalena

Paul covered his face with his pillow and cried as he remembered his father, his faith and his love. Gathering himself a few minutes later, he took the letter and quickly made his way downstairs into the kitchen.

Mrs. Miesner looked at his face and knew something was wrong. "What is it Paul?"

"My father," Paul's voice faltered. "My father has died," he said looking down at the letter in his hand. Tears began to trickle down his face.

Mr. Miesner got up from his chair at the same time Mrs. Miesner turned of the stove burner and came by his side. They both threw their arms around him and cried with him.

As they released their embrace, Paul stepped back and wiped the tears from his face. "I have to go and tell Ruth."

"Yes, go and take as much time as you need. We'll keep the light on for you." Mr. Miesner said.

"We'll notify the pastor and ask for a special prayer for you and Ruth and your family this Sunday," said Mrs. Miesner. They saw him to the door and watched him speed away on his bike to the town of Sottrum to give Ruth the dreadful news.

Paul held Ruth while she cried. "It is so very sad to think of him not here with us anymore. Even though we haven't seen him, it was just the thought that he was home, safe, in the same house we were raised in."

"Yes, I know, Ruth, I feel the same… I wish I would have written him more."

"He knew, Paul. He knew you loved him. Don't guilt yourself for not having done more. It was his time. We knew he was in poor health, but still…it strikes the heart."

"Yes Ruth, it does."

########

Time moved on - summer and fall made way to winter. Paul's schedule consisted of one day a week in trade school and 5 days a week on the job training. From where he lived in Boeterson to where the electrical company was located in Rothenburg was 10 miles. This wasn't too bad of a ride, but during winter it was a lot harder.

########

For Christmas in 1951, Paul and Ruth were able to get together and exchange gifts. They reminisced about past Christmases when both their parents were alive. They prayed for their sisters and brother alone in the big house, now without their father. They thanked the Lord in worship because although he was gone, they knew where he was. It was a Christmas when both were truly grateful for the birth of their Savior.

########

Another year passed. It was February, 1952, and Paul was excited for spring. He didn't make much money as an apprentice, but he had saved enough from working on the farm and over the past year to buy a motorcycle. This would be the year he would buy his first real means of transportation – a 98cc Fichtel-Sachs.

As a young man owning a motorcycle was a dream come true – there were many benefits and it made his life much easier. Traveling became a joy instead of burden. He also saved more time by being able to travel quicker to and from school and to job locations.

One day while traveling with his Geselle, the person who was in charge of his training, they came across a large pit out in the country. His Geselle had a 300cc Zundap motorcycle. The pit was made from a blockbuster bomb and was very large and deep – a two story house could fit in the middle and not be seen. During the war, after a bombing run, if the planes still had unused bombs they would dump them in the countryside. The Geselle thought it would be fun to ride down into it and up the other side. Paul watched as the Geselle road down to the bottom, but unfortunately he couldn't get back up the other side. Paul went for help and found nearby villagers to help him drag his motorcycle out of the pit.

Having a motorcycle and being young and adventurous, Paul found himself in many circumstances where he could have been seriously hurt. On one occasion, during the summer, he and his friends decided to go swimming at a local quarry. By the time they finished it was dusk. Driving through the fields on his way home, suddenly something told him to stop. Putting on his brakes, he looked down. Here, almost pressed against his throat was a barbed wire fence.

Another time the following winter, he took his hands off the handlebars for a moment. Instantly the bike went down after hitting an icy patch. Paul watched as tree trunks passed by his head several times as he spun out of control. He often found himself thinking of Psalm 91 when he came upon these situations.

########

Paul was an entrepreneur. Just as he found ways to feed his family after the war by selling stamps, mushrooms, and sawdust, now he thought of ways to make money to save for his trip to America.

He started a small electrical repair business: fixing toasters, televisions, radios and the like, building up a large clientele. In fact it grew to the point where he became concerned that it might interfere with his apprenticeship. He also realized it was time for him to have his own apartment as Mr. and Mrs. Miesner complained about the coming and going of so many people at their front door.

After he found his own place, he also opened a propane gas station where people came and exchanged their empty bottles for full ones. Both businesses flourished and on top of everything, Mr. Toelke contacted him and asked if he would come and work on the farm on weekends because they were short of help.

It was a very prosperous time for Paul - so much so that many of his friends asked him, "Why do you want to go to America? Look at what you'd be leaving behind." They were right in many ways, but he couldn't shut down the pull inside of him. He was drawn to America – he wanted to further his education and knew that the United States would give him the best chance for this. Echoes of his father's stories of the opportunities, the beauty, the people, and of course the gigantic breakfasts...there was nothing that could deter him from achieving this goal. His mind was focused and set.

########

In 1952 Paul finally took the train to Hamburg to go to the American Consulate to apply for an immigration visa. Mr. Toelke was right – it would take up to 3 years for it to go through. He was given a list of 4 mandatory things he would have to comply with:

1. He would need to have a sponsor.

2. He had to be in good health.

3. He had to have a job lined up.

4. He would have to serve at least 2 years in the military.

A sponsor was no problem. He knew he wanted to settle in Baltimore, Maryland and that his church had connections there. He was already in great health and he knew that because of his electrical training, getting a job wouldn't be that difficult either. He didn't like the idea of going into the military, but if that's what it took – he would do it.

########

In November of 1953 the border opened (temporarily).[2] One still had to have an official reason for travel, so when Paul received a letter from Elisabeth stating that Magdalena would be coming to visit them, he knew it wouldn't be a 'visit' but would be to stay.

He again shared the news with Ruth who gave out a joyful scream upon hearing that her little sister would be joining them. Paul made arrangements with the Miesner's for Magdalena to take his old room. Through the help of church friends and relatives they saw the youngest of the Tittel family delivered safely to the doorstep of her new home. Paul and Ruth were there to greet her when she arrived.

"Magdalena, look at you - you're all grown up!" Ruth said holding her sister at arms length and looking her up and down.

"You've grown taller yourself since I last saw you, Ruth, but the biggest change is Paul. You're twice the size you were when you left Hartenstein!" Magdalena yelled as she gave Paul the biggest hug.

They talked for hours while helping Magdalena unpack and get settled into her new home. As the months passed they made it a point to visit every Sunday after church to catch up on what was happening in each of their lives.

########

In the spring of 1954 Paul finished his apprenticeship, took the tests and was legally ready to have his own business. He thought he would use the year he had left before leaving to further his study in a more advanced field in the same electrical branch. He was interested in working with larger motors. He found a man by the name of Johann Freese who tutored him in the repair of larger electrical machines.

Paul was proud of his training and all that he had learned. On a fall day in 1954, he had a friend take a picture of him and Johann working outside on one of these motors.

In January, 1955, Paul received his immigration visa. His holler of joy could be heard throughout the neighborhood. He spent the next several months getting his affairs in order, purchasing his ticket to America, writing

Elisabeth that he would soon have a new address, writing Christa that he would soon be visiting her and saying goodbye to the friends he had made in West Germany.

The caravan of friends, church folk, and fellow co-workers who wanted to see him safely onboard his ship, the SS Italia, amazed Paul. He looked back at the cars following them on the way to Bremerhaven.

"Looks like you're the man of the moment," said Johann while clinching a cigar between his teeth.

Paul laughed. "You're just jealous, Johann."

"Who would have thought half the town wanted to drive to Bremerhaven to see you safely on board your ship?" Magdalena said shaking her head from the back seat.

"It's nice they lessened the rules and regulations over the years. Anyone can come onboard the boat, although they can't go inside without a boarding pass." Paul informed them.

"Oh, that will be fun," added Ruth.

It wasn't long before they were all onboard the SS Italia. It was a warm day, but the sea breeze cooled the air enough. Walking on deck with his friends and family around him, he thought back to the picture of his father and uncles when they made their first trip and wondered if they felt like he did. "Totally bold, fearless and courageous with just a hint of fear," Paul chuckled to himself while he walked along with his sisters.

The whistle blew indicating that it was time for guests to leave. The large group of church friends and co-workers started disembarking.

"Promise you'll write us, Paul," Ruth said as she and Magdalena embraced their brother one last time.

"Yes, I promise. Not only will I write you but I'll send you pictures too. Don't worry, mom and dad, Elisabeth, Herbert, and Christa made it safely over, I know God will give me safe passage too."

Ruth let go of her little brother's hand. Reaching the dock, Ruth and Magdalena waved a last goodbye to Paul. She was sad to see him go, but saw the smile on his face and knew he was happy to be leaving. So, she smiled back and waved enthusiastically, cheering him on toward his new life in America.

Paul made his way into the ship. He had paid for a room with a porthole wanting to see at least a glimpse of the ocean when he was in his cabin at sea. There was a bunkbed, so he would be having another man stay with him for the 8 day journey. His curiosity was peaked as to who it might be.

Since he was first in the cabin he took the top bunk. He remembered when he and Magdalena shared a bunkbed and he always slept in the top bunk. A soft sigh escaped his lips as he thought of his little sister.

"Enough of that," he thought to himself. "There's a whole ship to see and I'm going to explore every part." Paul left his bag on his bed, but carried his valuables with him. First he went to the dining room and lounge to see where he'd be eating. Next, he talked a mechanic into letting him see the engine room. It was breathtaking to Paul – a dance of machinery in motion.

After walking around the deck several more times while the ship headed out of port, he headed back to his cabin and saw that his roommate had arrived. "Hello, I'm Paul Tittel," he said as he entered the cabin holding out his hand.

A bright blue-eyed, blond haired man turned to shake his hand. "Werner Schock, I see you've claimed the top bunk."

"Do you mind?" asked Paul.

"Not at all," said Werner.

Paul clambered up to his bunk and looked down at his new roommate. "So why are you going to America?"

"Opportunity, education…You?"

"Very much the same Werner," Paul replied.

Over the next 8 days the two became quite close friends. Finding many things in common and many nights they talked into the wee hours of the morning.

"It's hard to believe the journey's over," Paul thought as he and Werner stepped out on deck. They were nearing the Harbor. It was foggy but many people had come out hoping to catch a glimpse of her (Statue of Liberty).

As if on cue, as they passed by, the fog parted and dissipated at her feet. The sun blazed down upon her and there she stood; Proud, Beautiful, and Strong. Embraced by the arms of Liberty, Paul knew this was a country blessed by God, and because of this, he knew his life within America would be blessed too.

"Maybe the journey's not over, maybe it's just beginning," Paul thought back to his father's stories, specifically the prayer they prayed as they left this beautiful land years ago. He could almost hear them saying it again - soft as an ocean breeze, 'Maybe someday our children will come back.'

"I made it, ma, I made it, pa, I made it…thank you for your prayers," Paul said softly to himself as he looked to the horizon and his new life in America.

A Journey Completed: The true story of a boy's family through two World Wars, a horrible Cold War, and his journey to freedom.

1. http://www.lutheran-hymnal.com/online/aTLH_Hymns8.htm

"Praise to the Lord, the Almighty"
by Joachim Neander, 1650-1680
Translated by Catherine Winkworth, 1829-1878

Praise to the Lord, the Almighty, the King of creation!
O my soul, praise Him, for He is Thy Health and Salvation!
Join the full throng:
Wake, harp and psalter and song;
Sound forth in glad adoration!

Praise to the Lord, who o'er all things so wondrously reigneth,
Who, as on wings of an eagle, uplifteth, sustaineth.
Hast thou not seen
How thy desires all have been
Granted in what He ordaineth?

Praise to the Lord, who hath fearfully, wondrously, made thee;
Health hath vouchsafed and, when heedlessly falling, hath stayed thee.
What need or grief
Ever hath failed of relief?--
Wings of His mercy did shade thee.

Praise to the Lord, who doth prosper thy work and defend thee,
Who from the heavens the streams of His mercy doth send thee.
Ponder anew
What the Almighty can do,
Who with His love doth befriend thee.

Praise to the Lord! Oh, let all that is in me adore Him!
All that hath life and breath, come now with praises before Him!
Let the Amen
Sound from His people again;
Gladly for aye we adore Him.

The Lutheran Hymnal
Hymn #39

Text: Neh. 9:6
Author: Joachim Neander, 1679
Translated by: Catherine Winkworth, 1863, alt.
Titled: "Lobe den Herren, den maechtigen"
Tune: "Lobe den Herren, den"
1st Published in: _Erneuertes Gesangbuch_
Town: Stralsund, 1665

2. http://www.coldwar.org/articles/60s/Berlinwalltimeline.asp

Appendix

Brother Against Brother

The pictures as shown here are 4 soldiers of the same family. Two of them were forced to serve in the German Army and two served in the American Army. Carl, the brother of Clemens served in WW1. Fought in France and received a severe head injury. He was then 18 years old. Herbert, the brother of Paul was drafted into the Hitler Army at the age of 17, even so he was American by birth. He was sent to the Russian front and was captured when he was 18. He spent until 1949, 5 years in war prison camp in Siberia.

Clemens, the brother of Carl immigrated to the USA in 1923, worked on a farm in Minnesota for one year. After deciding farm work was not his specialty he joined the US Army in 1924. On the picture however Clemens is seen as a corporal in rank. During his 32 years of service his rank was the highest attained by a noncommissioned officer, his rank was Sgt. Major.

Paul immigrated to the USA in 1955. After 11 month in the country he was drafted into the US Army. He would have received a rank of Sgt. in 2 years according to his MOS however that was stolen from him by manipulation. He was stationed near the East-West German border. The same place where he escaped in 1950. He was on the frontline, facing that colossal Russian and East German Army.

Herbert, his brother who was born in the USA but by tragic events had to return to Germany with his family as a baby in 1929. If there would have been a conflict between the western allies and the Russian Army at the time of the Berlin Airlift or any other time, Herbert would not have been too old to be drafted into the East German Army by the Communists. Herbert and Paul would have faced each other in a terrible conflict.

Thanks to our heavenly father who prevented such things to happen. It has been throughout history, that many such incidents occurred . We only have to look no further than the US Civil War.

"Paul Gerhard Tittel: A Two-paragraph Biography"

Paul Tittel has a story to tell. As a teen he risked his life fleeing East Germany, escaping Communist indoctrination and starvation. Immigrating to the United States in 1955, he completed studies in mathematics and electrical engineering at Johns Hopkins University, then applied this learning as a research assistant and instructor in the Departments of Physiology and Ophthalmology at the University of Maryland School of Medicine.

There he published in professional journals and presented multiple papers in ophthalmology. Simultaneously, he was on the cutting edge of technology, building an analog computer that was utilized in dissertation research by multiple doctoral students. He holds several patents, and for more than sixty years was a church organist. He is author of *Never Alone: A Chronicle*, which relates his experiences in escaping death and oppression, and God's tender mercies that kept him. Indeed, Paul Tittel has a story to tell. It will reward every reader.

Made in the USA
Las Vegas, NV
19 March 2022